John James Tayler

Last series of Christian aspects of faith and duty

John James Tayler

Last series of Christian aspects of faith and duty

ISBN/EAN: 9783743367722

Manufactured in Europe, USA, Canada, Australia, Japa

Cover: Foto ©Lupo / pixelio.de

Manufactured and distributed by brebook publishing software (www.brebook.com)

John James Tayler

Last series of Christian aspects of faith and duty

LAST SERIES

OF

CHRISTIAN ASPECTS

OF

FAITH AND DUTY.

𝔇𝔦𝔰𝔠𝔬𝔲𝔯𝔰𝔢𝔰

BY

JOHN JAMES TAYLER,

LATE PRINCIPAL OF MANCHESTER NEW COLLEGE, LONDON.

"He, being dead, yet speaketh."

WILLIAMS AND NORGATE,

14, HENRIETTA STREET, COVENT GARDEN, LONDON;
AND 20, SOUTH FREDERICK STREET, EDINBURGH.

1877.

LONDON :
PRINTED BY C. GREEN AND SON,
178, STRAND.

PREFACE.

I HAVE at length yielded to the often-expressed wish of several friends that I would publish another volume of my father's Sermons. The only consideration that has deterred me from doing so hitherto, has been the recollection of his own words, constantly repeated to those who urged him to publish more, "that he would have entirely to re-write every Sermon, to put it into a shape in which he would think fit to offer it to the public." As this cannot be done now, I can but hope that the reader will remember the writer's opinion, and kindly overlook anything in the style or expression that may seem to be more suitable for delivery than for publication.

In making the present selection, in which I have been indebted to Dr. Martineau for considerable assistance, the choice has, with a few exceptions, been confined to Sermons written after the year 1851, and mostly preached (and in many cases written) within the last ten years of my father's life, so as to represent the views of his later, as the former volume did those of his earlier, years. I have mentioned at the end of each Sermon the year when it was written and the year when it was last preached, thinking that it may be interesting to some to be able to recal the time when they may have heard it, and to associate the voice and manner of the speaker with his written words. What he has himself said, on this and on other subjects, in the Preface to the series of "Christian Aspects" published twenty-six years ago, will, even at such a distance of time, still be the best introduction to the present volume.

H. E. OSLER.

HAMPSTEAD, 1877.

CONTENTS.

X.   PAGE

Contents.

DISCOURSES.

I.

Wisdom, the Fruit of Experience.

Job xii. 12 :

"With the ancient is wisdom; and in length of days, understanding."

THERE is a grand teaching in Providence which
is worth all that books can give. The events
which make up our lives, our intercourse with
mankind, our observation of the world, yield lessons so
clear, consistent and imperative, and indicate so distinctly a counsel and a plan pervading all things, that
a thoughtful mind will gather from its own experience,
enriched with the accumulated results of advancing
years, a more convincing evidence of the being and
government of an all-wise and righteous God, than can
be furnished by the greatest miracles of the material
creation. The fruit of this experience, treasured up in
well-digested conclusions, and expressed in a correspond-

ing regulation of the outward life, constitutes wisdom. Books alone cannot teach it; genius cannot anticipate it; the energy, enterprize and ability of opening life are often without it. It is the prerogative of years; it is the gift of length of days. There is something significant in the fact that moral excellence—the quality by which we most resemble Christ and God—is the latest of our attainments on earth, is slowest in coming to maturity, and goes on ripening and growing, when our other powers seem already to have reached their terrestrial limit. The highest efforts of intellect are often exhibited in the early part of life; Newton is said to have exhausted his rich vein before he was fifty; but the deep wisdom of the heart and life—the wisdom that arises from an experimental acquaintance with God and Providence, that teaches us what we are, and why we are here, and where we must look for our true happiness —the wisdom that dissipates the vain dreams of the imagination, and puts in their place the settled realities of eternal truth—can only be learned from the repeated witness of facts and the long teaching of successive years. How strongly and widely this belief is entertained by mankind, we have a proof in the language and institutions of the most celebrated nations. Seniority and wisdom have been considered by them as almost convertible terms. They have made age a qualification for office, and composed their highest assemblies and most venerable courts of the oldest men. Let us attend to the influences of experience, and consider what are the graver and more valuable qualities which it bestows on the human mind.

(1.) The flight of years alone—that quickened sense of the brevity and precariousness of life which comes over us when we have attained to middle age—brings with it some elements of serious wisdom. We see life in its true form and dimensions. We are no longer encompassed with visions, but look upon realities. The dazzling sunshine of the morning is gone; a vast, unknown, boundless future, veiled in gleaming mist, through which our inexperienced fancy shaped out to itself a thousand dim and floating forms of good and beauty, lies no longer before us; the fair illusion has passed away; and now, in the quiet light which rests on all things, we discern the horizon that bounds our little being, marked off in clear, sharp outline from the glorious canopy of heaven which is spread over it. We perceive at length where we are; we measure with more thoughtful eye the circuit of the field which God has given us to till; and we calculate how much our hands may yet accomplish ere the coming of that night in which our earthly labours must cease.

(2.) It is the natural effect of such reflections to take off our thoughts from theories and speculations which lead to no certain result, and to put us with redoubled activity on endeavours after positive good and practical usefulness. When we are young, we are full of projects and undertakings which the future is to realize; we are spendthrifts of time and opportunities of which we imagine the future can never be exhausted; we cannot bring up our minds to the point of execution, from the fond persuasion that some fairer occasion, some better plan, may yet present itself: and so years roll away, while our most cherished designs of usefulness as yet exist only in idea, and we find ourselves fairly arrived at middle life before we have entered with all our might on the great work for which God sent us into the world. This consciousness stirs up all serious men to new energy. They are deeply aware that no more time is to be lost. They acquire a stronger sense of the magnitude of life's duties, while they perceive that the space left for discharging them in is sensibly contracted, and feel that much of the strength and many of the opportunities which might once have been brought to bear on them, are now irrecoverably gone. It thus becomes a part of the wisdom of maturer life to husband the resources which remain, to brace up anew the languid springs of action, to bring the mind's best powers to the grave concerns of a moral and responsible existence, to discard dreams and encounter reality, to labour right earnestly in the cause of truth and virtue, and so prepare for the solemn change which draws every day more nigh.

(3.) We are qualified for more efficient exertion by another change which time brings with it. Length of years gives the thoughtful and observant a firmer conviction of first principles, running through life and indicating the design of Providence, and a quieter reliance on them, as ground that can never fail, established by God for the eternal support of His moral government. But the same experience teaches us also that the Divine plans, embracing the interests of myriads of creatures and extending over countless generations, proceed by a slow and gradual, though sure and unerring course;

and therefore we become less impatient for immediate results; we are less sanguine as to the good that will speedily and visibly arise from continued efforts in the cause of truth and virtue. But our faith in the final issue of things does not on that account fail; we are not, as in youth, thrown by sudden disappointment into the depths of despair; for we observe that the wise and good Father, under whose government we live, directs all things by fixed and general laws, which not only attain more certainly the ends successively accomplished in that sublime progression of good which is the great idea of His providence, but yield also in the course of their operation that salutary, though often painful, discipline which is best fitted to exercise faith, and form character, and train the spirit for a heavenly world. We learn to place a calmer trust in God, to rely on the tendencies which plainly manifest themselves everywhere towards higher and wider good, and striving in all things, with our clearest intelligence and best endeavours, never to work *against*, but always *with* God, to find in that simple consciousness a spring of unfailing cheerfulness and hope. These quieter and more patient feelings extend also to our judgments of our fellow-creatures. The idols of our youthful idolatry have turned out on a nearer acquaintance to be only men like ourselves; but, on the other hand, we have outlived many of our unreasonable and vehement antipathies. There are fewer, perhaps, in whom we could now put implicit confidence; none whom we can now look upon as infallible and perfect; but then we have more toleration and charity for all; for we see that all have their weaknesses, and none are wholly bad; that the finest intellects are limited by some prejudice, and the best and purest hearts overshadowed at times by a passing cloud of temper.   We make the best of the humanity which encompasses us, loving and cherishing its goodness under all forms, and doing all we can to root out the causes and heal the effects of the moral evil which so extensively adheres to it ; and when we are most sorely tried by the perversity and selfishness of the world—if we have drawn any lesson from the mellowing experience of life, we shall be better able to repress the feelings of irritation and enmity, to look up to Heaven and ask for a spirit of patience and forbearance, to call to mind our own infirmities, and say with the kind-hearted and ingenuous Peter, "I myself am a man."

(4.) Of all the attainments brought to us by increasing years, perhaps the most valuable is the better knowledge of ourselves.   He must have an overweening conceit whose high notions of himself are not beaten down by the mortifying experiences of some thirty or forty years, and reduced more nearly within the limits of reality. We find out by that time with tolerable certainty what we are capable of, and learn year by year to put a greater check on the ambitious projects of our youth ; and yet, if we are not conscious of gross folly or indolence, that experience yields more tranquillity than disappointment. It is an unspeakable blessing to feel content with our allotment in life, and with the measure of success which has attended it—to be reverentially grateful for such talents as God has committed to us, and to know that He will only demand a proportionate return.   If we would

only take a right view of life—such a view as length of
years naturally inclines us to take—half the discontent
and repining and envy which embitter it would at once
cease to exist. Why do we live ? Whence comes all
our happiness ? To answer these questions rightly and
practically is wisdom. And what does wisdom say,
from experience, are the grand ends of human life ?
Goodness, purity, affection—simply doing God's will,
and trying to make others happy. For attaining most
completely these ends, a very humble sphere of duty
and small allotment of intellectual ability—if faithfully
improved—abundantly suffice. And let us remember,
he who well improves what God has given, hearkens to
the voice within, and does right, is the truly wise—is
God's accepted child—and is in the sure road to heaven.
What a delightful and tranquillizing thought is this !
How all those distinctions which excite the evil passions of men, and fill the world with discord, at once
vanish at its presence, and leave our interest and our
reverence fixed on that sole distinction which has value
in the eye of God, and on which He has set the uneffaceable impress of immortality ! Just and merciful God !
Thou hast made the highest happiness of Thy creation
dependent on capacities which Thou hast given to all,
attainable by every humble and pious soul that is dili-
gent and faithful in cultivating them, and will lend
a reverential ear to the voice of the monitor within.
Cease, then, ye who understand the true work and dignity of your spiritual vocation, to be disquieted and
unhappy, because you have not the high intellectual
endowments, the clear reason, the flowing wit, the capa-

cious memory, the ready invention and the lively fancy, which God has bestowed, in this infancy of their being, on some few of His human family. Persist in goodness, and all these things—at least all the blessings and privileges they bring—will also come to you in time. For you are destined to a career of immortal improvement, and goodness is the means constituted by God himself for attaining to all the objects which it holds out in endless succession before you. Do you look with admiration on the efforts of any highly-gifted mind? Let no envy or discouragement mingle with that feeling. Know yourself, and be content. Reverence those high powers, not for the fleeting honour which they confer here below, but for the great and noble purposes to which they may be applied. Ask how their possessor uses them himself. Are they to him but the instruments of ambition, selfishness, passion, falsehood and wrong? Oh turn away from a spectacle which should only fill you with a pitying regret! But if he understands his mission among men, and exercises his divine faculty uprightly, to serve truth and goodness and shed abroad a spirit of heavenly beauty, rejoice that God has thus signally endowed a brother for the blessing and instruction of that great family to which you belong, and has raised him up as an example of what you and all men may hereafter become—rejoice to think that, in the glorious world to which you and he are equally tending, you also in due time—if you are true to your higher nature—will be advanced to be a fellow-worker with him and other pure and exalted spirits, in the sublime and as yet undiscovered purposes for which God has given you an immortal existence. If length of days has only given you a deeper sense of this consoling trust, and made you more aware of the worth and dignity of your moral nature, you have not lived in vain.

(5.) Similar tendencies of thought will weaken our attachment to the outward goods of fortune, and slacken our ardour in their pursuit. I do not mean to say it is ever desirable that we should become indifferent to the world, and lose our interest in its concerns and enjoyments; but if we have lived to any purpose—if we have not been wholly unobservant of the course of events—or if we have drawn any inference from our own and our friends' experience—we must have learned how unsatisfactory is the mere possession of wealth and elevated station, how disappointing is the result of gratified ambition, and what a bitterness rises up to the lips, in repeated draughts—bitterer at each repetition—from the intoxicating cup of pleasure. A revelation of the hidden meaning of things comes over the mind in middle life. The words of the wise enter our ears in youth like mysterious oracles. We have a dim feeling that they hide some great truth. But we hardly know what it is. It is brought out by the event which verifies them. Then at length we comprehend their full significance. Then they enter our hearts like a truth from God himself. What beautiful and solemn things are said to us in the Bible—and by the poets, those best interpreters, next to the Bible, of the mystery of life—of the worthlessness of riches, the misery of ambition, the deceitfulness of our wild imagination, the unperceived flight of years, and loss of strength, and failure of opportunities, and the quick approach of death! Perhaps we never disbelieved those words; perhaps we gave them the passing, not irreverent, heed of impetuous youth. But let any one compare the impression which then they left on the mind, with that which is made by them now, when every day is fraught with some experimental confirmation of their truth, and every terminated year seems to send them home with a more solemn impressiveness to the very depths of the heart. They come to us in youth like the fairy sound of distant bells, wafted, with a pleasing melancholy that stirs up strange, indefinite emotions, upon the summer breeze to the vacant ear; but now they come, distinct and solemn, with a voice that can no more be misunderstood, telling us of things to which our hearts bear hourly witness, and of which life, as it advances, seems to furnish only one unbroken exemplification. Yet it is not unmixed sadness that is the fruit of this experience. A calmer, purer happiness comes up to take the place of the bolder hopes and more eager interests that are fled. If life's lessons and opportunities have not been entirely neglected, treasures are left of which we never knew the full value till now. We fall back on the resources of our own minds, on the quiet happiness of our homes, on intercourse with friends whose worth has been tried by the vicissitudes of life, and on those pure pleasures of taste and intellect, of philanthropy and devotion, which can hardly be tasted in perfection, till time has chastened the imagination and subdued the heart.

Such are the effects produced by advancing years on all minds not wholly imbruted by sense and appetite, or absorbed by worldliness. Increase of age brings with it almost naturally more sobriety, forethought, moderation and contentedness. And such effects must be additionally beneficial when they are seasoned by piety and accompanied by virtuous habits. They furnish the first strong proof from experience, that life is a progression of good ; and that if the pleasures and advantages of one period must be relinquished, they are succeeded by others equally delightful, and as appropriate to the new circumstances which have been entered. This the young can only know by anticipation. Oh let them profit by the experience of their elder friends! Let them impress this great and eternal truth on their hearts, that virtue alone is true wisdom; that through every period of existence, purity and goodness of heart, rectitude of purpose, devotion to duty, and active benevolence, are the fixed conditions of happiness, the neverfailing source of that peace of God "which passeth all understanding"!

To the virtuous, a retrospect of life from any point in the course of it, though solemn and humbling, is not unattended with compensatory reflections. It yields the evidence of some progress in wisdom and goodness, some advance of the character towards the plainly discerned end of existence, and a conviction, thence arising, that life has not been bestowed entirely in vain. Must we stop here? Does not nature itself indicate, that progress, so far continued and capable of indefinite extension, looks on to something still beyond ? Christ, the prophet of humanity, confirms that anticipation, and tells us we shall live again. Oh let us cling to that blessed idea of endless progress in what is pure and good and happy! All that we can learn and do on earth but yields the rudiments of an immortal existence. We are born for heaven. Let us put our trust in God, and hearken to His voice, and accomplish His work; and He will at length give us the inheritance!

[Written, 1848; last preached (Upper Brook St., Manchester), 6th July, 1851.]

II.

The Divinity of Christ.

JOHN x. 30:

"I and my Father are one."

WHEN the celebrated Rousseau, in the middle of the last century, wrote thus: "If the life and death of Socrates are those of a philosopher, the life and death of Jesus Christ are those of a god,"—he gave utterance to a feeling which thousands of all sects, and not a few unbelievers themselves, have constantly experienced in reading that beautiful and wondrous tale of the Gospels. There is something in the presence of Christ which bows and commands all hearts with a power more than human. Poets and artists have felt this, and essayed in the highest efforts of genius to realize their conception of its mingled sweetness and majesty. A great scholar of the last generation, in confessing to a friend his difficulties about the miraculous, declared at the same time that he could never read of Christ without a feeling that he was something more than man. The late Charles Lamb, one not much given to the sentimentalities of religion, remarked once, in a society where he could open his heart freely, while his eyes glistened with deep emotion as he spoke, that if a certain Person were to appear in the midst of them, he could only fall down and worship, and kiss the hem of his garment. Amidst the tumult and fury of the last revolution in Paris, you will perhaps recollect the striking incident of the effect produced on the mob by the unexpected sight of a crucifix as they were bursting into one of the apartments of the Tuileries. Every head was instantly bared in the hallowed presence, and the hearts of that wild multitude paid a spontaneous homage to that great symbol of self-sacrifice and love.

Now what is this feeling of undefined reverence—this sentiment of involuntary religion—which enters every tender and thoughtful soul with the name and image of Christ? It is not wisdom alone, nor virtue, nor both combined, which excite it. Many have been the wise and the virtuous of earth who claim our profoundest respect; but we acknowledge them simply as men; we feel no disposition to worship them—least of all Socrates, the great moral teacher of the Greeks, so often confronted with Christ. We admire in him the subtle disputant whose keen logic and powerful irony dissolved the false appearances of sophistry and exposed to view the solid elements of truth and justice; but no devout influence accompanies his discourse and seems to hallow his life. Intellect is ever ascendant in him over faith and the affections. He grasps the rational principle of Theism, but wants its living soul. His whole character stands out, distinct and sharp and bright, like an orb without an atmosphere, unencircled by the glorious halo of religious consecration. Turn from the Memorabilia to the Gospels. How different is the impression produced! We at once perceive ourselves to be breathing a different air. The heart is touched. Conscience awakens from its slumber. Our aspirations soar above the earthly and the perishing. We have a sense of something heavenly and spiritual investing the mind and life of Christ, and going forth in his words of love and acts of healing power, which carries our thoughts irresistibly to the Sovereign Spirit of the Universe, and compels us as we read, in spite of ourselves, to confess some close, mysterious and ineffable communion between Christ and God. All have felt this who have had any faith left in their hearts. Those who have repudiated the ordinary conception of Christ, as God in the proper sense, often cling with increased tenacity, for that very reason, to the literal acceptance of the miraculous in his history, as an outward and visible evidence of that something more than human which their deepest impressions will not allow them to deny. It is this feeling—vague and undefinable but so strongly borne into the mind by the Gospels that none can wholly resist it—which believers of every shade of opinion intend to express when they speak, with an obscure but deep and true sentiment, of what they call the divinity of Christ. And it would perhaps have been well for Religion if Theology had left this feeling as it found it, loose and indeterminate, abandoned to the free interpretation of each believing mind. Logic, however, never knows its proper limits, and is perpetually encroaching on provinces that are not its own. When the simple fervour of the first age died out, and men lapsed into coldness and indifference, a purely intellectual interest was artificially kept up in the Church by endless disputes on questions that are absolutely insoluble, and by vain attempts to define in human phrase that which from its infinitude must for ever elude the grasp of human apprehension. The nature of Christ and his relation to God and man naturally became an object of deep attention, and so they must ever be with serious and meditative minds. But this is one of those questions which, depending mainly for its solution on feeling and spiritual temperament, no man can decide for his neighbour, and still less can the judgment of a majority in any particular age determine for all future ages. Two extreme views have resulted from this long controversy respecting the person of Christ. On the one hand, the system which takes to itself the name of orthodox has so exclusively exalted the divine element which all believers recognize in it, as to make Christ actually one in being and substance with the uncreated, infinite and everlasting Jehovah—the uncreated, born of a human virgin—the infinite, contracted within the limits of a finite individuality—the everlasting, subject to the penalty of death. On the other, those who apply reason to their faith, in natural reaction against this incredible statement, have brought too prominently forward the merely human attributes of Christ as the essential element of his person, limiting the fact of his direct communion with God to the special injection, as it were, of certain well-defined doctrines into his mind, accompanied by an outward power of miraculous anthentication, but denying all union with God beyond the needs of this particular case—denying that constant, general, unintermitting, all-pervading commerce with the Divine Spirit, which alone fulfils the idea of a true spiritual identity. "Christ was a mere man," say the extreme humanitarians, "inspired with the knowledge of some great truths, and empowered to work miracles in attestation of them." Theological warfare has chiefly raged between these opposite views and their associated doctrines. Here is the hinge on which the weight of controversy has turned. But there is something in the extreme aspect of both views which revolts our general Christian sentiment. We already perceive a searching on all sides after some broader view, which shall reconcile the apparent inconsistencies of these narrower ones, avoiding what offends us in each, and yet preserving the latent portion of truth which belongs to both.

Orthodoxy would not be unfairly described as the attempt to hold in union, by compromise and the blinking of undeniable consequences, ideas that are mutually repugnant and self-destructive. What is called the Athanasian Creed exhibits this tendency in its extremest form. But it pervades generally the doctrinal determinations of the Catholic Church. The tenet of the two natures in Christ comes under this category. It is expressed by that strange word, coined in the theological mint, God-man, i.e. perfect God and perfect man in one person. The difficulties and inconsistencies involved in this statement, if we try to conceive distinctly the several ideas of which it consists, are insuperable.

Perfect God must mean the whole of God and nothing but God; perfect man, the entire man and only man. The two natures are completely distinct. The attributes which enter into the essence of the one—eternity, infinity, absolute knowledge and unchangeable rectitude of will—exclude their opposites, which constitute the definition of the other: and if person mean, as to be intelligible it must, the possession of one consciousness and one will, it is evident that natures so immeasurably distant, so irreconcilably unlike, as God and man, cannot have a common subsistence in one person. But this doctrine, though it contain no truth itself, fills, if I may so express myself, the place of a truth, and represents a point in the order of thought where some truth ought to be. We must find this truth, not by the theological procedure of taking Christ fairly out of the circle of humanity, and of suspending him, as it were, half-way between heaven and earth, an unreality, an impossibility, something neither God nor man,—but by descending into the spiritual depths of our own human nature, that nature which Christ ennobled and glorified, in which he embodied the perfection and realized the ideal of humanity.

Man has been said to stand on the confines of two worlds, and, occupying already the highest position in the visible scale of being, to announce the transition to a stage yet higher, which is to come. Certainly, we discern in him two elements of opposite quality—two powers of conflicting tendency—the spiritual and the carnal; one inciting him to progress, the other detaining him where he is; one drawing him upward to heaven, the other dragging him down to earth. Paul has spoken of these powers—these laws, as he calls them, of our inner being, and of their perpetual conflict—with the intense conviction of personal experience; and every thoughtful, self-examining mind has felt the force of his words. Between these powers of the flesh and the spirit there is an unceasing strife for the mastery. One must rule, or our inner life is a perpetual warfare. One must predominate, to give unity to our moral being. Our intellectual and active powers are both instruments at the disposal of these commanding tendencies. They will obey the one or the other, whichever is uppermost, and will produce accordingly the worldly or the religious character. The carnal tendency is a part and an essential condition of our being as much as the spiritual, and works for good when the elements of thought and action which it involves are kept within due limits and made to subserve the higher ends indicated by the spiritual. It embraces all our natural appetites and affections, all our instincts of self-preservation and self-advancement, that disposition so deeply planted within us to revel in the pleasures of the present moment, and to extract all the enjoyment and all the benefit we can from the world that immediately encompasses us. In the spiritual lies the restraining sense of a moral law, the supreme authority of conscience, the deep inextinguishable feeling that we are destined for something beyond the present and the actual, and all those higher sentiments which fill us with the consciousness of God, envelope us with the awe of His presence, and in the grand idea of immortality indicate the final end of all our efforts and aspirations.

This spiritual element of our being marks our affinity with God. It is the witness of our sonship. It is the medium of our intercourse. It is the mysterious link which unites our nature with His. To make the spiritual law ascendant is the object of life's moral discipline; and were it fully attained, God and man would be at peace, would be spiritually one.

In Christ alone do we see the two tendencies progressively, and at last perfectly, harmonized, by the entire subjection of the carnal to the spiritual, and the unconditional surrender of both to the will of God. In all other men, the strife is visible to the last. With all their efforts, the work is still incomplete. The world has got too strong a hold on their affections. Passion and selfishness are unextinguished, and break forth with a fitful gleam at intervals. They cannot make God reign in all their thoughts, and introduce a perfect holy peace. They have achieved much for human frailty if they have rendered the spiritual tendency habitually predominant, and never intentionally wander from God. Christ alone could say of his human work, "It is finished." And in him, too, that perfection of obedience, that divine life, was truly a work wrought out by will and effort. We should wrong his excellence, and mar the effect of his example, if we regarded it as a gift from God. In Christ we pre-eminently see how virtue is accomplished by endeavour—how through toil and trial, through weakness and fear, the pure and true soul continually advances and is at length made one with God. We see the divine gradually triumphing over, and finally absorbing, the human. Yet how deeply is the human imprinted on all his history! What struggles he passed through! What terrors he vanquished! How fierce and fiery was that temptation in the wilderness! How insidious the worldly counsel of Peter! How sad those tears that flowed at the grave of Lazarus! How heavy and dark the sorrow of Gethsemane! But faith was ever at hand to restore the mental balance, and preserve the perfect harmony of his pure and trusting spirit with God. In this full and confiding communion with God as the source and principle of his whole moral being, we find, I apprehend, the true divinity of Christ, and the secret of that mingled reverence and love with which all religious hearts have honoured him. All spirit is of one nature, though possessed in various degrees. As partakers of spirit, men are the children of God. There is a measure of it corresponding to the moral capacities of humanity, which Christ alone, judging from the extant records of his life, seems to have filled up to its utmost limits, and so to have united our nature morally with the Divine. Through him the Spirit of the Father spoke clearly and intelligibly to men; for it is only a purified and exalted humanity that can interpret the Divine Mind. From him went forth the spirit that drew men by the attracting sympathies of faith and love to their Heavenly Father, and made them own His presence in the midst of them.

The divinity of which I now speak and which had its fullest manifestation in Christ, does not relate to the intellectual and constructive powers, to science or art; for these grow up and unfold themselves by their own laws and undergo a gradual development, one generation carrying on and completing the work of the last; and although these operations of the mind advance the general progress of the world, and are important agents under the providence of God, they are not essential to the fulfilment of the end of man's existence, considered as the subject of a moral government and the heir of immortality. When the moral nature is once impregnated with a religious spirit and actuated by a right impulse, all the energies of the intellect and the hand will take effect healthily, and accomplish some good and noble work; but without this higher guidance, they may be productive only of mischief, and supply little but incentives to crime. Man's moral and spiritual guidance was a necessity in the order of the world that needed early to be provided for; and it is not therefore surprising that the manifestation of God in Christ—in other words, the divinity of Christ—should be limited to the moral and spiritual attributes of man's nature, to those attributes which are the indispensable condition of his safe and happy existence on earth, without which, properly called forth and wisely directed, he can enjoy no inward peace, and knows not how to prepare himself for a tranquil and hopeful death. Every product of human genius and every effort of human heroism is, no doubt, in one sense a manifestation of God; but the soul which is the seat of virtue and religion, and where are deposited the germs of an immortal existence, sustains a more intimate and sacred relation to Him, and seems the fittest subject of His special influence and immediate instruction. The prophet, of all human beings, claims our highest reverence; for he is familiar with those secret things of God which reach to the deepest wants of the soul, and his word is wrought out in his life. Wonderful indeed are the workings of the Divine Spirit in the thought of the philosopher, in the melodious fancies of the poet, in the creation of the artist, in the invention of the mechanician; but these things have another divinity in them than the life and doctrine of Christ: that we recognize in the harmony of an entire moral being with God—in the harmony of its will, its affections and its endeavours, with the holiness, the rectitude, the truthfulness and the love, of the great Parent and Sovereign Mind of the universe. In all these things, Christ was one with God, and therefore it is that we pronounce his work and life divine.

And it is our own moral nature—a heart and conscience sincerely given up to truth and right and love—that can best appreciate the evidence of this divinity. Christ knows his own, and they know him. His sheep hear his voice and understand it, and they follow him. This sympathy with Christ's mind is the preparation for all true belief, and an opening into the real divinity of his nature. His miracles, grand and beautiful as they are to those who accept them as historical realities, confirm that deep and solemn impression, but only when they are interpreted in the spirit of his life, and less for what they are in themselves than as the outgoings of that rich and plenteous love which filled his heart, and the witness of that Divine Presence in whose overshadowing potency he lived. The divinity of Christ, as I have now explained it, cannot be proved by any logical arguments against which some sceptical difficulty might not be raised; but the devout heart feels, with a conviction which no hostile reasoning can shake, that his life and his spirit were filled with a pervading energy that could only come from God. It is not to be deduced as a specific inference from any one act or particular discourse or insulated event, but must be embraced as a general conclusion from our impression of his life as a whole, presenting us with a living embodiment of our highest conception of the divine in the human.

The true believers in the divinity of Christ are those whose hearts glow with a kindred fervour when they meditate on his teaching and his life, and who feel a virtue issuing from them which enters their souls and makes them better and happier men; they are those who are stirred up by his holy example to do like things and to live in the same spirit; who transcribe his moral image into their lives, and aim in habitual purpose and endeavour to be one with him, as he was one with God. By the multiplication of such hearts and lives, the whole Church will gradually become divine, and God, its Head and Founder and unfailing Protector, be all in all. Seek them not in noisy disputants and wrangling theologians, in narrow sectaries and intolerant bigots, in fierce contenders for a phrase or a form; but make wide your heart and your hope, and look for them in the pure, the upright, the loving, the truthful, the heavenly-minded of every sect,—among all, whatever their profession or their name, who earnestly cultivate the mind that was in Christ, who strive to render his spirit of truth and righteousness ascendant in the earth, who will enter into no compromise with falsehood and wrong, and, owning every man as a brother, put forth all their influence to draw out and foster whatever is divine and immortal in every member of the great family of God.

[Written, 1843; last preached (Little Portland St.),
2nd July, 1866.]

III.

Serious Aggregate Result of Small Sins.

—————

"He that is unjust in the least is unjust also in much."

WE are all too prone to overlook small things. What is great and striking attracts all our regard, while events of daily occurrence, though they make up the staple of existence, pass away unnoticed. An admirable foreign writer, in some recent pictures of domestic life, has well shewn how unnecessary it is to go to the adventurous and romantic alone for sources of the deepest interest—what treasures of the purest happiness, how many occasions of exercising the most exalted heroism and virtue, are shut up in every human lot—if we have only quiet and truthful hearts to see where they lie and to draw them forth for our use. It may not be unprofitable, as a counterpart to these very delightful and truly religious views of life, to point out another kind of blindness which not less frequently seizes the mind—that insensibility to habitual infirmities of temper and daily transgression in small things, which lulls us into the persuasion we are all that we ought to be, because not chargeable with heinous offences against God and man, although it is the aggregate of these petty sins which goes far to determine the ultimate value of the character, and disqualifies us for discerning and enjoying the many means of happiness with which every existence is fraught.

It is not sufficiently borne in mind that the distinction of great and small belongs mainly to our relative estimate of things, and can hardly be supposed to exist in the view of God—that the most important results flow from very insignificant beginnings, and that the mightiest agencies are the joint effect of myriads of minute and imperceptible influences. The earthquake and the pestilence which visit our earth at intervals, and sweep away thousands of human beings at a stroke, we stand in awe of, and put down among the terrible judgments of God; while we take no note of the silent operation of poisonous effluvia which may be issuing from the impure retreats of human misery on every side of us, tainting the very air we breathe, and converting the life of numbers into one languid and protracted disease. Some crime, into which passion or strong temptation had betrayed us, and which draws down upon it the condemnation and abhorrence of mankind, would at once reveal to us our frailty and our guilt; and against the frequent recurrence of such actions there is a protection in the deep-seated feelings and strong resistance of society; but sins against holiness and love, which do not meet the eye and thwart the interests of the world

—which prey in silence on the vitals of the inward man —may be persevered in with a callous self-complacency till the love of purity and truth is quite extinct, till the affections are all consumed, and the heart is hollow and cold, and the hideous skeleton that is left is only hidden from view in the decent clothing of a worldly respectability. It is with these pigmy foes to peace and virtue—so insignificant, when we look on them singly, that we treat them with contempt, but which attack us in the dark and weaken us by innumerable small wounds when we are off our guard—that the chief warfare of the Christian life has to be maintained. Some have thought the language of the New Testament, in inculcating the duties of constant watchfulness and self-denial, severe and exorbitant, and adapted rather to the circumstances of the first Christians than to the ordinary tenor of human life. And undoubtedly it has a breadth and a generality which require the qualifying influence of reason and experience in its application to practice. Nor, again, can it be questioned that they who truly love God, and have surrendered their hearts and wills to Him, will find their existence freed at length from every sense of constraint and fear and filled with peace and enjoyment. But this blessed state appertains to the maturity, and not to the commencement, of the Christian course in a world like ours. It implies fixed habits, settled views, well-regulated affections. It is the result of a discipline which not unfrequently must have been trying and arduous. If we reflect that moral excellence—in other words, the right tendency of our affections and endeavours towards God and man—has been made the condition of happiness, and that moral excellence is not a spontaneous growth, but must be achieved with effort and painfulness, in the subdual of much that is refractory, in the quickening of much that is sluggish, in the purification of much that is gross—if we remember that in the order of human development, "that is not first which is spiritual, but that which is natural, and afterward that which is spiritual"—and that amidst the crosses, temptations and duties of our every-day life this moral discipline has been constituted, and the qualifications for heavenly happiness must be sought and cultivated—we shall feel that our Divine Master spoke in truest accordance with the experience of every serious and thoughtful mind when he said, "If any man will come after me, let him deny himself, and take up his cross daily, and follow me."

Human amiableness and excellence have their roots in the domestic affections. A Christian household is the nursery in which virtue is best reared for its future duties in the world, and for the happiness which lies beyond the world. Whatever is purest and gentlest— whatever is most generous and disinterested—whatever is most delicate in the sense of honour and integrity, most refined in sentiment, most earnest and heartfelt in devotion—is the natural expansion and development of that sweetest and earliest affection which unites the hearts of parents to their children and of children of the same parent to each other, and which, springing up from the deep fountains of the immortal soul, overflows into the world, and blesses and sanctifies every other relationship of life. This is the divine influence which a Christian household should exercise on society; for home stands nearer to heaven than any human institution, even than the sanctuary itself. Here may the husband and the wife, from the permanence and intimacy of their relation, act on each other's views and character, and aid each other's spiritual progress; and here, in the cheerful discharge of their common and respective duties, prepare themselves and their children for the purer love and service of the heavenly Father. Here, in the spirit of mutual help and courtesy, and in thoughtful consideration for the comfort and happiness of their servants, may they nourish the dispositions and exercise the virtues which on a wider scale contribute to the well-being and improvement of society, and which, if every household furnished its due proportion of them, would speedily remove the worst evils under which society groans. But if such be the influence of home, how vast must be its corresponding responsibility! If such be the peace and the blessedness which it can yield, let us not forget that they arise from a thousand little nameless acts of quiet duty and self-denying love, that they are at once dispersed by the want of kindness and courtesy, and can only be preserved by a principle of cheerful piety and by continual watchfulness over ourselves. How much misery, for example, is inflicted on the members of a family, and what an amount of sin is actually committed in the ordinary occurrences of the passing day, by the outbreaks of an irritable and peevish temper! We are all so apt to offend in this way, that I shall be thought perhaps to have put the case too strongly. But how shall we estimate sin? Is not its very principle, giving way to our own ungoverned feelings, without consideration for others? and can we adopt a surer test of its malignity than the degree of suffering it creates? A person is vexed at some slight failure, some casual disappointment—it may perchance be the effect of his own thoughtlessness or want of punctuality, negligence in one sphere of duty being followed by its natural punishment in another: immediately—instead of bearing with calm and silent self-control the temporary interruption and inconvenience—he lets the influence of his ill-humour be felt by all who approach him. Every attempt to cheer and please is misinterpreted and repulsed with harshness. The kindest looks are met with a frown. The accents of affection fall unfelt upon the heart, or draw forth a reply of rude and hasty words. Gloom overcasts the social meal; constraint breaks off the cheerful talk; wife and child sit silent and sad; for the light of home is quenched, the spirit of heavenly peace is fled; and the author of all this misery—himself more wretched than the rest—incurs a double penalty for flinging upon others annoyances which he might have turned into blessings, had he patiently improved them. and kept them to himself. Now what can he offer in excuse for this gratuitous infliction of suffering? Will he allege the multiplicity of his engagements and the incessant occupation of his thoughts, which make him impatient of all interruptions? Will he plead constitutional infirmity, and say nature has made him what he is? These things are continually affirmed; and it is thought that such offences are venial, and do not detract from the general worth of the character; but it is in struggling with such trials of temper, and acquiring the mastery over ourselves, and causing the spirit of love and sympathy and kindly consideration to prevail over the fitful impulses of passion and fretfulness, that the moral discipline of our life consists—that discipline which strengthens the principles, and refines the affections, and fits the character for the benevolent purposes of God's providence. When any one is inclined to underrate and excuse these transgressions against the peace and harmony of a family, let him ask himself, what must be the guilt of conduct which thus wantonly strikes out so many hours of pleasant intercourse from the short span of human life, which stimulates into action the latent elements of discord in many patient and gentle hearts, which sacrifices without remorse the light-hearted gaiety of childhood, the unfailing trust and tenderness of woman's love, and even the faithful and obliging services of domestics, to the wayward humours of a proud, discontented, ambitious and selfish heart.

There are other sins, overlooked by the world, too readily pardoned by ourselves—less obvious indeed and striking than offences of temper—the amount of which, when gathered up from the silent records of every day, forms no unimportant element in the composition of a character—a love of ease, a study of our own luxury and self-indulgence, which makes unreasonable demands on the exertions of others, which expects in them sacrifices that we are not willing to share ourselves. This is a kind of selfishness which, disguised under a show of soft words and gentle demeanour, imperceptibly corrupts the heart and grows rapidly by being indulged. Such deference to our wants and wishes may be claimed on the ground of years or station, or may be spontaneously yielded by the affectionate respect of the young and dependent; but to throw ourselves willingly on these offers of assistance, still more to look for and exact them, and so to claim an exemption from exertion and self-denial, is a weakness which draws after it many evils—enfeebles the principle of duty, destroys the salutary consciousness of being fellow-labourers with the rest of mankind, inflates the mind with a feeling of self-importance, and gradually disqualifies it for the higher and severer efforts of virtue. Every one has his proper sphere of duty in the world; nothing should raise him above that sphere, and separate him from the trials and struggles that belong to it. By the kind but misplaced compliances of others, men are sometimes beguiled unconsciously into selfishness; so that while the language of flattery fills their ears, and all the outward marks of respect are heaped upon them, they are sinking by degrees below the moral level of the very persons whose submission and services they believe themselves entitled to expect.

If we extend our view beyond the circle of home into the world, we may observe a number of petty sins, the aggregate effect of which, though each individually is deemed almost too trifling to notice, tells very perceptibly on the value of the character and the general comfort and advantage of society. Men of talent and of many excellences have often been remarkable for a want of punctuality in business and for a general unfaithfulness in the discharge of minor duties. And they find many excuses for themselves; too readily they are often excused by others. They set off against these habitual deficiencies their great occasional exertions—the nobleness of their general aims—and the signal service afforded by them now and then to the cause of truth and virtue. But let us consider, of what is life made up? Of splendid bursts of genius and heroism? or of patient, noiseless, progressive efforts of daily wisdom and usefulness? Whence flow the order, tranquillity and happiness of society? By whom are the great designs of Providence carried into effect? The grand sum-total of the world's business is brought to pass, not by the irregular impulses of a few energetic spirits, but by the joint harmonious action of myriads of humble, faithful workers, who pursue the task set before them, and have no higher ambition than to perform it well. Compute the mischief and disorder that are oftentimes occasioned by one man's going wrong in the nicely-adjusted arrangements of human affairs. His coming up too late, or going in the wrong direction, or doing his work imperfectly, are failures which do not affect himself alone, but which derange the plans, increase the labours, multiply the difficulties, and perhaps hinder the success, of thousands who are connected with him. Every man in this life is so bound up with the interests of his fellow-creatures, that it is only by unswerving fidelity in duty that he can put away from himself the painful responsibility of having aggravated their sufferings and increased the weight of their labours. If we meditate on consequences, we perceive that these smaller sins, as they are considered, when habitually indulged in, are fertile sources of disorder and misery in the world. The noblest minds carry a spirit of high conscientiousness into every branch of duty. They make no distinction of great and small duties. They aim at excellence in all things. They will not tolerate slovenliness and inefficiency in any work which they deliberately undertake. Whatever is a duty at all, is a duty binding on them to discharge it well. They live as in the eye of God; and every task is executed as for His inspection and approval. When, on the other hand, the mind acquiesces in an irregular and imperfect discharge of ordinary duties, and sets this to the account of small and venial offences, it sins against itself, against its own peace and dignity, even more than against the world. It relaxes the effort, the watchfulness, the self-discipline, without which nothing great can ever be accomplished. It professes to be indifferent only about small matters, and to retain all its solicitude and exactness about those that are important; but habitual carelessness induces a general dishonesty of mind, a slurring over of distinctions, an easiness in satisfying the demands of conscience, which soon extends to the whole range of duty, and prepares a man for sliding unconsciously into violations of integrity, at the bare thought of which in the commencement of his career he would have turned pale.

In our intercourse with the world, to avoid giving offence, we are tempted to comply with established usages and conventional forms of expression, though we may not approve them, and though they do not express our real opinions. This is called an innocent conformity to the ways of the world in matters indifferent. But let us beware of the effect of it on our characters. Such compliances are small sins, the aggregate effect of which is very considerable. The habit of speaking and acting without correspondent conviction is of the very nature of sin. It makes life hollow and insincere; it perverts the understanding; it impairs the sense of right and truth; it withers up the affections; and makes the intercourse of men, not an exhilarating reciprocation of free and genuine thought, but a mere exchange of artificial signs, calculated for a given effect, and affording no indication of the real sentiments of those by whom they are put in motion. It is incalculable how much the little conventional dishonesties of our habitual intercourse corrupt the source of pure and noble feeling in the heart, and destroy that ingenuous simplicity of character without which true virtue is impossible. The surest sign of a commencing reformation of society will be a return to simpler manners, plainer speaking, and a more unreserved expression of individual opinion.

I have spoken of the accumulated effect of small sins on the character. There is another consideration often overlooked by us—the general effect of our own characters and actions on the moral condition of the world. We profess to be interested in the moral progress of our species. We express deep concern when instances are brought before us of the great wickedness of mankind. Does it never, then, occur to us to ask, What may be the influence of our own language and conduct on those who, as servants and dependents, are brought into the closest connection with us? If they observe that our words are insincere—different before strangers and in the free intercourse of our families—how can they put any confidence in us? If we forget the respect due from man to man in our treatment of them—if we apply to them harsh and degrading epithets, as if they were our slaves and not our helpers, born only to do our bidding and bear the arrogance of our temper—how can we demand the courtesy that we do not show, or expect to meet, behind our backs, with fairer measure than we have given? If we are oppressive and unjust in the pursuit of gain, seizing unfair advantages against the helpless and impoverished, extracting our very wealth from the poverty that crouches at our feet, how can we be surprised that discontent should prevail, and that wealth itself should be viewed with an evil eye? These are the influences of individual character which tell on the moral state of a community, and spread far and wide the elements of social disorder; nor can these general, diffusive influences, which are operating every hour and at every point, be counteracted and set aside by loud demonstrations of patriotic zeal or large donations to public objects. The money that has been wrongfully gained with one hand, will not change its character by being liberally dispensed with the other. Any tincture of injustice or dishonesty in our dealings with our fellow-men vitiates our whole relation to them, and is fraught with evil consequences, which no subsequent appropriation of the profits so obtained can rectify. If we never gave away a sixpence in charity, but at the same time never gained one dishonourably, our influence would be more salutary on the world, than if we distributed in profuse munificence the entire fruits of an unrighteous traffic. Nothing can compensate for the absence of strict moral rectitude. Men are tranquillized and satisfied by the experience of justice and humanity. Such qualities are the only source of mutual confidence and harmony. They lay the foundation of the social fabric, and without them it is vain to attempt the superstructure.

Whosoever allows himself to be unjust in the least, is involved already in the principle of sin; and there is no security that he would not, if adequate temptation and opportunity were thrown in his way, be unjust also in much. Christianity requires, that we surrender our entire lives to God, and aim at being excellent in all things. Virtue is not something extraneous to happiness, which we must cultivate only so far as is necessary to secure the favour of God, and then seek our happiness in other objects; virtue is in itself the source and principle of happiness, the sole means and condition of our present and our eternal well-being. Foolish, then, beyond expression is their choice who take up with a divided allegiance, and practice virtue by halves. Frail and imperfect, after all our endeavours, must our best service be; but there will be strength in a decided resolve, and peace in the consciousness of God's blessing. Faithful in that which is least, we shall best attain to faithfulness in that which is much; and having made a wise and honest use of the unrighteous mammon on earth, God will at length commit to our trust the true riches.

[Written, 1844; last preached (Upper Brook St., Manchester), 25th June, 1848.]

IV.

Quietness of Heart.

PSALMS xlvi. 10:

" Be still, and know that I am God."

THERE is a state of mind far more enviable than the insolent joy of prosperity or the wild ecstasy of unexpected success. We yearn after it amidst the agitations and excitements of a worldly life, when we feel the want of inward peace. Wearied with vanity, harassed with care, and sated with self-indulgence, we have a slight foretaste of its blessedness when we flee for relief to the Divine presence, and hear a voice speaking to our subdued and saddened hearts, " Be still, and know that I am God." This quietness of heart is the one great object of the wise man's earnest aspiration. It springs from the simple consciousness of having faithfully and unreservedly subjected our whole being to the law of truth and righteousness. It is the holy peace which brings its unfailing recompence to purity of mind and simplicity of purpose and uprightness of endeavour. Few indeed are they who habitually enjoy this inward tranquillity of soul. To most men it only comes at intervals, like glimpses of the distant heaven. The voluptuary finds it not in his weary round of palling gratifications. Not a feeling of it visits the eager accumulator of wealth, through long days of unceasing toil and nights of sleepless anxiety, consumed in watching the course of his vast enterprizes and hazardous speculations. You will not find it amidst the sharp-eyed, jealous struggles and wily calculations of the aspirant after place and political influence. These men may have what they call enjoyment, or imagine success, or clasp to their bosom as honour; and the multitude may envy them their prize. Yet if you knew the hidden secret of their bosoms, you could not call them happy. Inward restlessness and anxiety of spirit overcast the brightness of their outward day. They want the blessing of a quiet, peaceful heart; and ever and anon a voice comes to them from heaven in their better moments, "Be still, and know that I am God."

I enter no protest against a wise and healthy use of the good things of this world. The vigorous pursuit of riches and honours, and the hearty enjoyment of lawful pleasures, in the broad and open way of clear duty and high honour and human affection, I do not condemn. The hypocrisy which affects to despise them is as odious as the corruption to which undoubtedly they often lead. But it is the state of the mind within which gives character and value to all things without, which furnishes a sure criterion of their moral relation to us, and determines the extent to which they can be beneficially desired and accumulated. Peace of mind is the sole condition under which any outward advantage can become a blessing. Do your gaieties yield no kindly cheerfulness to your spirit? Does your wealth add no largeness to your heart, no liberality to your views? Does your ascent in the scale of honours make you no freer than before from mean and low solicitudes, nor inspire you with a nobler enthusiasm for the service of justice and freedom? Be sure that the one thing needful is yet wanting; and that without it, everything else, in whatever abundance it may exist, will remain but as a heavy, cumbrous instrument oppressing the powerless hand which cannot wield it. Do you, on the other hand, observe that, with your advancement in the world's honours and advantages, your heart becomes lighter and more kindly—your sympathy with goodness and your interest in others more warm and earnest—your admiration for things noble, beautiful and holy, a more intense and absorbing passion? You may comfort yourself with the reflection, that your life is in .harmony with the eternal laws of Providence, and that you are pursuing objects which a wise man and a Christian has no reason to disclaim.

Consider well the conditions on which alone this inward peace can come to you and abide with you. Its first prerequisite is, faith in the high purposes of your being, and devotion to God. Keep uppermost in your mind the glorious belief, that your whole life is surrounded, watched over, conducted and taken care of, by a Being in whom perfect Wisdom co-exists with perfect Love; and not in the way, be it remembered, in which rocks and trees and streams, and oceans and continents, and the wide realms of organization and instinct, are kept in their place, and preserved in their course, and held to their function—without consciousness and sympathy, without free response to the impulse which they have received, without any voluntary compact between them and their Creator. You occupy a far more exalted and glorious position in this universe. You can spontaneously ally yourself with God. You can freely put yourself into harmony with His laws. You are permitted to choose and adopt the conditions on which His blessing can be surely obtained.

Understand this privilege, and exercise it. Give yourself to duty; be devoted to right and truth ; and fear not. The world's sovereign law will then be on your side. The world's omnipotent Ruler will then be your friend. Though everything outward should perish around you, though neither honours nor riches nor success should crown your efforts in this visible scene, your mind will be safe amid the havoc and confusion. Its inward peace rests on foundations which nothing outward can shake. When sounds of terror pierce your ears ; when sights of woe pass before your eyes ; when your hands fail, and your heart faints, and you quake and shudder at reverses and calamities which seem to be overwhelming all that you hold dearest and most sacred—lift up your soul to God, and you will have peace. His voice will be heard above the storm: "Be still, and know that I am God."

There is always peace for the pure and upright mind. Men who are not thoroughly honest and true deserve the perplexities and distresses which they are sure ulti-

mately to incur. Under professions of regard for principle, and of zeal for human welfare, they are secretly
serving themselves and working for base and selfish
ends. Even while men applaud them, they have no
inward peace. Their world is all without. They find
but a blank at home. And when the trick is discovered
and retribution comes, and the tongues that were loud
in their praise are sharpened with bitter invective
against their detected falsehood, their woe is complete
and their disgrace crushing. There is not a place to
which they can retreat for peace and comfort. Abroad,
the world rings on every side with execration. Within,
they encounter self-reproach. In heaven they behold
an alienated and condemning God. Not so the pure-
minded and faithful. Their peace is found in conscious
innocence. From the misapprehension and prejudice of
men, they can appeal to an all-seeing Judge above. They
rely on His unfailing retributions. They are sure of
justice at last. That thought makes them patient under
wrongs, and forbearing under provocation, and gentle
towards the arrogant and the proud. Or if nature prove
too strong for grace, if irritation and resentment should
be gaining head and threatening to burst forth, they
hear their Father's warning voice, and are hushed into
quietness: "Be still, and know that I am God."

The earnest prosecution of some great object in life
preserves and cherishes a quiet heart. We might at
first view suppose it would have just the opposite effect.
But genuine earnestness is always quiet. Bustle and
restlessness are sure signs of its absence. When we
pursue an object for its own sake, for its intrinsic beauty

and nobleness, for the place which we see it fills in the order of Providence, or for some spiritual affinity which we feel it to possess with the impulse and fitness of our own souls, we are never uneasy and restless and dissatisfied. A moral spirit sobers and tranquillizes the mind in which truth is earnestly sought and right loyally served. The very effort and aspiration carry with them a secret joy, continuous and unceasing, which could not be exceeded by that of the most triumphant success. In all the greatest objects of human pursuit—scientific and philosophic truth, social amelioration, the establishment of justice and freedom, or the realization of some ideal of artistic beauty—we cannot but feel that, as the object is infinite, the complete attainment of it is beyond our reach; and that consequently the mere act of labouring after it, with some small consciousness of steady approximation, is reward and blessing enough for man in this life. It is the things extrinsic to the object itself—fame, riches, popular applause, worldly influence and dominion, tempting men to follow it with a feigned or divided homage—which fill the heart with doubts and jealousies and fears, and dispel the holy peace, where genius in its brightest moods, and virtue in its noblest aims, find their fittest abode. Thoroughly in earnest with its work, filled with some great conception, or intent on tracing out the laws and consequences of some vast principle, the mind enjoys a serene and absorbing quietude which the ordinary sources of human restlessness and anxiety, while that intense application of thought endures, seem impotent to disturb. Especially is this the case when a religious feeling exalts to its highest pitch the enthusiasm for art or science or the public weal; that high inspiring sense of immediate dependence on God with which a Fra Angelico or an Albert Dürer handled his pencil in the delineation of some angelic or saintly group, or a Milton or a Wordsworth exercised the faculty divine of immortal verse, or a Newton or a Herschel brought the movements in infinite space within the range of his observation and theory, or a Howard or a Clarkson devoted his energies to the redemption of the wronged and the wretched from helpless woe. In the prosecution of such glorious tasks as these, hindrances, enmities and jealousies, failures and disappointments, weakness, sickness, poverty — all may tempt and try and vex the spirit; but the great idea, the cherished purpose, the noble aspiration, still remains to animate and console. It dwells in the heart as a spirit of the holiest peace. To work with God in bringing forth the hidden beauty and beneficence of this lower world, in unfolding the ideas or accomplishing the results of which He has given the hint and supplied the incentive, but left the development and the execution to be the pride and the glory of man—this is a vocation so exalted and sublime, that the consciousness of it leaves no room for any mean and irritating feeling in the soul. Impatience and fretfulness, envy, discontent and fear, die away in that grand and solemn Presence. The best minds know and feel they are but journeymen under the great Master Artist of the universe. They work with His tools, and under the conditions which He has prescribed. They must await and obey His orders, and take the work as

He gives it them. Their support, their confidence, their inspiration, is in Him. On His breath they live. "Their Father worketh hitherto, and they work." In every rising of impetuous desire and outburst of passionate eagerness, they are conscious of throwing themselves out of communion with Him. Till that holy bond is knit again, they are powerless for beauty and for truth. The jarring of evil passions mars the inward harmony out of which all genuine inspiration flows. Their Father's voice recalls them to the peace which they have lost: "Be still, and know that I am God."

What is true of the most gifted and conspicuous, is true also of the humblest and least distinguished, of God's servants. If they do His work, as His work, with a full feeling of its value and beauty in relation to themselves, they will have peace. They will do it as unto Him, with fidelity and earnestness, and accept its outward adjuncts of worldly advantage, as they come, with gratitude, and in sure reliance on an unfailing supply of all things needful for the discharge of duty; but without impatience and disquietude. They will be still, and lean on the hand of God, and know that under all circumstances He will suffice for their peace.

Quietness of heart is further cherished by a spirit of love and sympathy. Selfish cravings and malignant passions are its greatest foes. Look into your heart. What are you conscious has been, and still is, the most frequent and troublesome disturber of its peace? Do you not find it in the selfish competitions of vanity or interest? in invidious comparison of yourself with other men? in discontent at your own position in society? in fancied neglect of your own merit? in jealousy of your neighbour's greater success in the world? in envy of his superior powers and more eminent distinction? Now, what is the sure result of this? You are gratuitously surrounding yourself with points of annoyance on every side. Wherever you turn, you come into contact with something that pains and vexes you. And observe, this misery is wholly of your own creation. It proceeds from your own diseased mind. If it were anything outward and positive, belonging to time and place, you might flee from it, and have peace. But you carry it within you; and wherever you go, there your tormentor is sure to be. Dismiss, then, these dark and wretched phantasms. Scatter them before the kindly, genial light of love, freely admitted into your breast. Feel that you are one of God's great human family; that brothers and sisters are living round you on every hand, assigned their several tasks and furnished with their respective instruments, to draw forth and circulate more abundantly the latent wealth and blessing of the world. Throw yourself heartily into their interests and their enjoyments. Make yourself one of them; and take your part among them cheerfully and energetically in promoting the general weal. Begin to serve them, and you will begin to love them. Cease to be anxious about yourself, and let things quietly take their course in the way of duty. Others, in return, will think of you; and the warmth of a brother's affection will attract and cement your hearts. A peace, a contentment and a joy, which you never suspected, will spring up around your steps you know not how, and transform the wilderness of selfishness into a blooming paradise of love. Oh! think of this human world, with its endless pursuits and manifold conditions and its myriads of toiling and suffering men, as under the guardianship and parental blessing of a just and merciful God, who through its varied scenes of trial and discipline and sorrow and sin is testing principle and fashioning character and ripening, in a thousand mysterious ways unsearchable by us, the elements of the heavenly world. And when its deep sorrows afflict and its dark sins appal your soul, do not despair; when its perversities provoke, and its ingratitude wounds, and its pride and its selfishness and its tyranny rouse and exasperate your spirit, cast it not aside with scornful indignation; do not retaliate, do not blaspheme; but remember God bears with these things, nor is deterred by them from steadily and unchangeably pursuing His purposes of love. Strive, then, to be perfect in mercy as He is perfect. From arrogance and deceitfulness, from hard injustice and oppressive wrong in the world, fall back on the peace of your own heart and on your trust in God. His voice will meet your prayer as it ascends and soothe your troubled spirit into repose: "Be still, and know that He is God."

This inward discipline will bring with it effects that abundantly compensate all the pain and cost of its acquisition. A quiet, loving heart clears the moral atmosphere, and disperses the clouds that darken the judgment and cast a chill over the affections of selfish and worldly men. Under the serene influence breathed through life by a sweet and gentle spirit, impulse is deprived of its disturbing force, passion is softened down into energy, and prejudice takes the harmless form of earnest conviction; the sentiment of duty comes forth in all its clearness and strength, and, sustained by the genial purity and tenderness of the affections, puts will in its true attitude, and inspires it with a prevailing tendency to truth and right. Life becomes less stimulating, but not more insipid. All its great interests remain as strong as before, to engage our sympathies and invite our exertions; but the sting of evil is taken out of them, and they furnish fewer provocations to ambition and jealousy and discontent. Life's darker shades melt away in the warm and sunny glow which the spirit's own brightness throws over it. For the world is the mirror of the soul. At one time it gives back the purity of quiet and loving thoughts; at another it reflects the troubled, racking clouds of pride and selfishness and worldly fear. Now first, when the heart is at peace, are all the faculties opened to perceive the greatness of truth and to feel the attractiveness of beauty. No more agitated by passion and distracted with care, the soul surrenders itself in a blessed repose to the holiest and most delightful influences; and when poetry infuses its harmonious imagery into the soul, or music draws out the immortal spirit and almost translates it to the spheres—when art displays its magical creations, or Nature lifts up her hoary mountain brow, and spreads the verdant carpet of her vales, and deepens her forest shades, and pours out her streams and lakes and seas in gorgeous variety before the raptured eye— owns in silent gratitude the benignant Presence from which all these things take their being and derive their beauty—and bowing down before the invisible throne, and feeling the soft breath of the eternal love—hears the voice that comes to it in grand and solemn accents from on high: "Be still, and know that I am God."

When tried and tempted and suffering—trembling under sin, conscious of weakness, and smarting from remorse—we enter our closet and shut the door, and pray to Him who seeth in secret, and unburden all that lies on our hearts, and cast off all false pretences, and strive to know and see ourselves the very beings that we are—when we lift up our hearts with a child's earnestness and simplicity to the Father, and remember His mercy, and throw ourselves on the riches of His love—we feel our fears abated, our hopes encouraged, our holy resolutions confirmed, our inward strength increased; in Christ's name we beseech Him to pity and forgive; and that voice of comfort once more is heard: "Be still, and know that I am God."

When the weight of advancing years hangs heavier on the drooping frame, and we see how soon we must lay down our burden in the grave—when death comes out more visibly from the dark, deep shade of eternity, and seems already planting his icy foot on this warm and living world, and human weakness would fain start and turn away in terror from that last, mysterious, unknown, impenetrable change—oh! let us take with us to the solemn verge of being the same quiet and trustful heart which has been the best reward of our faithful endeavours in life; let the consciousness of a Father's presence bless with its holy peace the awful moment of transition; and when the ear is closed to the last sounds of earthly joy and woe, that voice of comfort will be heard again: " Be still, and know that I am God."

[Written, 1851; last preached (Hampstead),
15th March, 1863.]

V.

The Unity of the Spirit.

Jᴏʜɴ xvii. 22, 23:

"That they may be one, even as we are one: I in them, and Thou in me, that they may be made perfect in one."

THESE words have ever struck me as perhaps the most beautiful, the most delightfully consolatory, the most richly suggestive, of the many beautiful, consolatory and suggestive words of the Bible. They express (so my soul apprehends and feels them) the fundamental truth of Christianity, and, through Christianity, of all pure, permanent and spiritual religion. They assert the unity of all spiritual existence from men through angels up to God himself. There is but one spiritual brotherhood above and below; we are all God's children; God is the Father of spirits, who in the broad page of universal history, for our comfort and instruction, has set forth Christ as a living type and exemplification of our human relationship to the Parent Spirit. Consciously or unconsciously—in open sympathy and sometimes through seeming antagonism—the soul of every true worshipper is formed in the loving, trustful spirit of Christ. For this cause we bow our hearts and our knees unto the Father of our Lord Jesus Christ, of whom the whole family in heaven and earth is named.

Were this spiritual unity perfect—did every conscious, reflecting spirit throughout the universe know its place and keep it in the great hierarchy of intelligences, and live and work in humble, faithful obedience to the laws which are imposed on its appointed sphere and particular form of operation—the heaven after which we aspire would be realized; the kingdom of God would have come already in all its glory and its power: as it is the marring of this same unity—the disruption of the grand, pervading harmonies of the spiritual universe, through the blindness of our self-will and the lawless abuse of our free-agency—which opens everywhere beneath our human world, that dark abyss of hell, into which all cold, unbelieving, selfish, carnal natures inevitably drop, immersed in a flood of soul-consuming misery, where they struggle in vain to grasp a blessing which they cannot reach.

To build up this spiritual unity from age to age—to restore it and complete it when broken—to arrest and subdue the disorganizing tendencies of selfishness and violence which threaten to shake it to pieces—is the proper work of the Spirit—the spirit of truth and comfort; that spirit which we are solemnly promised shall dwell for ever in the hearts of the children of God. There is no doctrine of Scripture more unspeakably important, none that has been more generally overlooked and misunderstood—and quite as much by the rationalizing as by the enthusiastic portion of the Christian world, than this doctrine of the Spirit. It is the full and clear apprehension of this doctrine which can alone unite us in a bond of living sympathy with the risen Christ, and keep ever open for us a direct approach to his Father and our own. This only can make Christianity something more to us than a beautiful tradition of the past—a present reality, a still existing fact, rich at this hour in spiritual blessing and strength to every believing soul. For the fundamental trust out of which Christianity springs, and of which it is only the most emphatic expression, is this: that this mysterious universe in which we find ourselves living and breathing, dim, evanescent points of conscious existence, is enfolded on every side in the loving embrace of a Parent Spirit, who permits His offspring, within these limits, for their own high discipline, the free choice of good and ill, but who comes with a directer aid and blessing to the souls that earnestly seek Him, hearkening to their prayers, and accepting their aspirations, and giving them such response as their stage of mental development will as yet enable them to comprehend. The law of spiritual intercourse is well expressed by James: "Draw nigh unto God, and He will draw nigh unto you." For God is no distant Deity, dwelling apart in solitary, unapproachable grandeur. He is daily and hourly in the midst of us, kept off from most intimate communion with our hearts only by our blindness and sin. He comes freely to all who seek Him. He is an ever-present help and blessing to our world; which, when we look upon it in the light of Christian faith, we cannot so much regard as the effect of a single act of power in the eternity which is past, as an ever-issuing, and from moment to moment unbrokenly sustained, product of His omnipresent and creative Spirit. From the impulses of that Spirit man's highest thoughts and noblest efforts —all, under its guidance, working together towards a common end—age after age proceed. Sympathy with God's chosen servants, as we can yet converse with them through their recorded words and works—the consciousness that we too, according to our measure, are labouring at the same providential task and are partakers of one spirit—is the most powerful stimulus and encouragement to perseverance in well-doing which our minds are capable of experiencing. This is that great and glorious Communion of Saints, binding together in one common inspiration the good, the brave, the truth-seeking, and the devout of all times and of all lands, which it is a privilege to be permitted to enter—that general assembly and church of the first-born, where God's elect are all spiritually gathered in one, and their scattered voices, mingling as they ascend, unite in a general chorus of homage and thanksgiving to the universal Father, sole Object of the final aspirations of all His children, sole ultimate Fountain of all holiness and truth. Of this inspiration, which takes up the human soul into living communion with God—this spirit of devotedness to God's service, of which the lives of all holy men and prophets are more or less completely an expression—we behold, according to my interpretation of the human histories of our planet, a master-type in the life and person of Christ—that final union and harmony of the human and divine which it should be the one object of our efforts and our aims to realize in ourselves and in the world. In all things it helps our human infirmity to have a glorious standard set before us—to see the possibilities of human virtue made real. Christ is to me the centre and connecting bond of this Communion of Saints. He sums up and unites in one bright focus those scattered rays of the Spirit which pierce everywhere through the thick darkness of the ages, interprets their broken lights and fragmentary revelations into coherency, and explains to us through the divine teaching of his life what is the purpose of man's existence here, and what is the future to which it points hereafter. The Spirit collects and effuses all its richness in him. Through him we enter into deeper sympathy and a more genial co-operation with those feebler expressions of it in the lives of holy men and prophets which from the beginning anticipated, and since his appearance have perpetuated, his great work on earth. By faith in him, by earnest sympathy with all that he did and taught for God's glory and human weal, we come into possession, according to our capacity and desert, of the same spirit which was "given without measure to him." By him, from the beginning to the end of the world, we are all made one in God. It is one and the same spirit which at last reconciles and harmonizes the warring minds of men. He in whom that spirit pre-eminently dwelt, he who was pre-eminently one with God, has broken down—if we only understood his words in their deep, essential meaning—the partition-wall between all our sects and parties and most ignorant divisions. He is our true peace. He came from heaven to heal our miserable schisms. He came, and, with words of ineffable sweetness and power, preached peace to them which were afar off, and to them which were nigh, that "through him we might all have access by one Spirit unto the Father."

Now this doctrine of the spiritual unity designed by God to pervade and bind together all things, is not an unfruitful speculation, but is fraught with the most valuable influence for our whole cast of thought and course of action. If by deep and fervent sympathy with that trustful and loving spirit which shone forth so conspicuous in Christ, we can make ourselves in aim and effort truly one with the beneficent Sovereignty of the Universe, how must the very consciousness of that sublime dedication of ourselves inspire and elevate our whole being!

Set out, then, in the very morning of your lives, without any lurking reservation on behalf of what is base and selfish, with a frank and manly determination to look simply for what is right and true in all things, and to make unswerving loyalty to those high interests your single rule of conduct. This is the only way to know God's will and do it. You may not find it at once, but you have set your face in the true direction to find it. Much nearer to God and His eternal truth is he who errs with a loving honesty and simplicity of heart, than he who sees more clearly, but uses that better light for a selfish purpose. Moral wisdom is comprised in two emphatic words—holiness and love. Holiness restrains, love impels. Holiness curbs and guides our inferior appetites and passions, subjects them to reason and conscience, and confines them within the limits which the governing law of the universe obviously prescribes. From the root of holiness the purest love will spring, stirring all our natural impulses and spontaneous affections into sweet and genial action, filling our hearts with the holy sympathies of home and friendship and virtuous attachment, inspiring us with a lofty enthusiasm for all that is glorious and beautiful, and urging us to put forth all our energies in the defence, assertion and encouragement of whatever is just and upright, noble, pure and true. To earnest and aspiring natures there is continually present an ideal of what ought to be as the sovereign law of their existence. As they dwell on it and contemplate it, it glows into clearer brightness before their mental eye, and it becomes the one object of their lives to pursue it—to do God's highest will, thus ever more and more plainly revealed to them, and at whatever expense of effort and self-sacrifice to bring up the dull and mean reality of life in themselves and in the world to the glorious ideal which they behold in God. This it is to work in the spirit of Christ—to be one with him, as he is one with God.

This, I say, is not a visionary, unpractical view of life, fit only for the talk of divines and the rhetoric of the pulpit. On the contrary, it is of all views of life the most directly and most obviously practical. It offers the most effectual means of overcoming the manifold obstructions and difficulties which beset on every hand our passage through the world. What must we all do to succeed in anything? Would you possess yourself of an abstruse science, you must give up your whole soul to it. You cannot master it with a divided attention and a sluggish interest. Would you become eminent as a scholar or a soldier, as a lawyer or a divine, as a merchant or an agriculturist, you must not be disheartened by difficulty or shrink from self-denial, but throw all your energy and enthusiasm into your chosen pursuit, and live for it; you must not cease from your exertions till you have surmounted all obstacles and achieved your object. But these are only inferior and transitory pursuits, subordinated to a grander and nobler end, in the view of a religious mind—valuable relatively, and to be prosecuted with earnestness so long as they engage us, but enduring only for a time, and to be abandoned when age comes, or competence permits us to relinquish them. A higher end remains for us, which embraces all these lower ends in its comprehensive grasp—the doing of God's will for the furtherance of truth and right, and for the bringing out of the endless beauty and goodness which are latent in all things, in and through those appointed tasks of duty which bind us each to our place and function in this wide universe—a work the very consciousness of which confers grace and nobleness on all the inferior works that are included in it and subservient to it—a work which can never terminate, which is imperishable as the soul itself, and will endure into the boundless future which awaits us after death. There is no happiness equal to that of self-devotion to a great and noble end. Success is not indispensable to blessing here. An earnest soul can never be joyless and dry. If we can only feel that we are working with and for God—that no virtuous effort will be finally lost in the grand issues of His universal providence—*that* simple consciousness will lift the soul above all that is mean and depressing in the sad experiences of the world, invest with an almost heroic grandeur the every-day warfare of life, and draw a holy joy, which calms and purifies the soul, from the bitterness of disappointment and the toils of poverty. A moral sickness sometimes comes over young minds on their first acquaintance with the deceit and hollowness of the world. They begin to distrust and depreciate all things. They doubt the semblance of virtue. They quench the ideal which a liberal education should have taught them to cherish, in the low and sordid realities which immediately encompass them. They close their eyes to a broader and nobler, and in truth a far juster, view of things. Not finding everything as it should be, they omit to balance the evil with the good, and suspect pretence and falsehood everywhere. They cast off prematurely the joyous and trusting enthusiasm of youth, and, unhappily for their own enjoyment and a right appreciation of the world, anticipate by many years the cold caution of age. They invert the natural order of the seasons, and turn the spring into the autumn of life. Now I say to all young persons, as you value the possession of a calm, a pure, a noble nature, guard against this cold suspiciousness of soul. It cuts the nerve of all noble and heroic action. It dries up that inner fountain of religious enthusiasm out of which whatever is best and greatest in human nature must flow. If it escapes some errors, it will miss the most glorious of all success. Believe in truth; believe in virtue. They are not shams, but realities. Do not think the world is stronger than God in the conflict with falsehood and wrong; and when you have once taken a course which you know is right, however it may be thwarted and opposed, feel certain of victory at last, because God is with you in it. Despair and distrust wither the best of causes. The world will take you at your word, and not set a higher value on any interest, however sacred, than you set on it yourself. If you love truth, if you honour humanity, if you think right and justice and freedom indispensable conditions of the world's progress and happiness, then serve these interests with such energy and confidence as if you felt that they could not perish; as if you knew that the eternal law of the universe was bound up with their preservation and their triumph, but felt and knew at the same time, that the God whose child you are, and the Christ in whose spirit you desire to live, had left that preservation and that triumph dependent on the fidelity, the effort and the self-sacrifice, of free and responsible men.

To be one with God and Christ through the power of the Spirit in the way which I have now described, not only cheers us under the discouragements, and helps us over the difficulties, of life, but pours a positive increase of peace and blessing into the soul. All nature brightens to the eye, all truth assumes a higher significance, all beauty is invested with a diviner glow, under this religious influence. To be one with God through Christ—think what that implies! To live in conscious and purposed harmony with the supreme and omnipotent Intelligence, through the spirit of love and trust and obedience—what a state of privilege is that! "For God is love; and he that dwelleth in love dwelleth in God, and God in him." What we need for the attainment of that thorough earnestness in all our pursuits which creates a pure and healthy relish of existence, is religious inspiration—the feeling that God is ever with us, that we are ever working in and for Him. Give man this, and he is equal to everything; he is above all sorrow and all care; he is strong for good as the blessed angels in heaven. It is the curse of a worldly, selfish, over-civilized age, that it will not, or cannot, give itself up to this simple, childlike love and trust, this unreserved and unquestioning devotedness to God. Take the spirit of Christ with you into the world, and you make every pursuit and enjoyment in it religious; you convert its whole sphere of business and interest into a living sanctuary of devotion. A few young persons, deeply penetrated by this spirit, and going forth into the world under the power of it, may advance the highest interests of their kind—may become, in their future spheres of action, without busy pretension or noisy display, simply through the silent influence of their sentiments and examples, reformers, in the noblest sense, of their country and their age—elevating its moral tone, dissipating its prejudices, healing its sorrows and redressing its wrongs—calling out into more abundant productiveness the seeds of good and beauty which are everywhere slumbering in the deep bosom of society—not backward, when occasion demands, to lift up a fearless voice in support of their country's honour and weal, and stretch forth, if need be, an energetic arm in defence of insulted freedom and violated right. Oh, my young friends, cherish this generous, this Christian enthusiasm! Let it not be starved out of your souls by the mercenary, self-seeking and paltry ambition of the world! You are summoned to a work in which the good and noble of all past ages are with you. Christ is with you in it. God is with you in it. It is a work which will bring you into vital contact with the greatest reality and deepest life of the universe. For what is more real, more living than truth, justice, beauty, virtue? Seize this work, I implore you—you that are now entering life—it is your honour, your privilege—and devote yourselves loyally and faithfully to the high duties and noble responsibilities which it brings with it. Give to them the richness and the strength of your ripening and your maturer powers. And when age at length creeps over you—when the eye is no more bright with the fire of youth—when the tongue is no longer fluent and persuasive as of yore —when the step falters, and the frame bends, and the hand is powerless for action—you will be cheered by the reflection that, while power was yet in you, you thought and spoke and laboured earnestly for the good of your kind. And do not suppose that your work is then done and your recompence already complete; do not suppose that the seeds of good which you once scattered on earth, you shall never behold ripening into a rich and glorious harvest. Look rather on these symptoms of bodily decay as friendly intimations that the old tenement is crumbling down to set the imprisoned spirit free—simple warnings,

seasonable and not unwelcome to the virtuous mind—
that the dark curtain of death is about to drop for a
moment on this fair, but fading and evanescent, pageant
of earth, only to rise again on a brighter and a more
enduring scene, where you will dwell for ever with
Christ and God—Christ in you, and God in Christ, that
all may be made perfect in one!

[Written, 1854; last preached (Little Portland Street),
8th March, 1859.]

VI.

Reciprocal Influence of Piety and Benevolence.

1 John iv. 7, 8:

" Behold, let us love one another: for love is of God; and every one that loveth, is born of God, and knoweth God. He that loveth not, knoweth not God; for God is love."

THERE is the closest sympathy between the religious and the benevolent elements of our nature— between the spirit of piety and the spirit of love. It is true that there is a form of religion which consists in fear; and fear is always associated with selfishness. A worship based on fear represents the lowest stage of the religious life; when men's passions are so fierce and strong that they are only to be restrained by the prohibitive threatenings of the divine law, or their regards to self, whether personal or national, are so intense, that it seems their chief object in approaching the Deity to secure for themselves or for their own people a monopoly of His protection and blessing. Man forms God in his own image; his religion is the reflection of his own moral nature: but when his worship has once been defined and fixed—when it is stereotyped, as it were, by sacerdotal authority, in consecrated rites and established dogmas—his religion then re-acts mechanically on the nature of which it was at first a living and spontaneous expression, and perpetuates by an artificial force into later periods of mental and social development those views of God and of His relations to our human world which belong to the infancy of man's terrestrial existence. As actually constituted, religion has too often checked the free unfolding of our moral and spiritual faculties. It has contracted instead of expanding—it has tied down instead of lifting up—the soul, of which it is, or at least professes to be, the actuating sentiment. Too often in this world men have become wise, large-hearted and noble-minded, in spite of the faith which they had inherited from their fathers. They must break away from their priest to render a free service to their God. Now love is a more congenial sentiment to the human heart than fear, and occupies continually a larger place in it, as man's nature grows freer and richer, and extri-. cates itself more and more from the superstitions and the tyrannies which darkened and crushed his earlier career. To this natural expansion of the soul, religion ought to correspond; and so the genuine faith of the heart and the conscience ever would; but the priest and the sectary interpose and say, "No; this is not my faith, the faith in which I have grown up, and to which I have habituated myself; and as it is not my faith, it must not be yours." Blessed, therefore, beyond all power of human utterance, was the mission of that heavenly Teacher who gave to our race a religion founded on that "perfect love which casteth out fear;" who repudiated in his whole life and doctrine that low and narrow selfishness on which the ancient priesthoods rested—and too many Christian churches, following in their wake, still rest—their strongest appeals to the human heart; who taught us to worship, in the one only God, a Father—a Father of boundless compassion and infinite benignity; who united all his followers in one great family by the bonds of a common faith and charity; whose new and special commandment it was, that they should love, as he had loved, with a pure, disinterested, self-sacrificing love; and who set an indelible mark on his religion, that it might never be mistaken through all coming time, in those memorable words, "By this shall all men know that ye are my disciples, if ye have love one to another." Whose soul has not at times been utterly wearied and worn out by the strife of theologians and the hostilities of sects— willing to take wings like a dove, and fly away to the wilderness, that it might be at rest? "Gentle and holy Jesus!" we are ready to exclaim, "where is thy spirit fled? Who has transformed it into the spirit of bitterness and persecution? Wert thou now to re-visit this earth, thou couldst not recognize the church which thine own love breathed into existence." Happily for us, the life of Jesus has been preserved, as a standing witness against his church. If we want to know what is true religion, we find it in the religion which Jesus himself lived; we find it in that spirit of love which filled his whole being—in that spirit of meekness, patience, humility, trust and self-devotion, which has drawn the hearts of all men in loving reverence towards him, as a perfect type of human religiousness — as the most beautiful expression ever vouchsafed to earth of a holy life and a noble death. *Our* Christianity is Christ himself. When taunted by human intolerance with misbelief or unbelief, we point to the Gospels, and say, "Here is our religion: to this eternal law of Love we appeal from your fallible and presumptuous judgments; and by its blessed light, in spite of your censures, we will humbly strive to live and die."

There is a profound depth in the apostle's words; mark them well: "Every one that loveth, is born of God, and knoweth God. He that loveth not, knoweth not God; for God is love;" and again—"He that dwelleth in love, dwelleth in God, and God in him;" "There is no fear in love; but perfect love casteth out fear; because fear hath torment. He that feareth, is not made perfect in love." He that feareth, cannot yet know the Father, as He is revealed in Christ.

How is it that we ever come spiritually to know God? to feel Him present with us as a living reality? Is it when the fear and the selfishness of this world lie heavy on our prostrate hearts? Is it when the folds of sense are bandaged thick around our higher vision, and we believe only in the things which affect the needs of the outward life, and we are oppressed with fear lest these should be taken from us? No; such are seasons when we have all felt that God was far from us; that He had shut up the light of His countenance, and left us alone in the world. But there are other and better moments than these (happy they the tenour of whose lives is made up of them!), when everything we see, and all that we experience, is felt to be a revelation to us of the spirit of a Father; when the grandeur and loveliness which surround us in creation—the many noble actions and beautiful lives which stand out to us from the page of history—the great purposes of social progress and human development which are silently accomplishing themselves from age to age and from land to land—the thrill of delight struck into our souls by every word of eloquent wisdom, by all true poetry and genuine art—the sweetness that distils on our hearts in giving forth and in receiving every gush of pure affection—the holy peace which fills the life in the faithful discharge of duty and the honest service of truth and right—when all these things are daily and hourly witnesses to us of an unseen Presence which inspires and ennobles and blesses our existence, and assure us with a depth of inward conviction which reasoning could never produce, and human words are inadequate to express, that the God in whom we live and have our being is Love; and our souls, expanding into sympathy with His boundless benevolence, desire no greater happiness than to be one with Him, and to work with Him in the promotion of all things pure and beautiful and good.

This spirit of love is the religious birth of the soul; it is the light in which we first truly see God; the influence under which we first become truly conscious of Him as the real and only Life of the world: for then it is that we dwell in God, and God in us. Every lingering shade of atheistic feeling fades away before this inner effulgence of the loving soul. Man cannot be the only or the highest thing that loves in this vast universe. There is—there must be—in it some great, deep Heart of sympathy, the infinite counterpart of our faint and feeble human love; for we could not be so moved and awed by unreality and deadness; and till we feel this —till we feel that the holy tenderness which comes over us at the sight of boundless oceans or setting suns or starry skies—that the strong sympathies which seize us when we think of human sufferings and wrongs, and will not let us rest till we have done our utmost to relieve and redress them—cannot be explained by any curious network of nerves and fibres, by any laws of chemistry or mechanics, but is a living breath from the Omnipresent Love, working unseen but ever active beneath the material veil of things—we do not truly believe; the cold inference of reason is not yet quickened into a living faith; God is still a name rather than a power, a force than an agent, an operation than a person. Christ is the incarnate love of the Father; religion embodied in act. How we should love God, and how we should love man, and how both together make up true religion, first becomes plain and visible to us when we look on that beautiful and blessed life, and take its spirit to our heart of hearts, and resolve that by it we will endeavour to live.

A few obvious conclusions result from the view that we have now taken of religion as the spirit of love, and of Christianity as its truest manifestation in the life of Christ. These conclusions we may reduce conveniently under two heads: (1) Benevolence is the best expression of religion ; (2) Religion is the surest guide of benevolence.

(1.) It follows at once from the doctrine which I have been attempting to expound, that true religion has its seat and source in the heart and conscience of men. The question is, not what they believe, if they have only used their reason honestly to know the truth, but how they feel and purpose and act. If a man does not feel the awful greatness and all-subduing mercy of God, if he does not embrace the goodness which shines out in the life of Christ with a love which touches his heart and influences his will and flows into his own life, his religion is simple judgment or opinion ; it has not yet become a faith. The use of reason is auxiliary to faith; its office is to discern and discriminate what the spirit gives, and to harmonize it with light flowing in through other avenues of the soul. It cannot create the religious matter on which it acts ; it simply chooses and guides, restrains and directs. Christianity is in deep accordance with our spiritual sympathies and needs ; and its strongest proof is the witness which it carries within itself to every pure and loving heart. Place the life of a selfish voluptuary, of a mean and sordid worldling, and the life of Christ, side by side—compare the maxims which govern the conduct of the one with the spirit which animated the actions and teachings of the other—and ask any simple, earnest, thoughtful mind, in which of them he finds true religion and discerns the life of God. His answer will decide the question, for it is the answer of nature itself, and outweighs in value the grave, dull arguments of learned divines. The same considerations furnish us also with a test of true orthodoxy. Christianity is neither dogma nor ritual; of these every man may have as much or as little as he likes, if he will not disturb his neighbour; but the words which Christ speaks to *all* of us, and which *all* of us are alike bound to accept and obey—they are spirit, and they are life—the spirit of holiness and the life of love. Weary me not, then, with the vain janglings of sectarians and bigots about believing a little more or a little less. Does God care for these things when the heart is right, and the mind has honestly striven to know the truth? Shew me the man whose soul is filled with the spirit of the Father—whose religion is love—whose piety breaks forth, not in anathemas, but in blessings—who thinks the life and work of Christ of more importance than the metaphysics of his office and person—and, whatever name he may bear, though the bigot may set the stigma of infidelity upon him, I am sure that I see in him the authentic marks of a true child of God, and a faithful follower of His blessed Son.

But if benevolence be thus the test of piety, piety is equally necessary to impel, sustain and guide the work of benevolence. Christian love must be distinguished from mere natural compassion—that instinctive tenderness of heart which is sometimes found in conjunction with a low form of moral character. In this crude state it contains the material of Christian goodness, but it is not goodness itself. For charity, like all other graces of the soul, demands culture and self-discipline to be maintained in a healthy condition and exercise its proper influence. Instinct gives the impulse ; but reason and conscience, under a deep sense of religious responsibility, must work out the result. The compassion of instinct is not incompatible with selfishness. It may be little more than a weak intolerance of the sight of pain, which gives and weeps as much for the relief of its own as of another's suffering; and when it seeks the excitement thus afforded to the feelings, and delights in it, it degenerates into weak and idle sentimentality—of all conceivable states of mind, the furthest removed from Christian love. Christian love works from principle, not from impulse; its operation is steady, thoughtful and continuous, not fitful and capricious. It sets a high end before it; and in the works of mercy which it prosecutes, it takes a comprehensive view of the position and destiny of the nature which it seeks to relieve, and desires to elevate and bless. It contemplates man as something more than an animal, a transient dweller on earth, that eats and sleeps and toils and dies; it sees in him the possessor of a responsible and immortal soul; and these higher considerations temper its sympathies and guide its efforts. How to do most good to that which is in itself precious above all price—how, while relieving the body, not to debase and enfeeble the mind—how, while lightening the pressure of poverty, or assuaging the pains of sickness, or helping to advantages which are not yet within reach of personal exertion, not to relax one motive of manly self-reliance, not to quench one sentiment of generous self-respect, not to chill by one passing breath of weak indulgence the spirit of resolute, provident thoughtfulness—this is the problem which Christian charity proposes to itself, and which in many cases it finds more easy to propose than to resolve. The soul outweighs in value the body; man's temporal condition is of less importance than his moral and spiritual state; yet soul and body are so closely linked together here, that if one is starved and wretched, the other pines along with it; and universal experience testifies that piety and sweet and holy affections cannot flourish in the midst of filth, disease and rags. There is room, therefore, plainly for a charity which finds its objects in the outward circumstances and bodily wants of mankind; but to do its work wisely, it must be under the guidance of a principle; and that principle can only flow from religion. What is called charity sometimes performs its functions in a very negligent and mechanical way, without one earnest thought or one glow of sympathy—merely to get rid of a troublesome claim, or to satisfy the opinion of the world. There is more of evil than of good in this; it is indolence, selfishness, blind worship of the world. The charity which truly deserves the name—the charity which is of Christ—distributes its silent blessing, as in the presence of the Sovereign Love, with tender and considerate conscientiousness, balancing compassion with reflection, ever looking on the relief afforded to the body as a means of reaching the heart and healing the soul. Permanent charities, which constantly outlive the zeal in which they originated, are very liable to be abused. As often administered, they bless neither him that gives nor him that receives. No thought, no feeling, no sense of responsibility, accompanies them. The cock is turned, and the waters run—whether to waste or otherwise, is not noticed or cared for: and thus the once living spring of Christian love is often turned into a hard and soulless petrifaction. So many mischiefs have resulted, so much improvidence and pauperism have been nursed, so many absurd usages and false ideas have been perpetuated, by this abuse of established charities, that it is not surprising enlightened men should in modern times have taken up the pen against them, and gone to the length of absolutely condemning all permanent charities and fixed endowments whatever. The rigid political economists have stoutly maintained this view. But have they not gone too far in the opposite direction? Is not their own view a narrow and one-sided one? Is it possible to meet the constant vicissitudes to which our modern societies are so peculiarly exposed, without a corresponding provision of funds to meet pressing cases of undeserved misfortune or inevitable want, derived not merely from the momentary exertions of individual benevolence, but from steady and reliable sources? The proper remedy of the abuses complained of would seem to be, not the extinction of the charity, but the improvement of the administration—awakening those in whose hands it is placed, to a stronger sense of their religious responsibilities, and giving them, under the enlightened action of public opinion, a clearer perception of the proper object of their trust. Our religious and our charitable institutions have both been injured in some degree by the utilitarian tendencies of the generation which is now passing away. Man cannot be made the subject of the rigid deductions of abstract science. There are feelings in his nature which cannot be brought within the narrow limits of logical formulas. Who can calculate his deserts? Who can measure the deep wants of his immortal soul? There is something in our irrepressible instincts which repels such hard legislation, and says it cannot be just: and when we look on the amount of want and suffering which political revolution or commercial failure are daily, through no fault of their own, bringing down on countless multitudes—on innocent women and helpless children, on young men whose prospects have been blighted for ever by sickness or accident, on old men who have survived their strength without having been able to save the means of subsistence from the gains of former years—we turn with a sense of unspeakable relief from the cold and heartless maxims by which we are sometimes told the intercourse of fellow-beings should be regulated, to the sweet and natural love of the gospel, which reminds us that we have the poor and the wretched with us always, and commends them to our compassionate sympathy and care.

There is an appropriate and beautiful connection between the Chrisian Church and all those institutions which have the relief of human wants and the promotion of human well-being for their object. The spirit of Christian love foresaw that there would be permament liabilities to suffering and want in this changeful and uncertain world of ours, which no extemporaneous charity could adequately meet; and that they whom such liabilities overtake might not be left to accident and pine away neglected and forlorn, it set apart and consecrated in the name of religion ample funds for the relief of poverty and the cure of sickness and the comfort of old age. And it was a beautiful provision; it has gladdened many a sad and a weary heart, in spite of the abuses which human ignorance and indolence have permitted to cluster round it ! Hence have arisen all over our land, and in connection with every form of Christian faith, the decent asylum, the comfortable retreat, the seasonable aid, the elementary instruction which has so often led to respectability and honour in after-life. Misfortune must not be confounded with guilt. Poverty is a very different thing from pauperism. Let us do all we can to diminish guilt and to eradicate pauperism : but misfortune no one can avoid; and poverty—such are the changes of life—may be the lot of the richest among us ere he dies. Shall we, then, in the spirit of reckless innovation, sweep away every monument of the benevolent forethought of our predecessors ; or rather—inheriting their spirit while we reform and modify their ideas—put the institutions which they have bequeathed to us, whenever they require it, on a sounder basis, and administer them in accordance with more enlightened views ? A very serious responsibility attaches to the administration of all charities. They must not be handed over to the careless and indifferent. They cannot safely be divorced from the vigilant supervision of a religious spirit. The work of charity is the proper work of the Church. Here its faith and its piety find their fittest exercise. The Church then fulfils its highest and noblest function when it breathes into its members the deep spirit of Christian love, and concentrates their earnest thought on the wisest and the most beneficent application of the funds which either the periodical zeal of the present or the permanent endowment of the past has placed at their disposal.

[Written, 1856; last preached (Upper Brook St., Manchester), 4th January, 1857.]

VII.

Life in God and Christ.

———✦———

Galatians ii. 20 :

"I am crucified with Christ; nevertheless, I live; yet not I, but Christ liveth in me; and the life which I now live in the flesh, I live by the faith of the Son of God, who loved me, and gave himself for me."

I SUPPOSE we all of us feel at times, however deep may be our conviction of the essential truth of Christianity, some difficulty in realizing to ourselves the precise nature of our personal relation to Christ himself. Those who make him perfect God, the immediate object of the faith and worship of their souls, and those who reduce him to a simple man, only somewhat wiser and better than Socrates, would they candidly avow their actual feelings, equally experience this difficulty. The old archæological method, if I may so call it, of explaining everything in the New Testament by a reference to the manners and beliefs of our Lord's own time, and by an unqualified assertion of the utter disparity between that first age of the Church and our own, contracted the significance of Christianity into a single though very curious chapter in the long history of the past—a chapter which told its tale, like other chapters, to future generations, and was then supposed to have fulfilled its task and to be closed for ever; and hence he was regarded as the most enlightened interpreter of Scripture who could shew that Christ's teaching and ministry, the whole life and action of the apostolic age, though intended to exert a rectifying influence on the intellectual apprehension of religion, had no affinity with affections and made no appeal to powers that are ever dormant in the religious constitution of the human soul. The exegesis of that theological school conceived that it had then most effectually accomplished its work when it could demonstrate that the proper meaning of words in Christ's age had no corresponding meaning in our own. Nor was this defect of immediate authoritative application at all repaired by insisting with a proportionate earnestness on the miraculous accompaniments of our Lord's history; for the miraculous, as usually understood, is something wholly extraneous to the inward and spiritual life, and does not, till something deeper has been infused into it, bring the living God at all nearer to us; as we may convince ourselves from innumerable examples in ecclesiastical history, where the miraculous, though sustained by an astounding mass of testimony, because it is conjoined with another doctrine and a different kind of life, produces on us no impression at all resembling the miraculous in Christ. I ask, then, What is it that we all recognize as divine in Christ ?   What is the central fact of his history, what is the great, distinguishing element in his person, which make that history and that person unique and unparalleled in the annals of our race ?   What is the real point of attachment to him in all creeds? What is it that, through endless diversities of utterance and under discordant masses of doctrine and usage, has ever with unfailing attraction drawn the hearts of devout and earnest men towards him, as the spiritual ideal of humanity — something more, something higher and holier, than an eminently wise teacher, and faultless exemplar, and most benevolent social reformer ?   What is it that we should feel was wanting, if we were to substitute any one of these characters, or all of them together, as an equivalent for what we now, dimly perhaps, but with unmistakable depth of conviction, comprehend under the vague expression of the divinity of Christ ?

I wish to say a few words explanatory of this solemn but obscure relationship which we feel to subsist between our own souls and Christ, not as a mere historical personage that has long passed away from the earth, but as the representative of a permanent reality, a constant interest of our spiritual experience. I cannot, of course, in the short space of time allotted me now, exhaust this great subject. I can only indicate a few of its main points and grander bearings. But would all religious minds more freely exchange their thoughts with each other, every utterance of sincere conviction might contribute to a more distinct apprehension of what it is that we mean when we designate Christ's person and work divine, and give it a more powerful influence over our hearts and lives.

Our first general impression in meditating on the beautiful record of the Evangelists is this—that in some way or other God was more immediately present in Christ, working in him and with him, bringing His fatherly compassion and mercy through Christ into living contact with the opened and relenting hearts of His children. Such an impression, even in its vaguest form, is one of immense moral influence, and fraught with endless consolation to all who can once distinctly realize it to themselves as a fact. That a Being of infinite holiness and majesty should transcend the limits which seemed to separate Him impassably from His human family, and through His incarnate Word, His sovereign Wisdom and Love made manifest in a human soul and embodied in a human life, should seek out, plead with, admonish, convict, humble into contrition, and comfort with the assurance of forgiveness and acceptance, the myriads that had gone astray in spiritual darkness, almost to the utter loss of all sense of their heavenly parentage and immortal destination—what an idea is this—how sublime, how exalting! Yet it is an idea that with all its grandeur lies close to the deepest consciousness of the human soul—the consciousness that we live only in God, that the moral law is His voice within us, that every availing impulse to moral renovation and moral advancement comes to us from the breathing of His Spirit.

Nevertheless, intimately as this idea is involved in

thc general religious consciousness of man, the capacity
to embrace it as a truth, in the full and developed form
in which it was presented by Christ, implied a great
progress, and marked a new stage in the religious education of our race ; and the manifold expression of it in
thought and feeling, in literature, art and worship, dis-
tinguishes by the broadest features of contrast the Christian from the heathen civilization.

In heathenism, Deity formed a part of Nature, bound
up with its order and subject to its destiny, having distinct names and an appropriated mythology and worship,
as representative and symbolical of its mightiest agencies
and most prominent phenomena. When philosophy began
at length to attempt the interpretation of its fables and
tried to find out their underlying principle, it resolved the
popular superstition into a vague Pantheism, which made
God and Nature one. Whereas the Hebrew Monotheism
from the first recognized a God above Nature and independent of it, its absolute Creator and Governor; and
so far above even His chosen people, so unapproachable
by their highest aspirations, that, except in a few brief
gleams of affectionate tenderness in certain passages of
the Psalms and the Prophets which anticipate the spirit
of the gospel, it seems to leave a vast abyss between
God and the world, across which His creatures send
their adoring thoughts with no other feeling than that
of His overwhelming greatness and their own utter
littleness and absolute subjection.   Other monotheistic
religions have made the separation between God and
the world wider still.   In Islam, the sense of His overwhelming greatness is so oppressive, that it seems to

crush the free agency of man and to convert religious trust into passive fatalism.

Too much of this jealous environment of the Divine Majesty—necessary, perhaps, in the first ages to give its full development to Monotheism and to protect it from the encroachments of Pantheism—has passed out of Judaism into many of the popular forms of Christianity, though the spirit of Christ and its highest expression in the beautiful language of the Fourth Gospel are so strongly opposed to it. Modern Deism, taking its start from the traditional ideas of the popular Monotheism, which are more properly Jewish than Christian, has wrought out from them its theory of the universe; a contriving Intelligence at the head of the great cosmical mechanism; a mechanism, which having been once set a-going in accordance with the laws of an infallible construction, the same Power which framed it, left to itself, and then dwelt apart, in no direct communion with the human soul, approachable only from afar through a long intervening process of secondary causation.

With quite another view, the Christian idea is that of a Parent Mind, dwelling in the universe which issues from His creative Spirit and is sustained by His omnipresent energy; maintaining a sympathetic intercourse with His human family, listening and replying to their earnest utterances of prayer, inviting them to a mutual friendship and communion, which it depends on themselves to cultivate or permit to die. With all Christians, God is the Source of the moral law, the Power to whom we owe responsibility; the Inspirer of the trust and the hope in which alone the soul truly lives; the infinite

Ideal of all that we feel to be noblest and best in our own highest thoughts. According to the Christian view, God and man are in immediate contiguity, drawn towards each other by the closest spiritual affinities—affinities which do not annihilate, but ennoble and elevate, man's free agency. To live in harmony with God and work out His will, ever choosing and following what approves itself to reason and conscience as best, and through the effect of ever-deepening communion, to rise up ever nearer and nearer towards His own divine blessedness—this, in the Christian theory of the universe, is the proper end and destination of man. And it is the expression of this great truth in fact, its realization in a living person, which gives to Christianity its distinguishing peculiarity and constitutes its divine power. Christ is not so much the revealer of divine truth as proposed to the understanding—not so much the manifester of the Divine character as an object for the religious affections —not so much the exhibiter of a divine example for the enlightenment of the conscience and the regulation of the life (though he is all this, too, beyond any prophet or teacher that ever lived)—as he is the setter forth, in his own person, of the true relation between God and man, displaying to all time in the light of history what should be the posture, aim and working of the human soul in reference to God, to effect that spiritual union between the finite and the Infinite from which all high virtue, all deep religion, all true blessedness, must proceed. To have witnessed, only for once, the possibility of such an union, is an unspeakable gain to humanity; since it reveals, as nothing else could do, the sublimity of its destination. Whatever proceeds from a life that has enjoyed such intimate communion with God, that has drawn so much nearer than we can, with all our strivings, to the Fountain of infinite light, possesses an authority, and carries with it an assurance, which human reasoning and mere outward miracle could never give, on all those deep, mysterious themes which excite the solemn fears, the intense hopes, the unappeasable longings of mankind. We welcome it, as it shines out through Christ, as a gleam of God's light cast on the darkness of our human world.

But this union with God—how does Christ's history, that epitome of our immortal destiny within a few brief years, shew us that it is to be attained? Simply by love, by trust, by self-sacrificing devotion to God's will. So it is that man gives himself up to God, and becomes filially united with Him, by the love of whatever is good, by trust in whatever is just and wise, by self-sacrifice for whatever is noble, right and true. This spirit of loving, trustful self-sacrifice, contains the true wisdom and blessing of life. It lets us into the secret of the eternal Word; it lays open to us the spiritual mystery of the universe; and gives us power to turn all its discipline into blessing, by shewing us why we were placed under it, and how it must be used. In the language of an old philosophy, which has influenced that of the New Testament itself, this spirit is the Divine Word which was with God from the beginning, and in relation to man's spiritual nature was God. It is the Word that utters the secret or theory of God's moral creation. This Word is the heavenly wisdom which dwelt in Christ, and took full possession of his soul, and made him one with God; so that he became, in the language of that same philosophy, the incarnate Word of God. And this same spirit, the power and wisdom of God in the man Jesus, translated to the heavenly world, and becoming there a purely spiritual influence, constitutes the ever-present and undying Christ of the Church —the ideal of our humanity—oneness with God, sought by faith and cemented by the Spirit—the spirit of love, trust, devotedness, self-sacrifice, binding together Christ's true Church in all its forms over the whole earth, and uniting Christians of this day by a tie of living sympathy with the Christians of the apostolic age. Yes, it is one Spirit, one divine Word, one Christ, which is working now as then in the hearts of all devout and truth-seeking men, making them spiritually one with each other, one with Christ, and one with God. This spirit of self-sacrifice, so beautifully symbolized in the Cross, by which we unreservedly surrender ourselves to God, and live in and through Him, creates the true life of man. Not till we forget ourselves—not till we are crucified with Christ —not till we have resolved to live, not to ourselves, but to God—do we understand the true glory and blessedness of our being. It is not we who live, but Christ who lives in us. The old carnal, worldly, selfish life is put off; and a higher life, a life of God, not growing up through the coarse roots and fibres of sense, but coming down on the soul through love and faith from above, thrusts it out and takes its place. We have resolved to live no more selfishly for ourselves, but simply to do what is right and speak what is true—to live for others, and to live to God. In that resolve once earnestly made is the spiritual birth of the soul, its translation from an animal to a heavenly life. And how beautiful the humblest human life becomes when it is thus consecrated by a divine affection—when simple duty and the service of others become its governing aim—when self-sacrifice becomes easy and even delightful because it is prompted by love! God himself—with no irreverence be it spoken—sets us the example. His omnipresent agency is a ceaseless ministration of service and love. He dwells in the midst of us as one that serveth. Nothing is too minute, too obscure, too insignificant, for His unfailing care. The most delicate fibre in the structure of an animalcule is wrought with the same exquisite skill and the same benevolent subserviency to the sovereign good of creation, as the most glorious of the myriad suns which swim in the unfathomable depths of space, and the planets which trace their mystic dance around them; and when we look on it through the observer's glass, minute as it is, we experience an equal thrill of wonder and awe, because we feel that the same Spirit of wisdom and love is working in the least and in the greatest of things.

To be one with God, therefore, is to be one with His spirit of boundless benevolence and unceasing ministration to the promotion of good. God calls on us in the plainest language to work with Him. Only our sin and our selfishness stand in the way. When we can renounce these and turn to Him with all our hearts, the barrier is broken that stood between us. His Divine love, no longer intercepted by the perversity of our wills, rushes in upon the soul and melts it into tenderness and contrition, and the long-lost affection of a child for its forgotten Father; and that spiritual change takes place within which carries with it a sense of Divine forgiveness and the earnest of acceptance. In his own life Christ shews us what it is to be a true son of God. Sympathy with Christ brings us into harmony with God. Participation in his spirit gives us a share of his own divine peace. It is this spiritual link through him with the unseen world—this life in God which he imparts through faith to his true followers of every name, and which makes them, however outwardly distinguished, all inwardly one in him—it is this, crowning and completing the effect of his doctrine and his example, and making them not a philosophy but a religion, which impresses on his person and his gospel a character strictly divine.

I may possibly be charged with mysticism and enthusiasm for speaking thus. But I speak the simple language of Christian truth. It may be thought, perhaps, that I am holding up a visionary and impracticable excellence to the imitation of men. But I am not conscious of advocating anything wild and dreamy. I would only have Christians reduce to practice the principles which they notoriously profess. I affirm deliberately that the spirit of Christ, which is the spirit of self-surrender to God, is the spirit of wisdom and blessedness. The very world of sense is ennobled by the spirit of self-sacrifice. It is most true that all things have been created for our use and are meant to be enjoyed; but they can only be enjoyed as they were intended to be, that is truly enjoyed, by self-control, by the sacrifice of undue and unfitting self-indulgence to the higher end which the sense was designed to subserve. By keeping this end in view, we perfect the senses themselves, render them more refined and exquisite, and treat them with the care and consideration due to all God's creatures. Bringing them under these restrictions into the service of the loving and the beautiful, we compel them to yield an enjoyment temperate and pure (such as Christ himself disdained not to share at the bridal-feast of Cana in Galilee), which imperceptibly melts into and mingles with the moral and the spiritual. It is true Christianity to seek after God and strive to work with Him in our whole life. So long as God was believed to be widely separated from the world, and the world was looked on as something essentially corrupt and impure, so long it was natural that religion and the world should be divorced from each other, and shut up in distinct spheres, between which, it was naturally thought, there could be no mutual intercourse. But now, when God has shewn us in Christ in how close and intimate a relation He subsists with every pure and noble soul (the purer and nobler the soul, the closer the intimacy)—now, when we believe Him to be everywhere immediately present and operative in His creation, the deep, invisible life out of which all things spring, and from which they draw their form and working and beauty—that separation ought no longer to exist; the secular life and the religious life are now fused into one. Men no longer retreat into the cloister, to become religious; they think they best display their Christianity by active duty in the world. Everything becomes religious in the habitual consciousness of the Divine Presence. All life has a nobler feeling and higher aim infused into it by this spirit of Christian devotedness and trust. The world is too strong for all of us. We want something of this enthusiasm, this heroism, this sublime poetry of religion, to counteract the low ambitions, the petty jealousies and cares, the sordid, selfish, mercenary tendencies of our daily life. What a change would come over our world if the great impulses which move it were practically to take a Christian direction! If our merchants and our manufacturers, for example, in their successful pursuit of wealth, would regard the social influence conferred by their vast transactions and extensive establishments, as, partially at least, a trust committed to them by God, improving the condition of their dependents, elevating their tastes and refining their manners, and bringing them into more genial and friendly relationship with their superiors in station and culture! If statesmen, renouncing the crooked ways of diplomatic intrigue and the low arts of a factious and selfish policy, would recur to the manly language of truth, and aim directly, in the spirit of Christ, at the great ends of justice and humanity! If professional men, seeing why God has constituted society and placed its members in various relations towards each other, would never allow themselves, in the fiercest rivalries of ambition, to seek their ends by one moment's deviation from the path of strict honour and simple veracity! If artists and authors, feeling the true worth of their vocation, would disdain to court an ephemeral popularity by gratifying low tastes and awakening ignoble interests, but would strive to breathe into men's hearts a love for whatever is pure, refined, elevated and divine! Nay, if the theatre itself could be turned, as some nobler-minded men have endeavoured to turn it, into a nursery of generous sentiment and the best affections of the heart, by vividly realizing to ear and eye the varied lessons of human experience in the truthful delineation of manners or in the high tragedy of passion and woe! This renovation and ennoblement of our great social movements will never be effected by appeals to the reason alone, by considerations of expediency, or by an utilitarian calculation of possible advantageous results. The change, if it comes at all—and come, I hope, it may, and believe it will—must come from the awakening of a new religious enthusiasm, from a new outpouring of the spirit of Christ, seizing with a divine fervour the nobler part of men's natures, making them capable once more of self-forgetfulness and self-sacrifice, and substituting for the love of money and the love of rank, the frivolous competitions of social vanity and the mean struggles of a worldly ambition, the purer and nobler love of their country and their kind, the grander ambition to serve God, and in self-consecration to His service to develope those fruitful germs of strength, wisdom, knowledge, beauty and blessedness, which are buried deep in the world of nature and the world of man, and which nothing but our selfish strife and narrow-minded prejudice hinders from breaking forth into unsuspected abundance for the inconceivable enrichment of our race.

All periods of rapid social growth, when evils long allowed to accumulate have to be risen up against energetically, and must be cast out, demand, and are usually accompanied by, an access of religious enthusiasm. Such was the period of the Reformation. Such was that of the Long Parliament in England. Such was that of the expulsion of the French from Germany in the early part of this century. Godwin, himself an unbeliever, has noticed the tone of lofty enthusiasm which was conspicuous in the great men who figured in our civil wars, and which has shed an unmistakable grandeur on the usurpation of Cromwell. It was the sense of something higher and nobler than mere material interests, something more authoritative than the cold calculations of a mercenary intelligence—the sense of allegiance to a Gospel that spoke to the divine and immortal in man, which inspired the thought, and gave eloquence to the speech, and made strong the arm of that illustrious age, and in spite of the errors and the crimes of Puritanical intolerance and intense political antagonism, has stamped on it a character of uneffaceable greatness, and associated with it the memory of some of the noblest efforts ever made by our race for liberty and truth. And so it must be with every age that would leave behind it any monument worthy of the love and veneration of posterity. The spirit of religion must endue it with the power of heroic self-sacrifice. Christianity, instead of having done nothing for civilization, according to the doctrine of some modern philosophers, furnishes the only principle that can give it power and impetus to throw off its cleaving impurities and to expand into a healthier and nobler life. Christianity, instead of having exhausted its resources and done its work, as some scruple not to affirm, is only now entering on the full consciousness of its sublime mission. The Cross must again lift itself up from the dust, where it has lain so long, trampled on by the irreverent feet of a mercenary and voluptuous age, and scorned with contemptuous indifference by a selfish and ignoble philosophy. It must plant itself once more on the heights of humanity. It must breathe a loftier meaning and a deeper soul into literature and art. It must inspire philosophy with a more religious aim. It must base politics on high theory, and convert them into the beneficent science of social well-being. It must go forth, as an angel of mercy, to the wretched, forsaken and lost, and bring back the wanderers to their Father's house, till over this wide earth there shall not be one spot on which the light of heavenly truth does not fall—one solitary corner so secluded in its misery, that the voice of the Comforter does not find it out, and bring to it refreshment and peace !

[Written, 1858; last preached (Church of the Messiah, Birmingham), Good Friday, 14th April, 1865.]

VIII.

ᴛᎥᒍ Ꭲᗼᩤᨦᕊᝤᨦᨡᨡᨦᨥ ᦉᗼᨥᥦᕊ ᨙᗼᨥ ᗴᗴᨦᖋ ᨥᨦᖼ ᗴᗴᔋᕊᨦᨥᗴᗴᨦ.

The Transforming Power of a Faith in Christ.

———◆———

Romans xii. 2 :

" Be ye transformed by the renewing of your mind, that ye may
prove what is that good and acceptable and perfect will of God."

CHRISTIANITY has constantly manifested itself
in two predominant types or forms, to one or
other of which nearly all Churches up to this
time are capable of being referred. It has looked for
salvation—in other words, acceptance with God—either
from the undoubting belief of certain intellectual propositions, or from the scrupulous fulfilment of some outward law of duty. This distinction has been especially
conspicuous since the Reformation, and it subsisted
without any essential modification under the philosophical enlightenment of the last century. The great
divines of that remarkable period employed their treasures of learning and ingenuity, on the one hand, in
explaining and defending—in rationalizing, as far as it
was possible—the old metaphysical orthodoxy; on the

other, in shewing that Christianity, when stripped of its Jewish envelopment and traditional adhesions, was nothing more than a pure and beneficent system of ethics, enforced by higher motives and a more perfect example. The former preserved as Christianity whatever the thought and feeling of successive centuries had accumulated on the primitive elements of the religion; the latter explained away those elements themselves, and left little as a residuum but the universal suggestions of our moral and spiritual nature, expressed or implied in the acts and teachings of Christ, and encircled with a mysterious halo of supernatural sanction. Schleiermacher first, at the beginning of the present century, in his "Discourses on Religion addressed to the Educated Classes," with that penetrating insight and decision of purpose which always mark true genius, demonstrated unanswerably that neither the orthodox nor the rationalistic view had seized the essential principle and real significance of Christianity. He shewed that religion generally, and Christianity its purest and most concentrated expression, was neither something to be *known* nor something to be *done*, but the assumption by the believer of a peculiar attitude of mind—a certain affection of the inner consciousness—towards the Divine and the Infinite, from which, once become habitual, a new and higher moral life must of necessity flow; and that this reverential, trustful self-surrender of the soul to God was introduced, as it is still preserved, among men by a strong sense of spiritual relationship to Christ. As the proper distinction, therefore, of Christianity, Schleiermacher substituted for belief in metaphysical propositions and for practical conformity to a particular ethical code, a certain spiritual affection of the soul produced by trust in and reverence for a person.

This was a recovery of the true idea of Christianity; and it is in perfect accordance with the guiding law of human intercourse and social development. If you wish to elevate your fellow-creatures, to breathe into them a higher tone of sentiment, and incite them to a nobler course of life, you will not attain your end by simply convincing their understandings—not even by imparting to them the absolute truth (supposing any man could be sure that he had got it himself)—nor by holding up to them an outward model of faultless excellence, to be imitated with scrupulous fidelity in all its details. How, then, must any one who goes into the world with the purpose of a reformer, who desires to infuse into it a new spiritual life—how, I ask, must such a person proceed? Well, he must touch men's affections; he must awaken their interest and their sympathies; he must command their reverence; he must inspire them with trust in himself. He must reveal to them, in his own character and working, a view of life, a meaning in existence, of which, though they might never yet have dreamed of it, as soon as it is thus set vividly before them they at once perceive the justness, the beauty and the truth; some higher conception of man's duty and capacity, which, though a few dim glimpses of it might at times have flitted across their minds, they would never themselves have realized, and still less have attempted to put in practice, till they saw the possibility demonstrated in action. They must feel that the truth thus brought home to them is so great and deep a truth, that they are willing to put their confidence in him who thoroughly and consistently exemplifies it. They must reverence him, and believe in him, not from blind, irrational credulity, but for the best of all reasons—because they feel that the sympathy which unites them with him comes from the soul itself, and is based on a reality which they cannot doubt—because they are sure that the path in which they see him so much in advance of themselves, is the path of right and truth—and therefore, though he may take some steps and utter some words which they do not, and at present perhaps could not, fully comprehend, this will not weaken their faith in him—because they feel profoundly, through that unmistakable sympathy which unites all pure and honest natures, that these obscurer points in his conduct and language where their intellects cannot yet follow him, are nevertheless connected by the closest moral ties with those fundamental principles of his life which they *do* understand, and of which they have from their own personal experience the strongest assurance. It is this vast moral strength, conveyed to them by the confidence and devotion of thousands, who can believe in virtue and truth when brought home to them in a genuine form, which enables great and good men to carry forward multitudes of their fellow-creatures, by the power of an honest sympathy, to a state of moral, social and spiritual advancement, which they could very imperfectly have imagined, and still less perfectly have wrought out for themselves. How often in moments of doubt and despondency have we not longed for some authoritative voice to disengage the truth that is lurking among our deepest thoughts, from the perplexities and scepticisms which have entangled it—to bring out clear and full what we know is there, but what we cannot perfectly realize to ourselves, what we cannot as yet adequately express! How constantly do we wish that some great and powerful character would arise, to collect and embody the vague and uncertain aspirations of our time; by the force of an heroic example and a mighty will, to electrify our feeble volitions and torpid endeavours—to shew us in his life what is truly noble and divine in our humanity; and by the attractive force that ever inheres in true greatness of soul, to lift us out of the feebleness and the fear, the servility and the selfishness, in which we find ourselves languishing! The absence of great personalities to inspire the popular heart with trust and loyalty, to take up and put in train for wise and peaceable execution those vague hopes and desires of a better state of things which are floating without form or definite purpose through all men's minds—this is the marked and startling deficiency of our age.

Such trust in some great personal embodiment of eternal truth we pre-eminently need in the case of religion; some visible presence on earth, to interpret for us what is dimly working in our souls, to give strength and permanence to trusts which we could hardly sustain into life, if they were left wholly to our own unaided weakness. Here are we on earth; and the great God is above us in heaven. We want the power and stimulus of some human life that shall bring Him near to us; that shall express in the unfading lines of history the true relation between us and Him; that shall bridge over the awful chasm which separates the human and the divine.

Such seems to me the spiritual significance of the person of Jesus Christ; and it is necessary to its producing the designed effect of faith in our souls, that we should look on it as a typical expression of human religiousness—of the true relation between God and man. What we have, therefore, to consider in Jesus Christ, viewed as the spiritual Redeemer and Saviour of mankind, is not solely his outward life, holy and loving as it was, nor the doctrines which he delivered immediately to his countrymen, solemn and glorious as were the truths involved in them, but the inward principle working at the centre of his moral being, which pervaded that life and inspired those doctrines, and imbued them with a quality truly divine. Now, that principle was entire self-surrender to God, drawing after it such intimate communion between them, that it justified the words which would else have been irreverent and presumptuous: "I and my Father are one."

Right and wrong present themselves as possible alternatives to all human minds. They must have stood before the moral consciousness of Christ, as they stand before our own: his pre-eminence lay in the absolute choice of right as claimed from him by love and devotedness to God. The divine purity which enters into all our conceptions of his character, consisted not in exemption from our temptations and trials, but in the constant ascendancy of a holy purpose and a devout affection which overcame them. Had he been spared the temptation, or had he yielded to it, in either case his example would not have been complete. Would we, then, be like him, would we attain to his holy peace, his insight into things divine, we must be drawn by sympathy and reverence within the transforming influence of the Spirit that dwelt in him ; we must get at the formative principle, and then the effect will follow of course. We shall then learn that sin is to be expelled and the world vanquished, not by reasoning with ourselves, not by the painfully conscious endeavour to conform our actions and habits to the rigid rule of the most perfect outward example, but by self-forgetfulness, self-renunciation, entire self-surrender to God, entire, even joyful, readiness to do and suffer all things for the pure love that we bear to Him. Not that a strenuous exertion of the will can ever be escaped. Christ himself did not pass out of the unconscious innocence of childhood into the toils and struggles of manhood, without the intervention of that solemn scene of the temptation—without a clear consciousness of the alternative which lay before him—without decisive choice and resolute determination. But the victory then achieved over the powers of darkness, the absolute unreservedness with which, from that critical turning-point in his spiritual existence, he gave himself up to God and God's work, assured his future strength and future peace, and put him in full possession of the spirit which vanquished self, the world and sin. In this self-devotion to God, he stands forth to the eye of all time as the highest type of religious humanity, irrespective of class, condition or sex, of age or nation ; he reveals to us the end of man, and the conditions of its attainment. His Jewish parentage and citizenship furnished only the outward form and vehicle through which that diviner, that universal life expressed itself to human sense, and found its fitting place in history. If the truth which it speaks to us had been conveyed in a more abstract utterance, its impression on our moral nature would have been less deep and lasting. There would have been less for our sympathies and our affections to lay hold of. It is this close involution of the divine with the human and historical—the sense of living fact which it brings home to us—its breaking forth upon us through the clouds and the sunshine of our daily experiences, now gleaming through the joyous festivities of domestic life, and now throwing a shadow of holier sadness on our human griefs, which makes the beautiful history of Christ so refining and elevating in its influence on the soul; which touches within us something that we feel cannot be of earth; which gives substance to the fleeting and reality to the ideal, and makes us sure that we are here not dealing with speculation, but reposing on truth. What we have all of us a thousand times experienced in a work of fiction from the presentment of some noble and beautiful character, amidst scenes which display its purity, its integrity and its heroism, in contrast with the vileness, the falsehood and the selfish cowardice of the world—how our hearts go forth involuntarily to greet it with our reverence and our sympathy, how we dwell with almost a personal affection on those sweet images of human goodness, that reflection of what is divinest in our humanity

—this same experience comes to us when we read with open heart and reverent trust the history of Christ, but in an infinitely higher degree—because in that history we feel that we are contemplating a reality, the highest reality ever witnessed on earth—a reality heightened in its effect upon us by the hallowed associations which the worship of ages has gathered round it, and rendered still more solemn and affecting by the consciousness that here, if ever, at this culminating point of human history, the great Father of mankind entered into most intimate communion with our race, came down and dwelt in the midst of His human family, and laid the foundation of a new spiritual creation in their souls!

In Christ, then, we see no mere legislator for the intellect, whose enactments are to subsist in fixed and immutable forms for all coming time; no simply model man, as some pedantic precisian might conceive him, whose outward sayings and doings were to imprint their peculiar image on our own; but the embodiment of a spirit of love, trust, devotedness, of oneness of will and endeavour with God, sending out a strong attraction for whatever is of kindred nature in us, and binding our souls through affection and sympathy in intimate union with itself. Thus faith in Christ, sympathy with him, the cordial acceptance and appropriation of his spirit as something divine, something which unites us with God—the resolution of our self-will and worldliness and carnality into the simplicity and sweetness and heavenly-mindedness of his life—put us, so far as we have real sympathy and communion with him, into the same relation towards God as he stands in himself;

and his spirit taking possession of our souls, redeems them from evil, transforms them by faith and love, and reconciles them to God. Historically speaking, Christ seems at a great distance from us; and we approach him through the sometimes dark and tangled avenues of an antique and fragmentary narrative. But the link which really unites us with him is this spiritual sympathy; and it is a link which nothing can break. The divine affection which knits together kindred natures, transcends all intervals of space and time. It demands nothing but a medium of intelligence; and that medium from age to age it finds in literature. The wires of history are stretched by God's own hand in all directions across our planet, to circulate the living fire from generation to generation, and from land to land. The written gospel takes us to Christ; and what thrills and subdues the devout heart in the gospel record of his life, is the remembrance which it awakens in us of his surpassing love for men, of his suffering and self-sacrifice for their good, of his compassion for those whom the more favoured members of the human family had cast off and forgotten, of God's conveying to all of us such precious messages of peace and mercy and forgiveness through him. There is something in a mission and character like this which at once engages our best and holiest feelings in its behalf. As soon as they are presented to us, we perceive that there is an inherent divinity in them; for they bear with a healing influence on the deepest woes of human life, and exhibit precisely that kind of agency which we should expect the benevolent Father of mankind to employ for the succour and relief of His children. It is through the holiest of human efforts and the divinest of human charities that God speaks directly to our hearts, and gives evidence that He is with us still, even in the midst of this wicked and suffering world.

But let the meaning of these words be rightly understood. Faith in Christ is not mere sentiment—a passive self-abandonment to compassionate emotions and devout sensibilities. True faith demands an earnest determination of the moral nature, with a fixed attitude of the will, followed by corresponding practice; conflict with all wrong, resolute adherence to whatever is seen to be right. It rises out of weakness into strength; it begins in most men with an effort, a struggle; it terminates in the serenest peace. It is the unquestioning relinquishment of all personal ends and selfish gratifications, when forbidden by the higher claims of love and truth; it is to keep the spiritual eye sincerely open, not sealed in selfish apathy or soulless prejudice, but ever quick to discern whatever new demands God may see fit to make on our exertion and our self-sacrifice; it is to live to Him and for Him, ungrudgingly and fearlessly, in the full persuasion that he who follows truth wherever it may lead, and does the right and honest thing, whatever it may cost, is fulfilling the appointed end of his being; and that whoever pursues this loyally and devotedly, must be in the sure way to eternal peace and blessedness.

And let no one say that such a faith is unsuited to a world like ours—that it is visionary and impracticable. This is the faith for which our world is now secretly yearning; the want of which leaves it faint and sick at heart, miserable and wicked as it is. It is the very word of truth which the world is waiting to hear. It is the word of command which thousands are ready to obey, could only a voice be found strong and bold enough to give it utterance. This world will never be emancipated and transformed till a few earnest and believing souls, brave in the consciousness of God's sustaining Spirit, resolve to keep terms no longer with the conventional folly and falsehood, and the old traditional unrighteousness, by which it has been held in bondage so long. With all our profession of Christianity, there is a profound and deadly unbelief eating away the inward soul of humanity. There can be no real Christianity without belief in goodness and in truth; and we do not believe, because we have not the moral conditions of belief. True faith cannot co-exist with a want of genuineness and reality in the inward man. Would we give up our selfishness and our pride, our worldly ambition and our idolatrous worship of wealth for wealth's sake—would we return to the simplicity of true men, "transformed by the renewing of our minds" in the spirit of Christ—we should get the right point of view for comprehending this mysterious universe, and the faith would come to us which is wanted for its interpretation. We should first endeavour to dispose of the difficulties which encumber the present life—the dark and terrible realities which stare us in the face here—for a Christian's view of social duties is a clear and simple, because it is a moral, one. He has only to ask himself what is right and true, and do it and say it. To which of our great social interests, diseased and crippled as they all now are—our politics, our commerce, our literature, our domestic relations, and our religious institutions—to which of them, I say, would not the spirit of Christ, could we only bring it back in its genuineness, apply at once a healing and corrective touch? And when we have swept away from this world some of those foul enormities which now darken and defile it, we shall look forward with a clearer ken to the brighter world which lies beyond it, and find in the latent worth and nobleness and capacity of our race the justification of more exalted hopes and a sublimer trust.

[Written, 1859; last preached (Upper Brook St., Manchester), 3rd January, 1869.]

IX.

Compensations for the Sacrifice of the World to Principle and Conscience.

Matthew xix. 27:

"Then answered Peter and said unto him, Behold, we have forsaken all, and followed thee; what shall we have therefore?"

EVERY one must have noticed that the paths of a high-souled uprightness and of worldly success do not always run side by side. It is only the coarser virtues of prudence, industry and common honesty, of which we can uniformly affirm that, so far as they go, they yield a sure and certain return of worldly advantage. The actual and the ideal—what is and what ought to be—are rarely in perfect harmony. Those simple-minded Galilean believers soon found that it was no slight sacrifice to have attached themselves to the cause of Christ. Yet they did not repent of their choice. It was in no spirit of distrustful regret that they said, "Lord, we have left all to follow thee." And so it must ever be with those who would live to

the highest ends of their being. There is no middle
course. There is no dividing of allegiance between God
and the world. If principle be worth anything, if conscience be the greatest of spiritual realities, it should
hold out to the last extent of the demand made upon it.
It should not break when tested by a heavier strain.
We reverence such faithfulness, even when we fall below
it ourselves. With what profound sympathy, with what
spiritual profit, do we read of all the great examples of
self-devotedness to a high duty—of the simple truthfulness and fidelity of the first Christians—of the unbending
constancy of the Protestant martyrs—of the calmer, but
not less noble, heroism with which the best of men in
more civilized periods have relinquished the prizes of
the world, and even broken their social ties, to bear
an honest witness to the truth, to fulfil some stern but
imperative obligation, and to give impulse and strength,
by their personal loss and suffering, to the sacred cause
of humanity! Efforts and sacrifices like these, when
they are striking and splendid, stand out in characters
of light from the page of history, and seem to receive a
kind of posthumous compensation in the lasting homage
of mankind. But true virtue seeks not human praise.
There are innumerable cases akin to these, hidden from
the general eye in the obscure depth of private life, of
which the world hears nothing and knows nothing—
cases of quiet, silent, cheerful self-sacrifice to the conviction of what is highest and best, whose recompence
is wholly within, bound up in the steadfast trust that
all faithfulness to duty carries with it the sympathy
and blessing of an all-seeing Father in heaven. Some

minds perversely delight in dwelling on the wickedness of the world. Could we know all that is going on around us, were many a secret history laid open, we should perhaps find more virtue than we are aware of to set off against it. In the worst times there have ever been some pure and noble souls who have renounced without a murmur the paths of worldly advancement, because they felt they could not walk in them with perfect uprightness, who have preferred obscurity and neglect to compromise with the high principle of un-swerving allegiance to God. How beautiful was that life-long sacrifice—known but to a few, till death per-mitted its disclosure—of a richly-gifted writer in the last generation, fitted by temperament to enjoy with exquisite relish the refinements and elegancies of the most cultivated circles, who gave up everything—love, ambition, fame—that in an humble sphere he might pro-vide a home for one whom Providence had specially confided to his care, and shelter a sister's shattered mind from the shocks and blows of a scornful world! By the side of a life thus unostentatiously converted into one long act of self-sacrificing love, how poor and mean seem all our bustling philanthropy and noisy zeal, eva-porating on the platform and exhausted in a subscription list! We have known men who thwarted their natural bias and strongest predilections, and applied themselves resolutely to a difficult and distasteful employment, simply to fulfil, at this painful cost, some claim of honour and conscience which they felt rested on them. Others, at the bidding of the voice within, have relin-quished blessings dearer still, and have borne in silence through life the deep sorrow of an attachment that might have made them happy, had not duty, calling in an opposite direction, prohibited its avowal. If we turn to the other sex, how many a woman of the highest accomplishment, qualified by nature to throw the brilliant lights of her intellect and fancy on the speculations of the wise and the refined discussions of the tasteful and cultivated, when drawn by marriage into another and a higher sphere, has firmly resisted the incompatible attractions of promiscuous society, renounced without a sigh the gay circles where she was accustomed to shine, and consecrated to the rearing of immortal spirits and the culture of a preparatory heaven on earth, those special gifts which less conscientiously applied might still have glittered with cold, unfruitful lustre through a wider sphere!

In all such cases we witness a true Christian virtue. There has been a sacrifice of the world to something higher than the world. There has been a preference of duty to selfish inclination. They have left all—all at least that the world considers of value—to follow Jesus. The question naturally arises, which fell from the lips of Peter, "What shall they have therefore?" Is it all pure loss? Do they give up the world, and get nothing —nothing but words and vain fancies—in return? Have they relinquished the substantial for the imaginary? Are the children of this generation laughing in secret at the folly of their choice? Is there no compensation? Is there no reality in the mind itself, or within the range of its still subsisting interests and satisfactions, to set off against the distinctions that are forbidden, and the riches that are withheld, and the ease and luxury that are denied, by a renunciation of the world for God? This is a great question, which we must all ask ourselves some time or other. On rightly putting and rightly answering it depends no small portion, not only of the true wisdom and moral greatness of the individual life, but of the progress of the world at large in knowledge and freedom and true happiness. If we are prepared to act on principle, and to do what we are convinced is right, at all cost, even though what are deemed the prizes of life must be relinquished in consequence, what remains when these are gone? Often, it must be confessed, to the eye of the worldly, absolutely nothing— nothing that makes life, in their estimate of things, worth possession: a lowly position, a life of toil, narrow means, the neglect, perhaps the contempt, of the aspiring and the vain. Are you prepared for an alternative like this? In the face of the world, it requires some courage to say, Yes. Take it, however, with all that it may possibly involve; you know the worst in regard to this world; and then see what God may have in reserve for you if you are determined to be a true and honest man.

It is impossible for any one to sink into utter misery so long as he is conscious of striving to act out the supreme law of his being. The perfection of every nature consists in its effectual working towards its appointed end. Man was framed to co-operate in his aspirations and endeavours with the Sovereign Wisdom and Love. This is his distinguishing function, and conscience is the indwelling law which guides him in executing it. In the consciousness of tending towards this end and of conforming to this law, there is a sense of fulfilled obligation and of quiet self-respect, a peace within, which no accumulation of outward advantages, no gratification of selfish desires and worldly ambition, can possibly replace, and which, though it may not take the name of happiness, no man actually possessing it would deliberately exchange for what is called happiness. Painful effort, constant watchfulness, sharp thwarting of strong inclination, may be among the conditions of keeping hold of it; yet in spite of all, the earnest and awakened soul clings to it as its chief good. Nay, it may even be clearly seen that the pains which have to be endured, and the sacrifices which must be made, are the consequence of a social tyranny and injustice that ought not to be. Still, they are not shrunk from and declined. It is through the willing self-sacrifice of His faithful servants that God achieves His highest purposes. There can be no greater honour for man than to work with God for the overthrow of whatever is evil and wicked. The noble mind accepts the task, however painful and severe; and, in the midst of personal suffering and toil, is cheered by the thought that, through its simple faithfulness, myriads may be spared in times to come the sorrows and trials which must at present be its own. In all this, the world will see no happiness, no smooth and comfortable enjoyment of life, no stimulating excitement, no tumultuous delight; in place of these, it will note, perchance, the grave and earnest brow, the subdued spirit, reflection always at work, the energies never at rest, and shed over all a certain pensiveness of spirit that ill accords with the light and vulgar merriment of the unthinking crowd. This is what souls of the highest virtue seem oftentimes to receive as their portion for renouncing the world. Ask them if they are happy, and they will perhaps say, "No, for the world is not what we would have it be." Ask them if they are discontented with their position, if they would exchange it for any other which the world could offer, they would assuredly reply, "No, for we are happier far in suffering for truth and right, which cannot perish and must ultimately triumph, than in yielding to inclinations which draw us away from God, and pursuing objects which are condemned by the inward law of our minds."

There is another consideration of unspeakable weight. You have given up the world where the world is at war with right and truth; but you have thereby gained new power and freedom for your mind. It will now work healthily and vigorously. You have shaken off with a manly courage the prejudices and the falsehoods that dulled its perceptions, and narrowed its range of vision, and hindered it from looking freely around it on every side. You have broken with the tyranny of the world, and disowned its arbitrary law; and you have now nothing to do but to keep your eye open, and see truth wherever it lies, and follow it honestly into all its consequences. This you could not do while you were a slave to the world. It would have been a sin against the rigid conventionalism which governs it. As the world judges, you may have relinquished much. But what outward advantage can outweigh the blessing of mental freedom? You can tell us now, from your own experience, how close is the connection between an honest heart and a clear understanding. You can tell us what a privilege it is, what a compensation for innumerable worldly sacrifices, to be able to see things as they are, to call them by their proper name, and to treat them as they deserve.

Then there are our affections, that bright "consummate flower" of humanity, whose bloom and fragrance no changes in the outward world can touch. How often in the pure, sweet air of virtuous self-sacrifice do they ripen into a rare and delicate beauty which luxury and selfishness would have smothered in the bud! In holy love, in genuine, disinterested attachment, there is a silent blessing which human words can ill express. It repays ten-thousand-fold every worldly loss which conscience may have constrained us to undergo, but without which so incurred, affection itself would have been less pure and less sweet. The consciousness of having acted uprightly, and of carrying a pure heart within us, draws out of the inmost depths of the soul the finest essence of affection, and sheds it on the sharers of our hearts and homes with the delicious feeling that we are not wholly unworthy of their reciprocated love. Closely indeed are those hearts knitted to each other that have taken a common vow of unhesitating obedience to the highest law, and have renounced for it what they feel to be untruthful, impure and unrighteous, in the world. Their common hope, their joint inheritance, is no more now among the things that perish, obnoxious to chance, consumed by time, and withered by the chilly breath of age, but carried forward into a sphere which no casualty can reach, deposited with God, the faithful and unchanging, the sure Friend of the virtuous—laid up in heaven, that dim but steadfast reality, which never fades away from the inner trust of the soul, where pure minds will find the deep truth and reality of what they once believed in and aspired after, and will grow for ever in mutual attachment and in worthiness of mutual regard. A love thus chastened with sorrow, thus disciplined with trial, thus nourished with influences that distil into it like a dew from heaven, is a love sweeter and purer far than any which could grow up amidst the choking cares and entangling excitements of this world's selfishness and pride; and in its simple possession there is a rich compensation for the heaviest sacrifices ever demanded by high principle and enlightened conscientiousness.

Hast thou surrendered much which the world of man could offer thee? Remember what is left thee still in the boundless world of Nature and of God. Open thine eye on this beautiful universe. How does it gladden the outward sense! How does it thrill with a deeper and a holier joy the immortal spirit within! And all this is thine. No power of fortune can take it from thee. The woods, the waters, the everlasting hills, the eternal stars, are thine assured inheritance. Thou art the spiritual proprietor of this earthly paradise. Thy possession is better than his, who calls himself the owner of the brute, material soil, but feels not the living beauty which grows out of it and breathes around it. When those houseless missionaries of Galilee crossed the midnight lake, and they gazed on the placid beauty of the heavens mirrored in its waters, and in the awful silence of the encircling mountains, as the voice of Jesus spoke to the immortal sense within them, they felt the solemn presence of the Eternal Father—were they not more truly possessors of that glorious scene than the warrior race that with dull eye and unawakened heart planted their standards on the hills of Palestine, and believed its people were their slaves? So thou, envy not the rich man the name of his possessions, but in the spirit of contented and grateful enjoyment feel them also thine. For thee his fields are green and his woodlands sing and his brooks glitter in the pleasant sun. One thing only thou needest to make thee heir of all these things—a pure, unworldly and loving heart. The spirit of beauty and the spirit of goodness are near akin. Cast out all unclean affections, all pride, selfishness, falsehood and malignity from thy inmost soul, and it will become a chamber swept and garnished for the entertainment of all sweet influences and beautiful images. Whatever may have been thy worldly sacrifices, though thou hast left all to follow Jesus, thou art more than repaid even here below in the increased sensitiveness of an innocent and open soul to all the wonder and loveliness which are daily shining in upon it. Here is a book spread open before thee, whose contents can never be exhausted, whose interest never abates, on which thine eye may rest with ever-fresh delight, when no foul passion closes up the avenues of the spiritual sense, when no remorse tinges with a sadder hue the retrospect of life, when no conscious self-degradation casts its own dark shadow on the beaming countenance of God's bright and beautiful world.

Lastly, when all else fails, there is left for the upright the privilege of closer intercourse with God. By simple faithfulness, they have won for themselves a nearer access to His presence; they have broken through the obstacles which stand between most human hearts and the living God. Having preferred a good conscience to the world, they can open their hearts in prayer more joyfully and trustfully to Him who reads the conscience. Having relinquished self-interest for truth, they can enter into a more entire and delightful sympathy with the God of truth. Intercourse with sympathizing spirits —how refreshing and strengthening it is! How gladly we repose on the counsels of the wise, and accept the aid of the strong, and welcome the consolations of the affectionate! But suppose all these were wanting, we have an all-sufficient helper in God. The All-wise, the Almighty, the All-good is our Friend. We are not alone, for the Father is with us. In the language of Scripture, beautiful from its childlike simplicity, never trite though incessantly repeated—"If we seek Him, He will be found of us." The Universal Spirit will not and cannot abandon us. The Parent Mind will not withdraw Himself from the minds that are made in His own image, and have forsaken everything to become entirely His. Vain world! rob us of what thou wilt. Faith is mightier than thou. Let us only preserve the free access of children to a Father's throne, and we desire no more. We have more than thou couldst give. We have nothing which thou canst take away.

I have said nothing, it will be observed, of future reward, of recompence in heaven. My reason is this—

that the surest witness of the immortal life is the witness which a genuine, disinterested virtue carries with itself in the present life. A soul self-surrendered to God, bound by the strong tie of filial love to the Father Spirit, living for objects and inspired by affections that transcend the limits of this phenomenal existence, is to me an inexplicable enigma, if it does not find its solution in the assumption of a higher and to us invisible life, which will take up and carry on towards an indefinite perfection the rudiments of intelligence and goodness already developed here. For what do we constantly see? A process begun in the formation of character, but left incomplete. We have the discipline, but we want the result. We have the consciousness of a deep, inward fund of unexhausted capacity, which the most successful and the most protracted cultivation only partially brings out. There is something within us which points incessantly to futurity. It is the voice of our inmost being, which nothing can utterly silence. It is a fact proclaiming itself through all history, in every extant literature which reveals the inner consciousness of humanity. Let it shine by its own light. Let it stand on its own evidence. Why should we distrust it, though at present it should seem to utter its solitary witness amidst the silence of the outward universe? If this life means anything—if the words of the holiest men, of prophets and apostles, of Christ himself, are not wholly devoid of significance—it is a lesson, a discipline, a preparation. If any can anticipate its solemn close with quiet trust, it is they who have looked on life as one high service of obedience and loving devotedness, and have sacrificed everything mean and selfish to the grand idea and the divine affection with which it inspired them. To the base, the selfish, the sensual, the false, death, it must be confessed, wears a gloomy and uncomfortable aspect. But for the virtuous who have feared God and had no other fear, who have purified all meaner loves in the love of the Father—what shall they have for their stay and consolation in that last hour? This alone, but this in itself all-sufficient—deep trust in God's essential and unchangeable goodness, summing up and including all other elements of faith in that central one—illumined, as the shadows descend, by the light that streams through the ages from the cross of Christ—gathering round it the reflected brightness of those pure thoughts, those sweet affections, those noble and holy aspirations, which once made the happiness of earth, and now supply from memory the imperishable substance of an immortal hope.

[Last preached (Little Portland St.),
    22nd January, 1860.]

X.

Ҭhe Ground of Trust in a Prophet's Words.

———◆———

Isaiah ii. 10:

"Who is among you that feareth the Lord; that obeyeth the voice of his servant; that walketh in darkness, and hath no light? Let him trust in the name of the Lord, and stay upon his God.

THESE words have been thus rendered by a distinguished modern Hebraist: "Whoso among you feareth Jehovah, let him hearken to the voice of his servant. Whoso walketh in darkness, and hath no light, let him trust in the name of Jehovah and lean upon his God." By the "servant of Jehovah" is here meant the prophet who reveals the deep things of God and brings them home to the souls of men. It is a fine description of the commanding influence of a prophetic spirit on the trust and reverence of religious natures. There is a side of our moral being which connects us immediately with God. There are trusts and convictions latent in all of us, which we are conscious are no inference from our own reasonings, and which must therefore form a part of the spiritual heritage originally bestowed on us by God. The prophet is one in whom this spiritual side of humanity has received a more than ordinary development; to whom the great primary intuitions of a living God, a moral order, an unfailing retribution, an immortality of spiritual life, are ever present with a force and a distinctness which they do not possess in the minds of the vast majority of men; who is profoundly conscious of the divine source of those intuitions, who feels that they come to him direct from God, and who recognizes in that feeling and consciousness a solemn mission to impart them to the world, and to impregnate the dull and carnal mass of his fellowmen with a livelier sense of their relation to things unseen and eternal. The prophetic character in its essential elements is not limited to one age or country, or one form of religion. As there are individuals in whom we still observe it conspicuous, so there are races of men of whose history it has formed the distinguishing feature. It has been the special function of the Hebrew nation, in the grand providential order of the world's growth, to develope the spiritual element of humanity. Its prophetic literature, culminating in the New Testament, for depth and breadth of spiritual insight is without a parallel in the records of religious thought.

Now, it is a question which must often suggest itself to serious minds—What is the final ground of our trust in a prophet's words? Why do we acknowledge such an one as in a special sense the servant of God and a messenger from Heaven? There are two extreme views prevalent in the world, distinguished as belief and unbelief—the acceptance and the rejection of a religion from

God. The first of these views finds the proper credentials of a prophet in the exhibition of a knowledge and a power transcending the known laws of human nature, and stamping on all his words and all his acts the immediate warrant of divine authority. The second will under no conceivable circumstances surrender the absolute sovereignty of the individual reason, and, excluding all instinctive sentiment and spontaneous sympathy as illusory and dangerous, will admit no spiritual influences and incitements, and give its trust and reverence to no character but such as it can demonstrate to be logically conformable to its present standard of intellectual and moral rectitude. The first view uses reason simply to verify the offered credentials. When that task has been accomplished, it foregoes all further right to inquire or doubt. Its sole remaining duty is to submit and believe. The second applies at once its own assumed criterion to the doctrines and actions proposed to its acceptance as prophetic, and if they are found unconformable, rejects them as spurious, whatever power may have accompanied their original working in the world, and whatever influence they may still exercise over the best order of human minds. It is often supposed that the sole alternative lies between these two views, and that no third course is open to an earnest and religious mind. I shall attempt to shew that this is not the case —that we are not reduced to the necessity of choosing between a hard and naked Deism, and the compulsory acceptance as divine of the entire circle of a prophet's recorded ministrations, simply from the attachment to it of alleged miraculous attestation. I would here remark by the way, that the two views just described, though apparently at the widest distance from each other, do in fact agree in their fundamental principle. Both are rationalistic. Both make religious belief an act of the understanding, a deduction from intellectual propositions and impressions on the outward sense, instead of an inward affection of the soul. Both seek to produce faith by demonstration, differing merely as to the part of the process where the demonstration is applied. Both, therefore, are equally at variance with that principle of *trust*, of *confiding sympathy* with higher Mind, of *reliance* on spiritual tendencies at first dimly apprehended, but ever felt to be something real, exhaustless and infinite, which is the essential element of all religious feeling, of all true faith.

Any attempt at demonstration where the premises involve an element of the infinite, must necessarily fail. This is shewn by the differences of opinion among those who accept what is considered the conclusive argument of the miraculous. Some declare (and on the ground assumed they seem to me the most consistent), " When miracle on behalf of a prophet has been once clearly proved, we feel ourselves precluded from making any distinction between particular words and acts ascribed to him) for how, reason by the hypothesis being now in abeyance, are we to determine which are divine and which are not?), and we must, therefore, take everything proceeding from him as invested with equal authority." Others find this too hard a tax on their belief, and without avowedly abandoning their primary ground—the compulsion of assent by the force of supernatural testimony—they take some things, and reject others recorded of a prophet, simply from agreement or disagreement with their own private sense of what is right and true. But this is obviously admitting a new principle into the question, directly opposed to the one on which it was understood to rest, and, as left by those who adopt it in this form, of very arbitrary and uncertain application. For myself, I have long felt that neither of the views to which I have alluded goes to the bottom of this grave subject, lays open the true basis of our religious trust and religious sympathy, and explains the strong mysterious hold of a prophet's spirit on the deepest feelings of the human soul. To prevent misapprehension, let me say, that I question neither the mataphysical possibility, nor on sufficient evidence the historical fact, of some directer manifestation of divine agency than we are able to refer to any law at present accessible to us, accompanying a prophet's words under peculiar conditions of spiritual development—what we call, for want of some more appropriate term which would not imply the violation of eternal law, *miraculous* or *supernatural.* Such manifestations may have contributed in their appointed time and place to arrest the attention and deepen the reverence of rude natures into which spiritual truth would otherwise have hardly found its way. I only contend that, belonging as they do to a remote past, their importance as a ground of faith for modern believers is over-estimated and put in the wrong place. One consideration has ever seemed to me decisive that we cannot make them our ultimate basis of religious trust—and that is, that let them be accumulated to ever such an extent, and alleged on testimony ever so complete, they could never compel us to accept as divine what we felt was at war with the first principles of reason and our deepest sense of justice and holiness. In the last result, therefore, we believe in virtue of something on which outward miracle neither has nor can have any direct bearing whatever. To us of this day it can at best be but an after-confirmation—a seal visibly set by the Divine Hand on that which the Divine Spirit has already approved to our inward nature as true. The question still remains, What are the positive grounds of the peculiar trust and reverence excited in religious natures by a prophet's words and a prophet's life?

With all our holiest aspirations and highest aims, with the sense of duty in all its forms, there is associated a feeling of authority. We recognize them as something not devised by ourselves with a view to personal ends, but intrinsically good, belonging to and befitting our nature, imposed by some power which is above us. In all these states of mind, which are natural to us till they are reasoned away by sophistry or extinguished in sense and appetite, we have the witness of a Spirit to which our own is mysteriously related and feels itself responsible. Allied to this feeling is the consciousness of what we ought to be and yet are not; the vision of an ideal excellence which our practice does not realize; what we conceive and desire, but do not bring to effect; that spirit of unceasing aspiration towards something purer and nobler, which ever cleaves, even amidst frailty and transgression, to every earnest and thoughtful mind. Our moral nature does not awaken to full self-consciousness all at once. It often exists within us for a long time as a dormant faculty, an undeveloped element of future life, dimly presaging, and vainly grasping at, something which it cannot as yet distinctly apprehend. This is the mental condition on which prophetic influence powerfully acts as a stimulus to self-development. Our dumb thoughts become articulate, and our feeble wills instinct with a new vitality. Our dim and cloudy aspirations shape themselves into definite clearness through the vivifying power of words that go forth from an inspired soul, through the quickening spirit of those revelations of a higher nature which gleam out of the life of a prophet. It is this experience of a kindling influence and an attractive force, drawing out what is highest in ourselves, quickening it into distincter consciousness, and giving it new body and strength, which is the source of our reverence for virtue, our trust in it, and our sympathy with it. This reverence, trust and sympathy, extend, it must be obvious, only to that side of a character which is moral and spiritual. They do not include agreement in all its views, or the adoption of all its particular acts and opinions as direct objects of imitation. They are limited to that higher region of the soul whence flows the inner principle of the moral life, immediately connecting our nature with God. A character thoroughly impregnated with religious principle, whose practical goodness has its source in habitual communion with God, we instinctively trust in and revere. We feel that such a character from its spiritual position stands nearer to God than we, and must of course possess a deeper insight into those eternal truths which are a bond of mysterious sympathy between the human and the divine. However men of this profoundly spiritual stamp may be inferior to ourselves in the accomplishments of human learning or in mere intellectual power, we listen with justifiable deference to whatever they utter from the depths of their own consciousness in relation to religious truth—on all those points which lie beyond the reach of scientific proof, and find their sole evidence in the experience of a holy life or in the secret witness of the spirit itself. It is this feeling which lies at the bottom of the peculiar veneration inspired by the prophet, and of the deep trust that we put in his words. For the prophetic element—though we distinctively recognize it as such only in its more prominent and developed forms—is infused in various measures into human character; sometimes latent, not yet unfolded; awaiting the stimulus of circumstances to call it into action. Every wise and virtuous parent who wins the young to goodness through the force of affection and sways them by a deep moral influence, partakes of this character, represents the majesty of God to his family, and speaks with the authority of a prophet. Every high-minded and conscientious instructor who with the contagious ardour of an Arnold breathes into the heart of youth the love of all nobleness and excellence, or with the refined spirituality of a Channing, draws up the souls of myriads from the narrowness of human creeds into the wide sympathies of a divine love, works with a power that comes to him from God—works in a prophet's spirit, does that which mere knowledge and intellect and simple good intention could never do, without the impulse and sustaining enthusiasm of religious inspiration. Every friend who gains a religious hold on a kindred spirit, who quickens its purest affections and noblest aspirations, who counsels faithfully in the hour of temptation and trial, who with firm hand restrains the giddy step that would have plunged into misery and guilt, is a messenger from God, and exerts a prophet's holiest power. We are so formed that we naturally trust in and revere what we feel to be above us. Only worldliness and selfishness destroy that natural, healthy reverence, and put distrust and contempt in its place. In the scale of spiritual gradation there is no break. Wherever there is mind, from men through angels up to God, there is one nature, one operation : the difference is only of degree. Spiritual laws are everywhere the same ; and all who own them, and strive to realize them, and make them ascendant in their own sphere of influence, are engaged in a common work. Each as he ascends to higher stages of spiritual development, acquires the power of drawing less advanced natures after him, and bringing them through sympathy into closer communion with God. This is the specific influence of the prophet ; and in this large, general sense, we see how widely it may apply. In his function on earth the prophet stands nearer to God than ordinary men, but he is not beyond the circle of humanity ; it is through their common humanity that he acts upon men ; his life is not an exception to its laws, but the noblest fulfilment of them.

With veneration and awe we pronounce the hallowed name of Christ. To us, God in His moral relations with our world is fully manifested in Christ. From our present moral position we see nothing beyond Christ. He represents the highest form of religious excellence conceivable by us. In him we behold the divine and the human blended in perfect union. Hence it is that he draws all men, even the best and wisest, after him. Therefore it is that we look on him as the perfect Prophet, and call him, in the most exalted sense, the Son of God. Our longings after a spiritual ideal, the cravings of our spiritual affections for some definite object on which they can permanently repose, find their fullest satisfaction in him. We see in him what our nature should be in the highest of all relations—in its intercourse with God. We are conscious that in yielding to the attraction of his spirit, we are carried forward in the direction which we know that we ought to take— on towards God and the world of spiritual perfection where He invisibly dwells—and further than we are taken by any other prophet. His life, too, expresses more completely than any recorded example, an image of pure and perfect religiousness, transcending our highest spiritual demands, and ever yielding, the longer we dwell upon it and the more our own spiritual faculty expands, new glimpses of spiritual beauty through the broken and fragmentary indications in which it has been conveyed to us. These things are the proper witness of his prophetic greatness ; for this witness is imperishable, and speaks to the inmost soul of man. Because his is the perfect humanity through which the light of the divine streams out on our dark and carnal world, therefore it is that we trust him with a perfect trust, and love him with a holy love.

But true Christianity is, not to be always talking about Christ, heaping up elaborate proofs of his divine commission, and discoursing of his nature and miracles, but rather to live Christ's life and to breath Christ's spirit; to dwell with him in the God of Love; fervently doing all good, freely embracing all truth, and rejoicing with simple gladness of heart in all the beautiful things with which God's universe is so richly stored. The life of a true Christian is a perpetual trust, a holy sympathy, a ceaseless aspiration. Its sublimest consciousness is the capacity of endless progress. A voice within cries, " On, ever on ; immortality is before thee !" Amidst the bewildering din of present passions and present cares, those sweet and solemn words come to us with undiminished clearness through the long silence of the ages : " I am the resurrection and the life; whosoever liveth and believeth in me shall never die. " The old prophets led on our race step by step towards God. Christ has rent the veil, and shewn us the Father, and placed us at the very footstool of His throne. One with Christ, we are one with God; and God is all in all. Nothing can separate us from God. In God there is ground for perfect trust. Who can distrust the purposes of infinite Wisdom and infinite Love ? Here in the Father's presence we lay down our anxieties and dismiss our fears. Though we should walk in present darkness, and no light come to us from the world, our confidence in the name of Jehovah shall not be shaken; we will calmly rest our souls on the eternal God.

[Written 1860 ; last preached (Hampstead),
15th December, 1861.]

XI.

Access to the Father through the Spirit of Christ.

—◆—

"I am the way, the truth, and the life: no man cometh unto the
Father but by me."

IT seems strange, that after commemorating the
resurrection of Christ for more than eighteen
centuries and a half, the question should still
remain to be asked, For what purpose did Christ appear
on the earth? Yet if you put this question to the
members of different churches, or even to different
members of the same church, you would probably get
a different answer from every one. Under this apparent diversity you would nevertheless find at bottom a
certain unity of feeling, sufficient to establish the hold
of each on a common Christianity. For myself, when I
pass in review before me the various forms of opinion
on this subject, and attempt, as a believer, to realize
my personal relation to Christ, I can find no fitter

mode of expressing Christ's special mission to our world than this:—that he rose out of the moral darkness and confusion of the ages, as a great historical realization of the true relation between the Human and the Divine—that he shews us for ever out of the depths of time what must be the attitude of the soul towards God to enable it to apprehend spiritual truth, and to enter continually into closer communion with the Father. Through faith, which is only another word for spiritual sympathy—through the kindling action which a higher always exerts on a lower religious nature—Christ draws men's minds into unison with his own, and imparts to them, according to their faith, a portion of his divine life. It is a frame of mind rather than an intellectual conviction which we obtain from him. It is through the religious affections—trust, love, reverence, self-sacrificing devotedness—that the spiritual light is revealed. Knowledge is constantly on the increase, and is ever modifying the opinions which rest on it; but these affections never lose their value or significance; they furnish the spiritual feeling which must underlie every form and measure of intellectual belief, to give it a healthy action and a right tendency. It is these which constitute a living bond between the filial and the Parent Spirit. The child must of necessity bear some resemblance to the parent; all spiritual natures are allied to each other; but the more obedient and loving the child—the more guided by the parent's precepts and moulded by the parent's spirit—the more complete must that resemblance be. Hence it is that we know God through Christ as we can know Him through no other medium. The Eternal Word of the Father—what it is that He means and designs in man—delivers itself to the world through His Son. Hence the Son is the Way, the Truth, and the Life. No man cometh unto the Father but by him.

In this its characteristic doctrine of the Word made Flesh—of the manifestation of Deity in and through Humanity—Christianity is distinguished from Judaism on one hand, and from Heathenism on the other. Judaism embraced some great truths :—one God, His invisibility, His absolute sovereignty over nature as His own work, His solemn moral relation to the human race :—but it set an impassable chasm between God and man, on one side of which was the great Law-giver, and on the other His subjects; and hence it produced a state of mind in which a sense of awe and subjection and of the constraint of outward law was too predominant.   Heathenism brought Deity into closer and more familiar intercourse with mankind, and instead of separating it from the visible universe as a distinct and independent power, interfused it, as an indwelling, plastic nature, through every part of it, and gathered up each prominent group of phenomena into the idea of a corresponding godhead.   But Heathenism from its fundamental principle was involved in two pernicious errors on opposite sides.   When the popular sentiment craved and found a personal deity as the object of prayer and trust, it split itself to meet this want into a multiplicity of deities.   Where the philosopher, resolving diversified phenomena into a common element, discovered a central unity, it was an unity inherent in the phenomena themselves, essentially pantheistic, and, except in the case of a few gifted minds of the Socratic school, scarcely assumed a higher character than that of the vital force of the universe. Christianity retains what is good, and excludes what is evil, in the Judaic and in the Heathen form of religion, both of which had prepared the way for it. It asserts as strongly as Judaism the unity and spirituality and moral character of God. Like Heathenism, it bridges over the chasm between God and man, and brings Deity into living contact with humanity; but it excludes every tendency to pantheism—to the resolution of God into a mere law of the universe—by maintaining intact the idea of personality in God and man—by exhibiting the union between them, not as a fusion of essence, but as a growing identification of will, resulting from free choice and moral effort on the part of man. This great idea is expressed in the person of Christ. One complete example, realizing an idea in fact, teaches more than endless general precepts. Christ shews us in his own divine life, in the spirit which animated it, in the aims to which it was habitually directed, how men must approach the Father, and learn to comprehend Him, and enter into communion with Him. In this disclosure of the mutual relation of God and man, made to us through Christ's person and life, lies, as I conceive it, the proper revelation of Christianity.

The words of the text, taken by themselves and as they have often been quoted, might seem to imply that all are shut out from a knowledge of the Father but those who have access to Him through the historical Christ, and that consequently all Heathens, Jews and

Deists, however reverent, sincere and truth-seeking, are for ever excluded from the Divine presence. But if intrepreted in the sense which I have intimated, they by no means justify so narrow and intolerant a conclusion. They simply teach that a certain attitude and tendency of mind, closely allied to moral character and capable of culture and development, is a condition of apprehending God as He is in His spiritual relations to the human soul, and that Christ, as the most perfect expression in his life and temper of that mental attitude and tendency, is an infinite help, through the attractive force which goes out from him, towards its attainment. But wherever that frame of mind even rudimentally exists—and we recognize it in the noblest men of all ages, yea, in some of those in Christian times who have been ranked with unbelievers because they could not master the proofs and accept the conditions artificially imposed by theologians—there we find already an anticipated or an essential Christianity. Nay, when the soul still remains cold, hard and sceptical, open to doubt but inaccessible to conviction, a change may come over it under the chastening discipline of life which will rend the veil and reveal to it the living God. So that to none do these words of Christ forbid the hope or exclude the possibility of final communion with the Father. They only indicate the way in which all must seek it—sympathy, conscious or unconscious, with the spirit of Christ. Now what is this spirit? How happy would it have been for the church and the world, if, instead of battling about creeds or perplexing themselves with metaphysical incomprehensibilities, men had studied and cultivated this spirit, and under its transforming influence had striven to be one with Christ as he is one with God! The Christian spirit centres in the conscience. Here is its living root. The eternal distinctions of right and wrong stand before it with an awful authority, as the expression of a law, intimately inwoven with its own essence, yet not created by itself—independent of and anterior to itself, yet felt to emanate from a kindred though infinitely transcendent nature. Fidelity to that inward law is the spontaneous impulse, as it is the most sacred obligation, of a Christian spirit. The habit of obedience—increasing conformity between human effort and the higher will which commands it—strengthens the consciousness of personal intercourse with God. Moral law can only act on mind, and it must issue from mind. It is unintelligible without the assumption of will both in its author and in its subject. The being who enjoins holiness must himself be holy. He who forbids ill-will and hatred must himself be merciful and loving. Seen through the obligations of the moral law, God is an object of reverence and trust; and these are the affections, so conspicuous in the mind of Christ, through which we first draw nigh to God and discern Him. Under their influence we are conscious of something which has an affinity with our inmost being, behind and beyond the phenomena which act on the outward sense. As we gaze on this wonderful universe—its silent, starry heavens, its vast oceans and variously peopled continents, and its huge mountain masses with the dates of millions of years written on their hoary brows—we are struck with unspeakable awe as at a Presence which we feel is akin to what is highest in us, and yet cannot wholly comprehend. We are forced back on our own deepest consciousness to interpret it; and hence our ground of trust. We are sure, from the secret sympathy which spirit has with spirit, that the Infinite Being must possess in unlimited perfection whatever is best in ourselves—what constitutes the special glory of a rational nature like our own. Thus, amidst the reverence and the awe which take possession of us when we contemplate the unsearchable works and ways of God, we are sustained by the faith which springs from implicit confidence in perfect rectitude and love.

No doubt, wherever we look, this universe abounds with mysteries which we cannot pierce, and appals us with difficulties which Science must leave where it finds them. We have no resource but faith in the essential qualities of Mind, operating most freely and purely in the highest Mind. We can only solve the dark enigma of existence by looking at it from the moral point of view—by believing, in accordance with our own deepest consciousness, that the Infinite Mind cannot err; that the greatest apparent contradictions and difficulties in His administration of the universe are the measure, not of imperfection in Him, but of limitation in us; that they may be indispensable to the highest training of immortal natures; and that they are what they seem to us, as forming part of a system too vast in the far-stretching relations of its exhaustless perfection to be comprehended by us. This is religious faith. It strengthens and grows clearer by exercise. Its genuine expression is patient submission and perfect trust. Love grows out of trust, and finally expels all fear. Communion with God—personal intercourse of mind with Mind—results in the same deep confidence and sympathy, only infinitely exalted by the nature of its object, which a human soul reposes in a revered and long-tried friend. It is mingled love and reverence which bind us to him. We are certain that he designs our good, and will promote it to the extent of his knowledge and power; so that where we cannot follow his workings or see the reasons for them, on moral grounds we trust him still. Apply this state of feeling to God, with the immeasurable enhancement which results from its relation to an Infinite Mind, and you have the foundation for religious trust. The religious man serves not from fear or for reward, but from affection. This makes duty delightful to him. Reverence, trust and love, are the feelings with which he looks up to God, and in which he seeks communion with Him. It is natural to him to obey. It would be like wounding an implanted sense to disobey. He must be ever about his Father's business. This is his proper work and mission in the world. So he comes to God, and understands Him, and feels that He is a living reality. Such is the spirit of Christ. It is absolute self-surrender to the Father's will.

This state of mind is not reached at once. We pass to it through successive stages. Christ is first the Way, then the Truth, finally the Life. The fundamental condition of all religious faith is a spirit of reverence and sympathy. It may be as yet unaccompanied by any definite creed, even if such be ever attainable. But to look on the deep mystery of existence with a reverent awe; to sympathize with the spirit of beauty and love which breathes through heaven and earth; to leave things impenetrably dark, unassailed by our impotent questionings, under an humbling sense of our own ignorance and of the unfathomable wisdom of God; to feel that a pure, loving and trustful heart is the best interpreter of the Divine ways, and a faithful discharge of clear and obvious duty the surest guide to the Divine favour—this is the Way to eternal life. Happy he who has found it, and perseveres in it; and without losing himself in the thorny wilderness of a disputatious theology, sees in Christ the best expression of a religious life; and putting his mind into sympathy with Christ's spirit, follows him trustfully through the higher stages of the heavenly road! When the mind is once set in this attitude, and looks out on the universe from this point of view, the phenomena which meet its gaze brighten up into intelligibility; they assume a distinct relation to the moral part of our nature, and become spiritually significant. We see that this universe, so far as we are concerned in it, if it has any meaning, is a place of schooling and discipline for the mind. We read its moral purpose; and that is, to fashion our lives and characters into a capacity for something higher still. So interpreted, life becomes self-consistent; and in that self-consistency carries with it an implicit proof of the rectitude of the interpretation. Christ is no longer the Way—he is now the Truth—Truth in the highest sense. For when we have wearied ourselves to no purpose to solve the endless problems which this world offers to us

—when Science makes us feel every day more and more how little we know, by ever widening round us more and more the circumference of our ignorance—when Philosophy teaches us little but this, how she is able to raise questions which she cannot answer—it is a support more than human to fall back on the highest instincts of our moral nature, to feel that here we possess a truth breathed into us from our birth which cannot perish—a truth which, in its purest and most perfect form, has been realized for us by Christ—a truth which, in the midst of much scientific darkness, suffices for our inward peace, our present guidance, and our future hope. For whatever else be uncertain or mysterious, our moral consciousness abides with us as the nearest and most indubitable of all realities. If I can believe anything, it must be the witness of my own conscious spirit; and this tells me that I am a moral and responsible being, and that if I walk uprightly, I shall walk surely. Uncertainty in other respects, said a great and good man, only makes greater certainty here. In fact, the experience of some two or three thousand years has little to add to the grand and simple philosophy of Job: " Unto man he said, Behold, the fear of the Lord, that is wisdom; and to depart from evil is understanding." This trust is confirmed and deepened by acting on it— by making it the inspiration of our thoughts and the guide of our actions. Christ is then formed within us, and becomes more than a Truth—even a Life. The profoundest conviction can only grow out of experience. So long as we are dealing with intellectual propositions, we can never fence off doubts. We must have living communion with God, to be sure that He is. But a life based on religion can never question the truth of religion. It carries too many living proofs within it to doubt the greatest reality of its experience. We cannot associate the idea of doubt with the mind of Christ. It vanishes in his presence, like a thin mist before the rays of the sun. And why? Because his faith grew out of his life, and his life was an habitual communion with God. There were a few dark moments when his suffering humanity distrusted itself; but it never distrusted God. Faith in himself was restored by faith in God. If we would have the faith, we must strive after the life, of Christ.

The two grand trusts of religion are—first, that this universe is watched over and directed by an infinitely wise and good Being, a Living God, a Father Spirit, the Father of all human spirits; and secondly, that death in the course of human development is not the final extinction of conscious being, but only the appointed process of transition for the individual soul to a new stage of more complete retributory existence. Let us only be assured of these two great truths, and we can well spare the arbitrary assumptions and shadowy speculations of an artificial theology. We shall then have all that we need for our warning and our encouragement, for our guidance and our hope, on earth. All other doctrines will cluster in due relationship around these central trusts, these fundamental convictions of the soul. But these truths, like all the deepest, must be spiritually discerned. We must come to them through the mind of Christ, or we shall not discern them at all. They are neither of them capable of such strict scientific demonstration as would exclude the possibility of objections which the religious mind might not feel of any weight, and yet the mere logician could not answer. Nor ought this to surprise and pain us. It is not that these truths want certainty, but that their certainty is of the deepest kind. They lie so close to the human consciousness, that they lose their proper character when we attempt to separate them from it, and pass them through the ordinary processes of reasoning. They are essentially subjective, and can with difficulty be viewed objectively. If we do not feel them, we cannot prove them. It is by putting the mind in a certain position or attitude towards the system of things visible and invisible, that we catch, as it were, the point of view under which spiritual truth reveals itself. If that position be not assumed, if that point of view be lost, if the mind, from whatever cause, be wanting in reverence and trust, all the science in the world will not make it religious, and demonstration will be lavished on it in vain. Perhaps, when the understanding has been fruitlessly assailed for years by logical proofs, and has stood out hard and obdurate, some deep sorrow, some wounded affection, something that touches and softens the heart, will open a passage for the Spirit of God to the inner sources of the moral being, and the man will feel what he never felt before. Love and gentleness, ever waiting for God's seasons—never obtrusive and assuming, never wanting in a brother's genial sympathy, when there is no moral distaste or disqualification for the highest truth—will always be found more effectual in the conflict with unbelief than hard pertinacious argument or the overpowering eagerness of a polemical theology. The favourite studies, the predominant modes of thought, the habitual frame of the mind, the aspects under which the universe is constantly surveyed, have far more to do with belief and unbelief on these momentous topics than strength of understanding, or range of knowledge, or even purity of life. There are truths of sentiment, if we may so call them, as well as truths of intellect; and the truths of religion are pre-eminently those of sentiment. If the understanding be not stimulated by the right feeling, it will not grasp the object sought. We are startled to painfulness when we first learn that so comprehensive an intellect, so pure and noble a spirit, as that of Alexander Humboldt, should have had no clear assurance of the great truths of religion. But we remember that his brother William, his equal in learning and genius, and still more profoundly versed in the history and nature of man—whose studies had been moral rather than physical—was a firm believer in the being of God and the immortality of man. Yet even he felt how strongly this last belief depends for its clearness on the frame of mind with which it is associated; and in one of his letters he expresses his earnest hope that it might never depart from him. Happily, he retained it to the last, and it was a consolation to him in his dying hour. How do these differences of opinion among the wisest—this partial eclipse of the brightest of intellects—make us feel the value of the spirit of Christ; so humble, loving and pure, so congenial to our natural affections, so in harmony with our deepest and holiest instincts! In religion, above all things, we discern the natural equality of men, and the great truth that lies in our common human heart. Here the humblest and simplest sometimes see more clearly and feel more deeply than the wisest. Faith is a wonderful faculty, and when strongly excited pierces far into the invisible. The first believers had witness, to us inexplicable, of the heavenly existence of their risen Lord. It was to them more than a belief—it was a fact. They never doubted that their beloved Master was risen from the dead, and had gone to his Father. Oh! that we could recover some portion of their vivid faith! that we, like them, could live as seeing Him who is invisible! that we in spirit could be partakers of our Lord's resurrection! that we could look on death as but the passage to a higher life! and that when dear friends are taken from us, we too could feel, without one passing shade of fear, that we are only resigning them to a Father's arms! Let us habitually cherish the spirit of Christ, and his faith will be ours. Because he lives, we shall live also.

[Written, 1860; last preached (St. Mark's, Edinburgh),
4th January, 1863.]

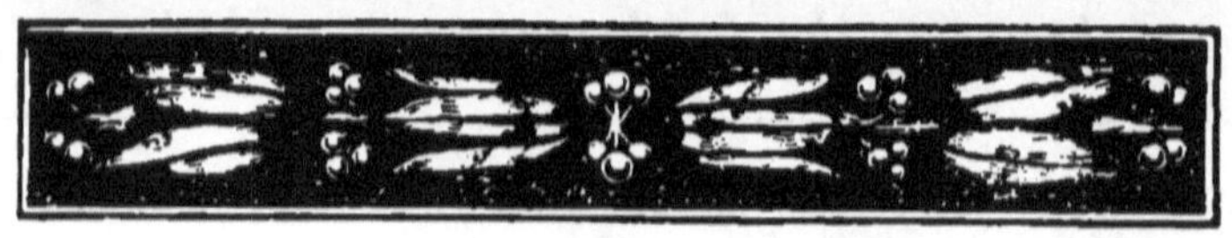

XII.

Affliction the Healer and Sanctifier of the Soul.

JEREMIAH xvii. 14 :

"Heal me, O Lord, and I shall be healed; save me, and I shall
be saved: for thou art my praise."

WE live in an age unrivalled for the progress of
scientific discovery and the accumulation of
material wealth; and it is impossible not to feel
proud of the intellect which is daily bringing to light
some new truth, and of the energy which is daily adding
to the resources of human productiveness. Nature lies
at our feet, subdued by the will of man; and it seems
no unreasonable hope that she may in time yield up to
us all her secrets, and place all her powers at our disposal. It is not surprising, therefore, that sanguine
minds, comparing our age in this respect with the most
brilliant periods that have preceded it, should become
almost dizzy in contemplating the possibilities that seem
to await our race on earth, and seek its entire future in
this direction alone. There have been—probably there

still are—enthusiasts who look to scientific intelligence, and a better organization of industry under its guidance, for the perfection of humanity—who expect by these means alone to annihilate the ills of life, to abridge and equalize labour, to expel pain and sickness and poverty, to fill our allotted term of years with an uninterrupted flow of grateful sensations from the cradle to the grave —in one word, to convert this world of stern trial and painful discipline into a sensuous paradise. Should this possibility be for a moment admitted, reflection will shew that its realization could not issue in any happiness that deserves the name. For our nature has two sides; and this is only one of them. No state could be blessed in which the springs of moral interest and spiritual aspiration were wanting. Science would lose all its beauty and nobleness, were its worth to be estimated exclusively by its material applications. No doubt, it is a grand thing, and one of the conditions even of moral and spiritual advancement, to be able to wield for our good the great physical agencies which encircle us, and to multiply and diffuse the materials of external well-being. But experience proves that the ease, the comfort, the luxury, which result from abundant wealth, when unchecked by other influences, tend to corrupt and enfeeble the human mind and render it incapable of its highest attainments. Providence itself, with the conservative wisdom which pervades all its arrangements, has set a limit to the enervating tendencies of material prosperity. In easy circumstances, mankind rapidly increase, and their numbers soon overtake, and then exceed, the means of ready and comfortable subsistence;

and now comes back the necessity for care and thoughtfulness and self-denial and painful exertion—now begins once more that struggle for existence, that fierce competition, that stern battle of life, which, while productive of great suffering to multitudes, stimulates men's faculties to the utmost, developes within them resources and energies till then unknown, and if wisely and honestly directed by the natural ascendancy of the strongest and most intelligent, will find out some cure for the most pressing evils of the time, and bring back again a season of comparative tranquillity and enjoyment. Regarded as a whole, and taking large periods of time into view, this is very much the history of human society; such are the ever-recurring cycles of connected change through which it passes on its onward way: and though that is a shallow philosophy which thinks it can wholly explain the existence of so much evil in our world, and refuses to admit any mystery in the wonderful scene of things where we find ourselves placed, this much we can at least see, that if our race is not to be stationary, but progressive, it can only become so through the agency of what we call evil—through the intervention of so much pain and uneasiness, so much dissatisfaction with the present and the actual, as shall suffice to stimulate a self-control and a self-assertion, an effort and an aspiration, from which our natural love of ease and enjoyment would otherwise have shrunk. The remark applies to the individual as well as to the species. What I desire for a few moments to call your attention to this morning is this: that there is a certain healthy balance between the two sides of our nature, the side towards

God and the side towards the world of sense, which must be maintained if we would fulfil the clearly-indicated end of our being; that the blandishments and seductions of a smooth-flowing and prosperous life, and not less the pain and uneasiness resulting from the pressure of narrow circumstances, can only be kept from corrupting and degrading us by the constant presence in our minds of those high spiritual considerations which hold the final end of our being distinctly before us, and make us feel the difference between what we are and what we were intended to be; and that this spiritual frame of mind is best preserved in us by a large inter-mixture in our lot of trial and suffering, of what the world often looks upon as absolute evil—not the evil that flows from self-abandonment to sloth and selfishness and sensuality, and perpetuates the degradation and moral impotence out of which it springs—but the beneficent sorrow which heals and saves—the sorrow from which no pure, faithful and loving soul can be exempted—the sorrow which overtakes the wisest and the best—the sorrow by which wealth may be sanctified, and poverty is often blest. This is what we should pray for—not outward prosperity, distinction and success—these are the simple accidents of our earthly existence —but the moral discipline, apart from which life's highest purpose will be missed; the wise and chastening Hand under which we may be reared into better and nobler beings; children of God, not wholly unworthy of the immortality which He has held out to us. "Heal us, Lord, and we shall be healed; save us, and we shall be saved: for Thou art our praise."

I suppose we have all found that hours of sadness, when not occasioned by a moral fall or too deeply involved in the complications of worldly anxiety, have often brought with them a serene and holy blessedness, which was more precious than all the joys and triumphs that the world could give. Not that the mere privation of any outward good is in itself desirable, or would be gratuitously sought by any healthy mind; but when misfortune, sickness, disappointment, or the death of friends, cuts off our ordinary supplies of interest and enjoyment from the world, we are inevitably thrown, if we have enough of spirituality within us to seize them, on resources that are not of the world, and we learn now, as we could have learned under no other experience, how solid and lasting they are. We find now that the greatest realities lie on this side of our existence, and not on that which connects us with the world. Sorrow opens to us glimpses of a higher being, as the immeasurable grandeur of the universe is only revealed to the bodily eye under the solemn shadows of night. In all our intercourse with the external world, however prosperous, unless it be seasoned and guided by high moral principle, we are soon overtaken by a feeling of satiety and emptiness; we feel that the satisfactions which it yields us are superficial and inconstant, and do not spring from the essential root of things. Have you never marked the deep note of melancholy which thrills through the strains of the most epicurean poets? How it betrays their inward sense of the evanescence and worthlessness of the very joys they celebrate? What an expression of oppressive weariness perpetually escapes the lips of those, all whose projects of wealth and ambition have been crowned with success, who have conquered the world, and after all not found in it the contentment which they sought! It is from such men, and not from the tried and the suffering, from those who must toil to live, that you will hear the confession, that there is nothing in this world worth living for. Even Science, when it lives for Science only, and does not grasp the higher spiritual truth in which it should terminate, sits down at last disconsolate and sick at heart on the height of its accumulated achievements, and sees round it only a wider prospect of bleak and comfortless desolation. But let sorrow turn the mind in upon itself, and send out its thoughts in the direction of invisible things, and it will discern the traces of a deeper law—a law of truth and holiness and love— underlying all that is transitory and phenomenal, and giving it its true significance; but itself imperishable, founded in the necessary and eternal relations of things, and cleaving to the immortal essence of all Mind. Here, if anywhere, is the great reality of our mysterious existence. This is a truth which lies nearer to us than all other truth. Whatever else may be delusion, this is a fact inseparable from our very consciousness. To fulfil the moral law revealed within us; to strive to be pure and just and merciful; to reverence conscience as our highest authority, and let ourselves be moulded to its requirements by the constraining influence of trust and love—this is, this must ever be, the proper aim of our being; this is the only intelligible answer to the question, Why are we here? Happy he whom sorrow

has taught this, and left his mind calm and open enough
to discern the transcendent claims of that highest law,
and to feel its nearness to himself! He will then learn
—perhaps for the first time—the deep meaning of those
words of Jesus, "Blessed are they that mourn, for they
shall be comforted." When the full consciousness of
this spiritual destination descends on a man, he becomes
a new creature—without a figure, he is born again. He
walks the earth with a quiet dignity and collectedness
of soul, as one whose deepest being is rooted in reality,
and who has got hold of imperishable truth. He lives
no more in a world of shows and shadows. He looks
on things with a disenchanted eye, and estimates them
at their true value. His inward vision is opened to discern a holier truth and a diviner beauty than reveal
themselves on the surface of the world. He is conscious of his nearness to the great central heart of love
which warms and cherishes all things ; and though he
may be stripped of much that the world covets and
frets after, he has a healthy relish of existence which he
never tasted before, and enjoys a peace which is new to
him—a peace which the world cannot touch, and which
is beyond the understanding of the selfish and the vain.
We speak of the sacredness of sorrow. It is a beautiful
expression, full of the deepest meaning. Religious sorrow sanctifies humanity as nothing else can. Not without a profound instinct of appropriateness does the
collective heart of Christendom reverence the holiest
of our race as "a man of sorrows and acquainted with
grief." It is the designation of one who lived the
closest with God, and saw the deepest into His eternal

law. Our highest conception of a saint is that of one who has come out of affliction purified and strengthened. Even in a work of art, how surpassingly beautiful do we find the countenance in which the expression of a calm intelligence and a quiet love is heightened by the traces of sorrow and the lines of earnest thought, beaming with the holy radiance still left on it, of inward conflict overcome and sanctified by the tranquil might of the Spirit!

Where our own interest and enjoyment do not for the moment blind our perceptions, we ever find that it is the expression of the spiritual overpowering the coarser manifestations of the carnal and the secular, which gives its most striking beauty and nobleness to human character. I have often thought that the poem and the novel, when they embody the feeling, as they often do now, of the highest genius of the age, furnish, in the various measures of interest which they excite, no unfitting test of the relative worth of things, and so convey the finest moral to the mind. Characters that impersonate luxurious ease and successful ambition—the very things most coveted by the world—if they have no other qualities to recommend them, serve but as a foil to set off the brighter objects associated with them—a dark and heavy background, to bring out in bolder relief the energy, the heroism, the fortitude, the self-denying affection and resolute principle, which throw into the narrative all its interest and its animation. Placed beside these higher qualities, how tame and ignoble they look! And the contrast teaches us where the true glory of our humanity is to be found—not in the smooth flow of worldly prosperity; not in high position and the vain glitter of social distinction; but in the grand toil and struggle of life, amid its stern trials and crushing sorrows; in the dark and troubled scenes which call forth its holiest affections and noblest efforts, which test its faith and its love, which bring out the "hidden man of the heart" in its undisguised and naked simplicity, and shew that its reliance must ever be, not on the "seen," but on the "unseen," and that the secret of its strength lies in truthfulness and manly adherence to duty.

I have said that sorrow turns our thoughts within, and teaches us to find there the governing law of our being. But it does more than this. It carries us beyond ourselves and the law under which we live, to the Being who created us and put us under that law. One of the strongest feelings which possesses an earnest mind is the sense of disparity between his practice and his ideal. Whence comes that ideal? He did not originate it, for it lies beyond him. Yet it must have its fulfilment somewhere; for he feels that it is the greatest of realities, the highest law of creation. Where, then, can it find its fulfilment but in Sovereign Mind— in a God? His own mind needs this support out of itself. His feet rest on the solid earth. But has the material side of his nature alone a footing in reality? His spiritual aspirations mount incessantly upward. In these, his highest thoughts, he is alone. No human spirit can go with him into the trackless depths of the infinite. He yearns for the recognition of a Father Spirit. He sighs for communion with something stronger, wiser and holier than himself. And is there no reality beyond himself on this the highest side of his nature? Does vacuity meet him here? Does he, with all his conscious infirmity, complete the scale of possible intelligences? When he asks in deep anguish of soul—in the dark loneliness where the world has left him—Is there no God to comfort me?—shall he hear for answer nothing but the eternal silence? No, it cannot be. There is a logic mightier than man's, before which all his sophistries vanish like mist before the sun, that assures us it is impossible. A spiritual necessity, when our nature is left to itself in the solemn shadows of affliction, and is not artificially stimulated to combat bad arguments, compels us to believe in a God. Our highest being would want its complement without Him. Alone with Him we have all that we need. Wisdom and love flow into us from Him. He is their Source, not we. We are but the channels through which they glide. Through Him we are linked in a holier bond with the great family of man. The sorrow which humbles and sanctifies us before Him, fills us with a tenderer and gentler sympathy towards them. Our human love becomes purer and less selfish through communion with Him; and so our religion descends on our morality, to elevate and spiritualize it. We are healed by the cleansing touch of sorrow, and made fit for the presence of God. The two worlds are brought into harmony, and the balance of our being is restored.

There is one hope to which our nature clings with intensity in the hour of sorrow—the hope of renewed existence beyond the grave and of final re-union in some more glorious state with the loved and lamented dead.

Sorrow which demands this holiest solace, strengthens in us the views and tendencies of mind which lend it the clearest witness and firmest support. It casts into shade the dazzling brilliancy of a sensuous life, and opens out a prospect on the other side of our being, into the vast mystery of spiritual things. Proof, in the ordinary sense of the word, is here out of the question; but there are realities too near to us for proof. For my part, I believe the voice of the human heart, when its utterances are the most sincere and the affections which fill it are the purest and the most divine. Those who have lived most purely and divinely, and in closest communion with God, have spoken most trustingly of the hope that was in them. The words of Christ, so calm, so deep, so clear on this solemn theme, outweigh with me all other considerations, and, coming from him, give me a faith which I feel is not, and cannot be, of this world. Years strengthen this faith, though they make it less demonstrative. We talk less, for the very reason that we believe more. The feeling which in earlier days overflowed in sentimentality and imagination, now sinks inward and penetrates to the depth of the soul, and dwells there in the reverent silence of a holy trust. And what need have we of that trust! How many within the last few months have passed away, whom we would fain have kept longer with us! How busily within that short space has Death been unpeopling the earth of its best and noblest inhabitants! And not yet does he stay his arm; not yet is he satisfied with his triumphs. Not only the dear friend and beloved companion, those who blessed our homes and brightened our daily intercourse, have been taken from us, but public sorrow has augmented private grief. The great historian[1] has dropped his eloquent pen, and gone to his last rest among the illustrious dead whose fame he had helped to swell. The accomplished authoress[2] who blended so exquisitely the finest sense of art with the gentlest feelings of humanity, whose aim was ever to refine and elevate the tastes of mankind, and whose last labours were consecrated to the wise and enlightened ennoblement of her own sex—she too has been summoned from her sphere of earthly duty, and left a great work to be carried on by those who understood her wishes and sympathized with her benevolence. Later still, as if death were making a clearance of the great and good of our earth, the tidings have reached us of the departure of another honour to our race—the intrepid foe of slavery, the manly asserter of truth, the fearless denouncer of hollowness and hypocrisy in every form—one whose religion stood not in empty forms, but however darkened, like yours and mine, with partial error in the sight of the unerring Judge, was the genuine, outspoken utterance of an unseared conscience and an honest heart—one whose death in the very bloom and blossom of his genius, far away from the land of his birth and the scene of his toils and triumphs,[3] will be remembered by an age more candid and dispassionate than this, as the martyrdom of a noble spirit to the cause of humanity and truth. All these have passed ·

---

[1] Lord Macaulay died 28th December, 1859.

[2] Mrs. Jameson died 17th March, 1860.

[3] Theodore Parker died at Florence, 10th May, 1860.

away, and earth seems darker and more desolate for their departure. But let us not wrong their nobleness, or bring discredit on the hopes in which they lived and died, by unchristian sorrow and faint-heartedness. They have joined the illustrious society above, and left us a glorious example below. The moral air we breathe is fragrant with the memories which they have left in it. Wise and good men will never be wanting to carry on their work; and even the humblest and feeblest may catch something of their spirit, and feel themselves nobler and better for the consciousness of sharing in the same humanity with them. Let us only be earnest and faithful, and the heavens will soon clear again over our heads. The same God who wrought with them will work with us. He purifies and strengthens us by these trials of our faith. The earth will gleam out again with its old beauty from beneath the transient cloud that has darkened over it, and look brighter and smell sweeter for the drops of sacred sorrow that have fallen on it.

[Written, 1860; last preached (Octagon Chapel, Norwich),
26th June, 1864.]

XIII.

The Dead Letter and the Living Spirit.

LUKE ix. 60 :

"Let the dead bury their dead; but go thou and preach the kingdom of God."

IT is a condition inseparable from the growth of
an historical religion, that in the course of its
development it inevitably assumes forms both of
intellectual apprehension and of outward expression in
worship, which, however truly representing the conviction of the age of which they were a spontaneous product, are apt, through the inherent tenacity of things
once adopted, to survive into a period when they become
forms and nothing more, and, like the dead branches of
a tree, must be cut off and cast away, to allow a free
and full expansion to the vital principle of the parent
stock. The first Protestants, who groaned under the
accumulated superstitions of centuries and wished to
fling them off, went straight to canonical Scripture for
help, and substituted its authority—coming direct, as

they believed, from God—for the authority of the old Church. They saw truth undoubtedly, but only half the truth; they did not see, what the Quakers of the seventeenth century clearly saw and beautifully taught, that there is an authority higher than Scripture itself—the Spirit of the Living God which speaks through it.

Any thoughtful person who looks at Scripture from the point of view which the present state of knowledge not only justifies but necessitates, will at once perceive that the demands of a self-consistent Protestantism are not satisfied by a simple repudiation of the traditions of the Romish Church, and that within the limits of the New Testament itself there are forms of thought and modes of belief evidently shaped by the intellectual and social conditions of that first age, which carry with them no spiritual authority to our minds, and are interesting and important to us simply as the providential vehicles through which the spirit of eternal truth flowed into and purified the grand commingling streams of universal human thought. In the mere letter of Scripture, as well as in the decisions of ecclesiastical councils, there are dead branches, no longer bearing fruit or abiding in Christ, which must be taken away and thrown aside, if we would get at the vital sap which can alone nourish our souls and make them grow. It has been the weakness of the popular Protestantism to accept Scripture in every part, in its ever-varying forms as well as in its underlying spirit, as a consecrated, unassailable whole—to attach as much importance to the retention of what is perishable as to the assertion of what is eternal; nay rather, with the perverseness peculiar to theologians, to lay the greatest stress on the most doubtful and disputable points, to set the most difficult questions on the very threshold of the Church, and say to the earnest and the truth-seeking, "Solve these, or you shall not enter in"—and by absurdly making it a point of orthodox honour to concede nothing, to endanger everything.

But are we to be for ever suspended on the deplorable alternative of believing everything or believing nothing? Must we for ever live among dead men's bones in a theological charnel-house? Is the spirit of Christ to be for ever identified with its secular forms? Shall we not rather each of us say to his own soul, "Let the dead bury their dead; but go thou and preach the kingdom of God"?

What is this kingdom of God, then? It is a spiritual condition; the sense of spiritual relations; the consciousness of subjection and responsibility to a spiritual authority. It is the profound feeling, not wholly explicable in human words, and darkened at times by passing clouds of human doubt and fear, which every pure and noble nature permanently cherishes in itself, of some mysterious kindred with the Infinite Wisdom and the Infinite Love, of which this visible scene of things, with the events that are continually sweeping over it, is the significant expression—the recognition of our instinctive worship of the good, the beautiful and the true, as the utterance of a paternal voice within us to guide our discursive intellects and control our capricious wills. To live in the habitual consciousness of this spiritual dependence and responsibility—to feel that we live, not in ourselves, but in Him by whom alone we live—to strengthen that feeling in the spirit of prayer and devout aspiration—and to obey its impulses without worldly fear or selfish regards in the steadfast aim and endeavour of the outward life—this it is, in the largest sense, to be a subject of the kingdom of God. Now observe, this belief, this conviction, grows up within us, and will at times force itself into expression, in spite of our worldly doubts and worldly fears; it is a natural fruit of the organic working of the inner nature that we possess. As it is not produced, so in its essence it cannot be affected, by anything external to us. Any influence from without bearing on our spiritual condition, can only obtain admission as it meets a responsive trust and sympathy from within. Any attempt to build up a religious faith on the so-called demonstrations of physical science, must necessarily fail, because the premises and the conclusion belong to different spheres of thought which have no logical connection with each other. Scientific theories of the universe are undergoing perpetual change; no one can tell what form they may ultimately assume. To bind up religion with any one of them, is to make it as assailable and fluctuating as they. The premises on which religion stands are shut up in the soul itself, and partake of its own immutability. Amid the ceaseless revolutions of scientific theory and the changes which society is constantly undergoing, our moral and spiritual nature endures unaltered—in its deepest wants and closest affections, its trusts, its hopes, and its aspirations, ever one and self-consistent. It is itself an eternal witness to the truth by which it lives. While our nature retains a conscience and a heart, religion can never forsake it. But though mere science cannot succour our religiousness when it is overwhelmed by doubt and fear, and intellectual teaching can only guide it when awake, not wake it when asleep, it is not inaccessible to the gentler influence of sympathy and love. The seeds of higher thought latent in it open at the touch of the Divine Spirit, through whatever channel conveyed, and sprout into unsuspected life. Contact with a kindred nature awakens and unfolds its own; and beliefs, which left to themselves might have slept for ever, start up into consciousness at the welcome bidding of a brother's voice.

This sympathy between religious natures is not intercepted, though the doctrinal medium through which it is expressed may be widely different in each. Whatever forms of utterance it may adopt, the influence of the religious sentiment on other minds will be in proportion to its depth and its perfect genuineness. Hence we sometimes experience the profoundest religious emotions from the words of those with whom we do not doctrinally agree. It is the recognition of a common spirit working through a different intellectual medium in them and in us. When a human soul enters into the closest communion with God, gives itself up to that divine inspiration, and speaks and acts under its habitual influence, we all feel the sublimity of the presence which it realizes among us, however rude and plain its speech, and however contrary its conception of things outside the soul to the demonstrated conclusions of the philosopher.

William Penn was a scholar and a courtier; George

Fox an unlettered rustic; yet Penn has left on record that the most awful impression he ever experienced was that of Fox in prayer—the contemplation of a human spirit absorbed for the time in the Divine. In a still higher degree, this is the secret of our feeling towards Christ. It is the unmistakable presence of the Divine in that grand and beautiful life which commands our reverence, and attracts our sympathy, and inspires our trust. Yet that Spirit, so intimately one with God, communicated with our human world through the popular conceptions and hereditary beliefs of its own day. No intelligible intercourse with the men among whom it wrought would have been practicable in any other way. It was the medium through which the Divine Spirit came into living contact with human realities; and all this Scripture has recorded with simple faithfulness, just as it occurred in that distant Jewish age and Jewish land. Had Christ's mission been cast in another age and another land, it must have taken another outward form, it would have spoken another speech, it would have left behind it a very different history. Yet the Spirit revealed would have been unchanged. The same wisdom, the same love, would have spoken in other words to the same human conscience and human heart. The same hope, the same trust, the same aspiration, would still have been breathed into the human soul.

How obvious is this on the slightest reflection! Yet how constantly is it overlooked in the popular idolatry of the letter of Scripture! The Spirit which spoke in all its fulness through Christ speaks still—speaks to you and to me, in answer to our prayers and in proportion to our faith. The fountain of inspiration which gushed forth so richly in the apostolic age is not closed; it is open and flowing still—it flows still into every pure and loving and devout heart which turns to Christ and asks his blessing. It is this Spirit still present and working in the midst of us, and not the works of an ancient book—which, however precious, is only one among manifold effects of its earliest operation—that connects us at this day vitally with Christ; makes us through all time living members of his eternal Church; makes us one with God as we are one with him—children of God in the same degree that we are brethren of Christ. And now mark, what has Theology done? It has consecrated the letter, which is only a form of the past, and despised, as mere natural religion, the spirit which is everlasting. It has lost sight of the human ideal, first in the historical Jew, and then in the dissolving light of a divine effulgence. To exalt the factitious greatness of Christ, it has surrounded him and his earliest followers with a magic circle, which nothing purely human is permitted to cross; has closed up the fountain of the Spirit—shut off its renovating streams from the ages—and left for us who still call ourselves Christians, the cold, intellectual contemplation of a remote historical event and the bewildered interpretation of a mysterious book.

This distinction between the spirit and the form of a historical religion, so conspicuous and yet so perpetually disregarded, it is of the utmost importance for the preacher of Christianity to keep in view, if he would leave the dead to bury their dead, and go forth to preach the kingdom of God in the fulness of its present meaning to the world. If he is not wholly unequal to his task (and the most gifted cannot be wholly equal to it), he must feel it one of the highest, as it is certainly one of the most solemn and responsible, that can be confided to a human being. Its worth depends altogether on the mode of its execution. If discharged with a high purpose of truthfulness and self-devotion, it is the noblest—if gone through with dull, mechanical routine, it is the meanest—of human employments. It has to mediate with a reconciling fidelity between the ever-changing forms of our external civilization and the ever-shifting aspects of a progressive science, and the eternal verities that are lodged deep in the human soul and proclaimed in the written word. The preacher or the prophet—for they are essentially one and the same —has to shew mankind that, however they may advance in knowledge, in power and in wealth—whatever unexpected command they may obtain over the material resources of creation—the moral conditions of our well-being remain for ever unchanged. There never can come a time when love and purity and honour and faithfulness and veracity will cease to be the grace and glory of our humanity. There never can come a time when the most exalted of human souls will cease to long for communion with something higher and more perfect than themselves, something to which they can look up, something in which they can place a filial trust. There never can come a time when the thoughtful spirit will be able to look on this vast universe without a sense of wonder and mystery which must breathe into it devout and reverent awe—there never can come a time when it will anticipate the inevitable event of death without solemn and earnest thought—without a welcome of the glorious trust, which no doubt or fear can ever finally pluck from the human soul, and which Christ uttered as the indwelling conviction of his—that it can only be the appointed mode of transition from a preparatory to a more advanced existence. These are themes which derive an imperishable interest, and furnish the prophet with an unfailing inspiration, from the changeless unity of our spiritual nature—an unity which, as it finds its witness in the universal consciousness, no scepticism can deny, and no revolution in our views of outward things can ever destroy. This is the great truth which the prophet has specially to guard, and which he must preach with courage and faithfulness, however the ears of a worldly and selfish generation may for the moment be closed against it. But in guarding the deep fountain of spiritual truth, he will not have to exclude any other truth, come from what quarter and under what shape it may. In the spirit of Christ, whose image is ever before him as a living embodiment of true religiousness, he will hail every new discovery of science, every fresh result of scholarship, as phenomena which themselves become religious through the light cast on them by the soul—seen in faith as but another disclosure from the Infinite Intelligence to our finite but ever-expanding capacity, of the form and order and working of His own ubiquitous activity. Viewed from the central position of the soul, what sphere of human thought, what scene of human activity, does not fall within the range of the prophet's vision? The world of business and the world of politics, the outer and the inner world—arts, letters, science and philosophy—suggest his lessons and furnish his illustrations and verify his words. Life and death, things present and things to come, all are his—for he is Christ's, and Christ is God's. He clothes all things in the light of the Divine Spirit which shines through him. To his eye, it rests upon them as a glory from above, making them all beautiful through its revelation of their hidden worth and sublime significance as a discipline for the free, immortal soul.

From a work in itself so noble, and furnishing so many opportunities for the exercise of the highest faculties and best affections, and for the dissemination of the most elevating influences, who that felt himself in any degree equal to its discharge would willingly withdraw? The Christian Ministry, as I view it, not only imposes a duty, but confers a privilege. Yet the duty which it imposes is so high, and the privilege which it confers is so precious, that he only who feels that he has adequate strength to meet its solemn claims, can be justified to himself in accepting the one and enjoying the other. A time comes in the life of every man when he is conscious of a diminution of the vigour of earlier years; when the silent admonitions of growing weakness and the sharper warnings of sickness bid him husband and reserve his powers for such duties as still imperatively rest upon him; and, while the shadows lengthen on his path, to gather up with his remaining strength such fruits as past labours may have yielded him, "ere the night cometh when no man can work." I would not have shrunk from this work of the ministry, arduous as I feel it to be, had not the experience of nearly two years convinced me that I could not discharge it as I feel it ought to be discharged, combined with the adequate fulfilment of other duties of prior obligation. I have not come to a hasty decision. No doubt was finally left on my mind that I could not properly execute the double trust confided to me. If I retained one, I must relinquish the other; and I have chosen that for which I am perhaps by nature and previous pursuits best qualified—in which I shall still be engaged in a kindred work—endeavouring, with the aid of my beloved and excellent colleague, to train an abler and more active generation for the ministry from which I must now retire myself—opening to them with honest freedom the genuine sources of divine truth—striving, as best I may, to combine in their young, unsophisticated minds, as the essential condition of all healthy progress, intellectual courage with religious reverence and humility. In quitting this pulpit, it is to me an unspeakable satisfaction that I leave in possession of it my friend and brother, with whom I have found it such a happiness to be associated, from whom I separate with so much pain, and with whom, in a no less important work, I feel it my best consolation to be closely united still. May God bless him in the great work which lies before him here! May long years of health and energy be given him to fulfil it, as few like him have the will and the power to do! His fidelity will never fall below his gifts. May the fruit be proportionate to both!

With one other word I will conclude. My connection with this religious society has been brief and transient, yet sufficiently lengthened to bring me into many pleasant relationships, and to procure me many friends. I trust that these moral ties will not be wholly dissolved by an official disruption. I would hope, if I dared, that effects of a higher and more enduring quality may have flowed, at least in some instances, from this transitory connection.

I suppose there are very few men, really in earnest about the work of the ministry, who have not felt at times a deep despondency at the little apparent result from their labours; who are not humbled by the consciousness, how ill they have succeeded in saying what they meant to say, and in making others believe and feel what they believed and felt themselves. If this were mere regret for the failure of oratorical displays to produce the intended effect and excite admiration and applause, such selfish vanity would be justly punished with disappointment. But the sorrow of which I speak has a deeper source. It is a genuine, lowly sorrow, that with all our efforts God's truth has been so ineffectually served by us—that after all our pains to conceive and utter it aright, God's word has so often dropped powerless from our lips. One consolation, however, ever accompanies the earnest, faithful soul—the trust it may reasonably entertain, that no true word, no word that comes up out of its deepest spiritual consciousness, ever went forth from it wholly in vain. There can be no stronger inducement to simple-minded fidelity, to perfect genuineness and simplicity of utterance, than this one trust. Brilliant generalities dazzle for a moment; then flash and go out. But whatever is individual and personal—whatever comes forth from the hidden man of the heart—is sure, sooner or later, in some form or other, to quicken into life some kindred individuality. The word which lies as a burden on your soul, which you cannot feel at peace till you have faithfully discharged—the word which brings with it to you all the weight and solemnity of a divine message—passes out of your mouth and wanders abroad, and finds entrance and welcome nowhere, till it encounters one whose case it meets, whose wants it satisfies, whose inward malady it heals. For him—perhaps that one solitary individual —you have spoken that word; and to know this, is your all-sufficient reward. The words that go forth from us, if they are true words, are like the seeds of plants blown about by the winds. Many seem scattered in vain and come to nothing; but one perhaps lights on a congenial soil, where it strikes root and germinates, and bursts into flower and bears fruit; and Nature's lavish expenditure is satisfied by that single return. Sweet is the recompence, after years apparently of unproductive toil, when the assurance greets us, as at times unexpectedly it does, that some wayfarer of humanity was cheered and strengthened on his journey by words of ours that fell accidentally on his ear—that God through us dispelled the darkness that lay on his soul, and breathed into him the resolve and the effort to lead henceforth a nobler life. What relationship between human souls can be so pure, so elevating, so enduring as this, which grows out of the root of our common immortality—which endures through this transitory life to ennoble our endeavours, and sanctify our trials, and render more sweet our sweetest affections—which carries with it to the grave a trust, a hope, an aspiration, not doomed to final disappointment, but destined to find its fulfilment at last in the mutual recognition and common blessedness which awaits us, if faithful, in some of the many mansions of our Father's house!

[Preached on resigning Ministry at Little Portland St.]

XIV.

Eternal Life of Good Men in God.

————+————

1 John ii. 17:

"The world passeth away, and the lust thereof: but he that doeth
the will of God abideth for ever."

SOME ancient authorities add these words: "even
as God abideth for ever." I do not suppose they
ever formed part of the original text; they are
probably an early gloss or interpretation. But they fill
up the sense of the passage, and shew how it has been
understood. They are a significant record of the feeling
of the primitive Church—how thoroughly it entered
into the great truth which pervades those beautiful
writings of the New Testament which bear the name
of John, that between God, the Eternal Spirit, and the
souls of good men, there is a close and ever-deepening
union, which death does not dissolve, but draws closer
still. In John, the life, the "life eternal" to which
death is represented as absolutely delivering over the
human soul, is never spoken of as an outward, future

good, capable of being conferred or withheld by any arbitrary decree, but as a certain habit or constitution of mind, growing up in the individual here on earth, and abiding in him, and inseparable from him, so long as that habit or constitution subsists. It issues from God, and is cherished by communion with Him; and, like God, its Source, it is imperishable. Christ, the mediator between God and the human soul, gives this life to his followers, because he possesses it himself in unlimited fulness through his perfect unity with the Father, and draws them through the attractive force of his self-sacrificing love into spiritual sympathy with his own divine life. The life which he received of the Father, that same life he imparts to them, that they all may be one; Christ in them, and God in Christ, "that they may be made perfect in one." As Christ himself speaks, in the fourth of our Gospels: "My sheep hear my voice, and I know them, and they follow me: and I give unto them eternal life; and they shall never perish, neither shall any one pluck them out of my hand. My Father, which gave them me, is greater than all; and no one is able to pluck them out of my Father's hand. I and my Father are one."

This is a doctrine of wonderful depth and richness. The more we reflect on it, the more we perceive how deep and rich it is. "The world passeth away," with all its short-lived splendours and vanities; but the soul of a good man "abideth for ever." It is united with God, and God cannot die. He is the Father of our spirits; and the spirit which has not through faithlessness and disobedience severed itself from the Parent Spirit, lives evermore through the inextinguishable vitality derived from Him. He who has once firmly grasped this great truth, and feels how it springs out of the profoundest consciousness of our moral being, is assured already of human immortality, and wants not the frail and tottering supports by which philosophy and theology attempt to sustain the sublimest trust of the soul. For the most certain of all certainties is the consciousness of my own responsible individuality. This is a reality which lies closer to me than all other realities. If I can be certain of anything, it is that I feel and think and have the power of voluntary action—that I live and move through something which is above myself and which is the necessary source of my being—that I am under a law which carries its own authority along with it—and that by reverent, trustful conformity to that law, I enter into more intimate communion with the Spirit from which it emanates. That Spirit Christ reveals to me as a Father; and the moment this revelation is made to me, I intuitively perceive the truth which it contains. It explains the relation in which I feel myself standing to the Author and Ruler of my being. I become conscious of affinity with that which is the Source of order, harmony and beauty in the universe. I feel that I belong, by what is highest in me, to that which is itself imperishable amidst perishable phenomena. This consciousness grows out of the very centre of my being—out of that which constitutes myself. I can sustain no religious relation to God but as an individual, with a personal trust and a personal responsibility; and all my reasonings on the Divine justice and rectitude, and all my expectations from the Divine mercy, proceed on the supposition that this personal individuality will be preserved. Moreover, it is my moral and spiritual, not my intellectual and creative powers, that constitute me a child of God. Human power and human wisdom are so absolutely incommensurable with the Divine, that they admit of no comparison with it. Here we are hopelessly remote from God, and must ever remain so. The finite here can never approach the Infinite. But it is different with Will, and all the moral qualities that depend on its exercise. Will is something which we possess in common with God. In the aim and tendency of our wills we may be ever drawing nearer and nearer to God, working more and more in harmony with Him to the extent of our actual insight and power—one with Him in the state of our affections and the direction of our endeavours, though eternally differenced from Him by the impassable chasm which separates the finite and the Infinite. Will implies personality; it is the ground of sympathy and intercourse between persons. The irrepressible instinct which impels us to pray to God and trust in Him, and in the higher stages of spiritual development to sympathize with Him and love Him, implies that God in this sense, as an all-perfect and all-mighty Will, is a Person. Our religious union with Him is that of sympathy between Person and person—between two natures made one, though infinitely different in all other respects, by a common quality of affection and will. Now it is precisely these moral attributes of God, involving affection and will, that we best understand, because they come most home to our individual consciousness, and we find some reflex of them within ourselves. The mysteries of creative and sustaining Power are placed beyond the grasp of human comprehension. What is the primal matter on which they act—how they mould it into organic form and working—how they project it into orbits of regulated sweep and velocity—how they express the grand geometry which defines the relations of worlds with worlds—how they furnish the principle of life and consciousness—how they bring forth successively more highly-organized types of existence—how they carry on through the ages the wonderful development of this vast Kosmos—these are things which we do not, cannot, and probably never shall, completely understand. Science can never go beyond phenomena. When it has reached the rudimental combination of ultimate elements, its researches must stop. It may exhibit results, but on the source and principle of action itself it cannot lay its hand. When it has pushed its inquiries to the utmost, it must always leave something which is unsearchable—lost in infinite depths which the finite cannot traverse—placed beyond those bounds which must for ever separate the human and the Divine. The wisdom of God and the power of God are therefore absolutely unfathomable by us. All extant phenomena discernible by the widest ken and minutest scrutiny of the philosopher's glass, are a very partial revelation of their exhaustless possibilities. But we do know, because our own experience is the witness here, what truth, what rectitude, what holiness and justice, and what mercy and love are ; and we feel that so far only as we submit ourselves to the guidance of these principles, do our lives result in order and harmony ; and that wherever we resist or contradict them, we involve ourselves in confusion and conflict, and come into collision with the sovereign law of the system to which we belong. Now these same qualities we perceive must exist in God, for His moral government is based on them—only to a degree of which we can say no more than that it is impossible for us to assign any conceivable limit to their perfection. If justice, veracity, benevolence, did not form the immutable foundations of His universe, it must cease to be a Kosmos and would lapse into Chaos. And if these qualities exist at all in God—and the deepest intuitions of our spiritual nature assure us that they do—in the Infinite Being they must themselves be infinite; and we may then, under all conceivable circumstances, calmly repose our trust in absolute Rectitude and absolute Love.

The moral attributes of God are not only those which we best comprehend, and which form a bond of union between our nature and His, but they are further the central attributes of His being, those which guide the operations of His wisdom and His power, and which— if there be a living God at all—we can see must of necessity be permanent and changeless. It is in them that the Divine immutability resides. No particular manifestation of Divine wisdom and power in the phenomenal world bears on it the stamp of necessary permanence, of absoluteness, of finality. We can easily conceive of other forms of existence than those which actually exist; for we can trace in the records of creation a constant succession of changing forms. But we cannot conceive of an universe constructed on a system of falsehood, wrong, cruelty and malevolence. Such a system must be self-destructive. Rectitude and truthfulness and tendency to the general well-being are essential conditions of permanent existence. So that the moral heart of the universe—the goodness, the holiness, the love, which are its inseparable attributes—cannot change; the possibility of existence itself is bound up with them. But the phenomenal forms in which the Central Mind manifests its conceptions throughout space, and the vast tide of events which the Sovereign Will is ever guiding and controlling through the endless channels of time—these are subject to continual change, and destined, so far as we can see, to illimitable development. Thus the aspect of the universe excites the idea of flux, mutation, transitoriness in the superficies of things, resting on deep central repose within—of varied action issuing from one fixed purpose of eternal love— of phenomenal variety as the living expression of spiritual identity.

To me there is something inexpressibly grand and consolatory in this view of the mysterious *state of I* to which our individual consciousness is attached— in the hold that we have, amidst the ruins of time, and the revolutions which are ever in operation all through space, on a moral unity which is imperishable. Mutability is the character most strongly impressed on everything phenomenal. The everlasting hills are silently wearing away, and depositing their solid contents in the bed of ocean. The mighty ocean itself shifts its place and varies its level, leaving new continents dry and submerging the old. Among the remotest stars of heaven mysterious changes are perceptible;—there are disappearances and new emergences and an intermingling of proximate lights of which man can give no account. Earth's bosom yields evidence of the diversified forms of existence which have successively tenanted its surface—of entire races of creatures that have been swept away, relinquishing their place to others that are its present occupants, and that will themselves give way in time to new developments of organized and animated being. Look where we may through the whole range of phenomena, nothing is fixed, nothing is permanent; all is changeful, fleeting, transitory. Within the narrower limits of human history the same experience repeats itself. The world's history is change—incessant change. Stronger races encroach upon and exterminate feebler. Ancient empires have passed away without a trace. Regions once populous and cultivated are a wilderness; and where the swamp and the forest anciently spread, there are now roads and bridges, and fruitful fields, and blooming orchards, and countless villages and cities. Arts, religions, languages, manners—all have changed, and all are changing. Is our individual life any exception to the universal law? From the cradle to the grave, it is a perpetual change. We bloom; we fade. We live; we die. Our fathers were, and they are not; and we shall follow them in our turn. Man's history is summed up with grand and simple pathos in the words of the ancient Preacher: " One generation passeth away, and another generation cometh." Were we to reason from phenomena alone, were there nothing beneath that which strikes the bodily eye, we might conclude that the universe was merely a linked succession of changes —production and extinction endlessly repeated. But through all these changes we discern a certain unity of type and plan which bespeaks a single Mind—indications of self-consistent rectitude of aim and a provident love issuing in preponderant good, which imply a moral character and purpose pervading the entire system of things, and intelligible from what is highest in ourselves —a persistency of benevolent aim, which justifies, amidst so much that is impenetrably dark and mysterious, the profoundest repose of faith on the absolute goodness, the perfect justice, the infinite love, which dwell immutably in the Central Heart of the universe.

It may occur to some, that reasonings like these are somewhat remote from the text with which we set out, and from the train of thought which would seem most suitable to the occasion which assembles us here to-day.[1] But it is not so. When we look back on the just and good who have been taken from us—when the minds which once cheered and brightened our social circle are eclipsed to us and translated to a sphere where our bodily eyes can discern them no more—when the evanescence and transitoriness of all that is earthly are brought home with a painful intensity to our consciousness—we naturally look around us for the traces of something stable and permanent in the midst of this vain and fleeting show; we ask ourselves what is the spiritual meaning and import of this mysterious universe;

---

[1] Originally written as a funeral sermon.

what is the relation of our conscious, intelligent and responsible being to that which is deepest and most durable in it; and, as we wait for an answer, the voice within and the word without take us to the Living God —our Father. Here is rest, here is permanence; here alone. The fashion of this world passeth away; but the truth, the justice, the mercy of God, do not and cannot pass away; they endure for ever. And this consolatory thought then arises within us—the same qualities which are changeless in God are the most durable in man. It is through our moral qualities that we are most closely united with God. These constitute us the children of God. As our Father lives, we shall live with Him. If there are any, therefore, of whom we can feel sure that they have passed through death to a higher life, it is the just and the good; for they are most like God in the only sense in which any comparison can be instituted between God and man—in the only qualities in which we have actual experience of living intercourse between us and Him. It is by our moral qualities—our sense of truth, our sense of right, our aspiration after excellence, our irrepressible tendency towards something higher than the actual, our exhaustless capacity of love—that we are related to the Living Power which is alone fundamental and durable under the ever-changing phenomena of the universe. Death can only bring us nearer to God. The qualities in which we resemble Him will have freer play and an ampler development when He is more fully revealed to us, and we see Him more clearly as He is. The characters of immortality seem to me far more distinctly impressed on the pure and upright heart and the holy life, than on the brilliant and original intellect. Genius is often wild, stormy and erratic in its operations; and, like the great explosive forces of the universe, when it has done its work and introduced the needful change, may be supposed.to subside once more within the ordinary limits of nature's operations, and to merge its individual existence in the resumed predominance of general law. But we can hardly conceive why the just, generous, devoted and loving soul should exist, except to serve God and to be happy in Him for ever. To live for God and with God seems the appointed end of its existence—the only end, as its own simple, noiseless example clearly shews, which gives a right direction to the working of the human faculties, and makes them immediately contribute to the general harmony and well-being of the world, and to the orderly and peaceable development of the Divine plans. I could draw an inference, therefore, in favour of the immortality of genius from its discovery of moral tendencies which it has in common with the simply virtuous; whereas from the indication of intellectual powers which ordinary minds share in an inferior degree with men of genius, I could not feel that I had equal grounds for the hope that they are destined for an eternal life in God. It is not, therefore, extent of power, but the rectitude of its exercise—not intellect, but spiritual-mindedness — not what the world calls cleverness, but simple fidelity to duty—not the resources of a highly-disciplined and richly-stored understanding, but the sweetness and purity of the affections of the heart—which point most clearly and steadily to a

higher life with God beyond the veil now drawn between visible and invisible things. It is the just, the
pure-hearted, the unselfish and the unworldly, that
we at once think of as the fitting inhabitants of the
heavenly world. It is of them that we say with Jesus,
in all the confidence of a devout faith, " Blessed are the
pure in heart, for they shall see God."

[Written, 1860 ; last preached (High Pavement, Nottingham),
21st February, 1869.]

XV.

Spiritual Vision.

"Jesus answered, and said unto him, What wilt thou that I should do unto thee? The blind man said unto him, Lord, that I might receive my sight. And Jesus said unto him, Go thy way; thy faith hath made thee whole."

THE wonderful works recorded of Christ bear on them a deep impress of moral and spiritual significance, and have been regarded, not unnaturally, by some as but types of a holier influence exerted on the soul. When leprosy departed at the touch of Jesus, it symbolized the cure of a more loathsome disease encrusting the inner life of man. When his voice re-animated the material dust, it prefigured the nobler resurrection of a spirit dead in trespasses and sins. When he turned water into wine, and fed multitudes with a few loaves and fishes, we have visibly represented to us, it has been argued, the dispensing of a spiritual element which slaked the thirst of immortal minds and satisfied the cravings for a bread that cannot perish. Without accepting or justifying this theory, as consistent with a true interpretation of the letter of Scripture, we may nevertheless unhesitatingly admit that it is the moral aspect of the miracles of Jesus, the spiritual lessons which they yield, and the view which they open into the interior of his own mind, which alone concerns us now, and can alone help to nourish a healthy faith in his religion.

Blind Bartimæus, spoken of in the text, exemplifies the case of thousands, who feel darkness resting on their mental eye, and would fain see the light if they could. As he hears the multitudes flocking past him, to gaze on the great Prophet of Nazareth, he deeply feels his own unhappy privation, that he too cannot look on the face of the Son of God. But his faith is stronger than theirs. He knows that he is in a divine presence. Though they rebuke him for his importunity, he only prays the more that he may receive his sight, and behold the revelation of heavenly love. It was this faith that made him whole.

What a depth of spiritual truth is opened to us in this simple narrative! Look around you. Not one alone here or there, but thousands are spiritually blind. They see not where they are. They know not whither they are going. A worldly, sensual, selfish life has sealed up their spiritual vision, and surrounded them with darkness. Happy are they if they come at length to feel their want, to perceive that the soul within is dark, and to understand the great truth uttered by Jesus, that "a man's life consisteth not in the abundance of the things which he possesseth." There are some in whom the sense of spiritual want—so far as we can discern—is never awakened. They are content with the animal life. Their thought and energy are only employed to enrich and embellish it. The very "light that is in them is darkness. How great, then, must be that darkness!" It is not of such that I now speak. To the Christian heart their state brings a deep sadness, an inexplicable mystery. Why should such men exist, we ask. We leave them to God. He will deal righteously with them. In His own time and His own way, He will pierce the darkness, and open the eye, and rouse the slumbering sense of the immortal within. I would speak rather of darkness that is felt, that is deplored, that makes desolate and miserable, that prompts the earnest prayer, " Lord, that I might receive my sight!"

I am putting no imaginary case. I am uttering the experience of thousands. Who ever communed deeply with his own soul; who ever interrogated earnestly the vast universe without; who ever penetrated through the superficial aspect of things to the infinite depths which enclose us on every side—and did not at times feel a dark, chill cloud of doubt and difficulty steal over him, which prompted the wish that this spiritual blindness might be taken from him, and broke perhaps into the very prayer with which the most remarkable man of modern times is said to have closed his earthly career—"Light, more light!" What a blessing it would be in such moments to feel the healing touch of a prophet's spirit, and to look with an open eye on the countenance of the Infinite Love! But such instantaneous miracles are not of our day. We must wait, and the needful cure will come at last. It is the first step in the right direction, to submit with patient trust to the inevitable conditions of an incipient and limited intelligence. As preliminary error ever fashions the way to ultimate truth, so doubts that come to us unsought, when not dishonestly suppressed or pusillanimously shrunk from, lead on to healthy and living faith. He who never felt a doubt, never effectually grasped a truth. It is the very sense of blindness that inspires the faith which is the source of spiritual light. There are men who will look on this Kosmos, and feel the want of nothing behind the phenomena which it offers to the sense—no holy, loving, sympathizing Spirit to hold communion with their own. They do not feel their blindness; and so long as that insensibility remains, they will never recover their sight. If they did, the prayer would go up for deliverance, and sooner or later it would be answered. It is a mistake to suppose that mere science can ever take the film from the spiritual eye. Not till the heart is touched with reverence and love, can science ever become truly religious. It receives rather than gives in this matter. It spreads out a glorious surface for the reception of the light shed on it by God's Spirit in the human soul; but for religious teaching, it shines with a reflected, not by a native light. Only in God's light do we see light. Not till we feel that the moral law, with all the sympathies and obligations attaching to it, is the first and greatest of all realities—the cause, the reason, the rule, the foundation of whatever exists and can exist—do we perceive that the universe would be impossible without a Mind, and that that Mind—possessed, from the very necessities of its nature, of the highest moral attributes which our own stage of moral advancement enables us to conceive—must be an object of unbounded veneration and trust. Just in proportion that our moral predominates over our animal nature—just in proportion that we feel the authority of a law which, we are conscious, does not emanate from ourselves—do we begin to see God and discern His spiritual relation to our souls: and that discernment is faith, and out of faith comes light. So our mental blindness is gradually dispelled; so the night that encircled us melts slowly into twilight, through which the great moral outlines of creation—its main purpose and general tendency—are already dimly discovered. In this spiritual twilight the majority of men live and die. They see enough to find their way without coming into collision with fatal error; but they want the clear assurance, the perfect trust, which would shine in upon them had their vision been fully opened by the touch of God's Spirit. Their faith is still rather an intellectual form, which they accept on another's warrant to supply their felt deficiency, than a living conviction of their own. In fact, till we have ourselves entered into personal relations with God; till sympathy with an Omnipresent Love has superseded the merely intellectual acknowledgment of a First Cause; till we discern a Father's agency in all things—we "see but in part," "as through a glass darkly," and we have daily need for the prayer of Bartimæus: "Lord, that we might receive our sight!"

Spiritually now, as physically then, the blind are healed by Christ. As the touch of his hand once opened the bodily eye, so for us at this day the touch of his spirit unseals the closed vision of the soul. Nor is there anything mystical in this statement. The constant laws of our nature explain the change. God works on us through our human sympathies. How infinitely richer and deeper is the truth infused into us by a holy life than by a religious discourse! The latter perchance satisfies the reason and silences reply; the former subdues and wins the heart and influences the will. It is the peculiarity of spiritual life that it must be imparted by spiritual communion. Words alone will not convey it: it cannot be taught. There are dormant elements of goodness in the worst and hardest natures, which awaken into new life at the kindling touch of a holier sympathy. They are drawn by an irresistible attraction of reverence and trust towards a higher manifestation of what they feel, however dimly, to be best in themselves. Displayed before them in that more perfect form, their faith in it is strengthened; they now believe in its possibility; and while its influence over them continues, they feel how healing it is. Now, this is a fact, not a doctrine. If you would subdue the unruly and reclaim the profligate, do not choose for your missionary the merely clever man—one who can talk and argue and dispute—but send among them the good, the truthful, the earnest man; one who has spiritual discernment and wide human sympathies; one who will bring his heart into contact with other hearts, and impart to them his own deepest life; he will bring back the wanderers, and gather them, if any one can, into the fold of Christ and God. All history proves the truth of this. See what an authority men of holy lives and perfect truthfulness and self-denying benevolence have acquired by the simple power of the Spirit over the roughest and fiercest barbarians. Nor is this transforming influence limited to personal intercourse. It subsists through tradition, and is transmitted by the written record. How many a young warrior in rude and simple times has had the passion of heroism first awakened in him by listening to the wild songs which celebrated the deeds of his forefathers! How many a mind of graver and more pensive turn has conceived the resolute purpose of self-consecration to a life of missionary peril and toil, in pondering over the chronicles which record the holy labours of a Columban, an Anschar, or a Xavier! Even in our own days, when there is so much to chill all lofty enthusiasm, and to limit our aims to material advantages and a worldly ambition, who has not known examples of young men snatched from the degradation of a sordid and selfish career, and diverted to a purer and nobler life, by simple contagion of the spirit that breathes from the biography of the generous and devoted Arnold! The influence of such books and such examples is wide, deep-searching and vast, beyond all calculation. It is through such subtile and silent channels that the Spirit of God traverses the ages from mind to mind, drawing the wise and good of all time into secret and often unconscious sympathy, and enabling them to combine with ever-accumulating force for the overthrow of evil and the establishment of the kingdom of God.

Now, if such be the metamorphic influence on our moral nature of all genuine goodness, even in its limited manifestations and while it does not as yet involve a perfect union of the human and divine, how profound must be its effect when it is set before us with no discernible imperfection and in unbroken communion with God, in the person of Christ — the ideal of our humanity, the revealer of the true relation of our nature with the universal Father; when we accept that person and interpret that revelation, not through the dim, uncertain medium of historical tradition and logical construction, but through loving and trustful communion with it—imbibing the spirit which it breathes, and appropriating, as far as we can, the life which it communicates! Faith is sympathy with a higher moral excellence than our own, and the trust which grows out of sympathy. In one word, faith is moral trust—trust in a person, in a character. Christ's whole life is an expression of perfect trust in God, and of the self-devotedness which springs from trust. In the view of Christ, the moral order of the universe had its source in the unerring will of God, or rather that will could not exempt itself from moral laws, and so impressed its own character on its work. This trust is the very sublimest that can take possession of the human soul. It is the unfailing source of spiritual light. It is the simple trust of a child in a Father. As we grow into the life of Christ through the entire submission of our hearts and wills to that spiritual law which he reveals, we imbibe more and more of that holy trust, and of the unspeakable peace which accompanies it. Through oneness with

Christ we attain to oneness with God. This great change in our spiritual relations—this trust, results, it must be obvious, rather from a moral affection of the soul, from its aspect towards God, than from the acquisition of any new truth; but though not a truth itself, it changes the character of all other truth, and sets it in a new light before us. Though originated not by reason, but by sympathy, it is nevertheless perfectly rational in its influence, since it harmonizes with and more thoroughly explains all that reason independently brings to it. It may be compared to the new meaning put into a scene of nature or an occurrence in human life by the interpretation of genius. The scene, the occurrence, remains the same; but we see in it what we never saw before, and what we now feel to be the highest truth, though without communion with more gifted spirits we should never have suspected its existence.

The advantage of religious faith over a mere intellectual or scientific reading of the universe, is this—that as it is founded on trust in a Person, on trust in moral character, it carries us over all those difficulties in creation and providence where mere reason would be constantly at fault. Whatever may be doubtful, no doubt can destroy the facts of my own conscious being. I know that I possess a moral nature and live under a moral law; and this knowledge, rooted in my inmost being, confirmed by the witness of the good of all ages, and interpreted by the death of the Martyr on Calvary, carries me up to the undoubting acknowledgment of an all-perfect Being who cannot possibly do wrong. Where I cannot see, therefore, or comprehend, I can still believe and trust. Though the mortal eye may be veiled in darkness, the spiritual eye can still discern unchanging light. The difficulty, vast and perplexing as it may be, results from limitation, not of Divine wisdom or love, but of human capacity. It is the inevitable accompaniment of a finite nature that has relations with the Infinite. Profound faith may even suggest the possibility that the most perplexing problems belong precisely to those parts of the Divine ways which, as they are the furthest from our present comprehension, are in themselves perhaps the most wonderful and glorious.

This is religious trust, the faith of Christ. How sweet is the peace which it brings to the soul! We live in God. We are children of the Infinite Love. Our Heavenly Father, who has revealed Himself in His Son, only asks our sincere aspirations and earnest endeavours after the right, and will Himself overrule to a remoter good our unmeditated precipitation into wrong —yea, the very follies, transgressions and sins which we deplore, repent of and renounce. Weak as we are, we are strong in Him. As His servants, we have courage to bear and do all things. Around us is this wonderful universe, where we can exercise our highest faculties in disentangling the web of laws which hold it together in organic unity, and gratify our most refined senses in contemplating the robe of varied beauty in which it is wrapped. Before us is spread a wide field of action, where the benevolent purposes of our Father disclose themselves to the unsealed eye of faith, and where He invites to co-operation with His own boundless goodness the energies and affections with which He has so richly endowed us, and the simple exercise of which is a source of the purest happiness. True, there is evil in this beautiful world—pain, sorrow, multifold and varied suffering; worst of all, selfishness and wickedness. But evil itself is an instrument of good in the hands of God; and if we understood our true relation to Him, we should feel it our highest privilege to be summoned to work with Him in abating and subduing it. Evil in some form cannot be separated from the discipline which is needed to prepare the finite spirit for the next stage in the endless life which awaits it. Let it not disquiet or perplex us. It is but for a moment, and is working out its own cure. Grapple with it bravely, and it will disappear or be transformed into good. If the pride and injustice and insolence of man should for one moment upset the balance of your mind, and irritate you into unseemly wrath, remember Whose presence surrounds you. One glance at the glorious heaven over-arching all, with the sun and the rain coming down on the evil and the good alike—one thought of that mysterious humanity where God has imaged Himself, and where He dwells in the unsearchable operations of His Spirit side by side with our infirmities and sins—will suffice to dispel all your bitterness, and bring down again the peace that you had well-nigh lost, on your reconciled and trusting hearts. See God in all things, and a new lustre will burnish the face of creation; a new spirit will breathe itself into your enjoyment of life; your eye will be opened to what you never saw before, and you will behold the face of Him who gave you your sight, looking benignantly upon you from every side.

It is the blessing of religious faith, that it makes our view of life one and self-consistent. It saves us from the perplexity and double-dealing of a worldly and selfish course. It produces the most beautiful attribute of moral character—simplicity and singleness of mind. If we have true faith, we can only have one allegiance and one law. It combines energy with quietness. We are to do right, cost what it may; and having done that, to await the issue in perfect peace. It transfers our affection from interests which are mean and perishable, to those which are noble and everlasting; from sordid avarice, from feverish ambition, from childish vanities, to objects which have engaged the efforts and the aspirations of the best and wisest of our race—the love of truth, the struggle for justice and freedom, the desire of human weal over all the earth. God is in these great interests, and they can never perish. As religious beings, we possess an affinity with God himself. The moral law on which He has built creation is older and more enduring than creation itself; and they who are formed in His moral image, and whose spiritual eye He has opened to discern eternal truth, will survive with Him the changes of time and the ceaseless transformations of the material universe.

[Written, 1861; last preached (Carter Lane),
11th August, 1861.]

XVI.

The Lessons of Time.

---

2 PETER iii. 8:

"Beloved, be not ignorant of this one thing, that one day is with the Lord as a thousand years, and a thousand years as one day."

THIS is a popular way of saying, that with God time has no existence at all. An old Greek put the same thought in other words when he said: "In view of eternity, a thousand, nay ten thousand years, is an inappreciable point, or rather the smallest conceivable fraction of a point." This is one of those primitive intuitions in which childhood and the infancy of our race often anticipate the conclusions of the philosopher. Time is a condition of the development of finite natures. It is predicable only of such natures as are limited, subject to change, and constantly passing out of one state into another. Time and growth are correlative. It is obvious, therefore, that it can have no application to a being that is infinite. It constitutes an essential distinction of the creature from the Creator.

Time is a power in God's hand, of which, as being above it Himself, He has an uncontrollable and exhaustless command. It is an element of which He can be lavish at will. Our old notions on this subject, determined by the letter of the biblical representations, were exceedingly defective. We were accustomed to speak of the beginning of time, and even ventured to assign its date. But so long as the Divine energy has given birth to finite and progressive life (and can we suppose it ever to have been inactive?), there must have been time; for time is the measure of the changes of life. Our ideas both of time and space have been wonderfully enlarged by the discoveries of modern science. Geological eras which have sufficed to the production of only one condition of planetary existence, almost transcend the bounds of chronological computation. Of space and time we see there may be an endless profusion in the working out of the Divine plans, without any encroachment on the vast surplus which remains. There is, perhaps, no consideration so fitted to impress us with the greatness of God and the littleness of man. But this subject has its practical as well as its speculative side. All things in this universe seem ultimately to subserve moral ends. They culminate in mind. Physical changes and successions contribute in their final result to spiritual development.

To speak now of time—I wish to shew its effect on the formation of human character. We are educated, we are trained for, we are developed into higher conditions of existence, by successive experiences; and such experiences supply the increments of time. We may say, therefore, that we are educated by time. But to produce this effect, experience must be noted and preserved. To turn time to good account as an educator, the mind must be kept open and observant, with ever-wakeful retrospect and forethought. It must not be shut up in the present. Its natural growth and development under the moulding hand of time are checked mainly by two causes—addiction to sensual indulgence, and absorption in the selfish cares of the world. These besetting sins frustrate the moral ends of life and take from time all its disciplinary influence; first, by so disturbing the calmness of the mind that it can no longer give back a faithful image of the world in which it lives; secondly, by preventing that comprehensiveness of view in which alone the just proportions and mutual relations of things can be seen. Sensual and worldly natures, in the progress of their degeneracy, lose all their expansiveness and recipiency, and dwindle down towards a mere point of animal and organic life. In an opposite sense to that in which it is predicated of God, being is with them a perpetual Now. God is above time; they are below it. Time rightly used connects us with God, and sweeps us onward to the bosom of His own eternity. To the mind that keeps itself free from these narrowing influences, and treasures up its varied experience, the world becomes continually richer in beauty and wisdom with the lapse of time. We read the same books, we converse with the same world, we look on the same nature, as of old; but we find in them now a significance which they did not discover to us before. In earlier days they spoke to the outward sense and kindled the imagination; they come to us now with graver aspect, full of deep and solemn meanings gathered out of many years, and carry their moral lesson deep into the inmost soul. Who has not reverted after a long interval to some favourite passage of a familiar author, and been surprised to find what new light rests on it, and what unsuspected truth it reveals? Who has not revisited some well-known scene, rich in associations with years long passed away, and found it clothed with a sweet and quiet beauty which the outward eye had never caught, but which is now shed on it by the spirit within? Time is needed to ripen our highest thoughts and purest enjoyments. Without its mellowing influence, they remain crude and sensuous. In the purest beauty, as in the deepest wisdom, there is a touch of sacred melancholy, needed to give them their true flavour — in which the consciousness of human evanescence, of death and eternity, has its share. The good that we have been permitted to do or to witness— the virtuous and the wise whom we have known and conversed with—leave behind them effects, unfelt perhaps at the time, which are enhanced by distance and consecrated by death, and fill the moral atmosphere of life with an imperishable fragrance. No beauty, no goodness, no truth, ever flashed through time, however brief its course, without yielding an influence that may be caught up and perpetuated by a spirit that is on the watch for it and worthy to imbibe it. These solemn influences deepen round us as we advance into years, and give to life, in our higher moods of thought, with all its sorrows and its meannesses, a grandeur and a glory which are not of earth. It is the balmy sweetness of evening, collecting and diffusing in that hour of calm the scattered odours of the day, and leaving on the soul a sense of rest and peace which is the foretaste of a higher life.

Time has lessons for the understanding, as well as holy emotions for the heart. We acquire under its teachings a juster estimate of things. Some enigmas are cleared up to us. What we once took on trust, is now justified by experience. We observe in the world many things that are at war with our first and most obvious sense of right. We see that it is not always the best and the wisest who are most prosperous in life. We notice how frequently impudence and unscrupulousness carry the day over delicate honour and high conscientiousness. Old prejudices keep their ground. Great truths make no visible progress. In youth, these things filled us with despondency, and we were disposed to murmur and complain. But time and experience bring with them a deeper wisdom, and put the world's order in a more satisfactory light. We discover that peace of mind, a true enjoyment of God's goodness, and the highest worth and nobleness of character, are not bound up with worldly distinction and success. We see that wealth and high place and splendid and luxurious living are beset with sorrows and trials which outward show cannot hide, and which it is a mercy to be spared; and that where men fix their ambition on these things as the great end of life, they expose themselves to temptations which few are strong enough to resist. We observe that genuine happiness and respectability are more within reach of all men than the world's estimate of good would lead us to suppose, and may be secured in every condition by a loving heart, a thoughtful mind, a faithful and earnest life. If any truth dear to us be discouraged or calumniated, we feel that its possession is the main thing—infinitely more valuable than any fame or popularity it might bring with it, and that the erring judgments of men cannot shake the foundations on which we know it to rest. Its low outward estate tests its intrinsic worth and tries our fidelity to it, and may be the ordeal through which it must pass to bring forth at last the richest spiritual fruits. If there be one lesson which time impresses with increasing force on the mind, it is the difference between the substance and the shadow of things—to hold cheap innumerable objects on which we once set our inexperienced hearts, and which the worldly and the frivolous still eagerly pursue—and to value, as the great thing which alone makes life precious, and apart from which its distinctions and successes are utterly worthless, all sweet and pure affections, all cordial friendships, duties well performed, opportunities wisely improved, knowledge and mental culture, social usefulness, and that inward peace which springs from firm trust in God and in the issues of His righteous providence—*all* under the ever-deepening consciousness of something grander and more enduring in preparation than comes to us through the perishable scenes of earth. Such are the rich and mellow fruits which are dropped, as time rolls on, from the branches of the tree of life into the lap of years.

The lessons of time strengthen our faith in the moral

government of God. It justifies itself to our widening experience. Life carries with it a constant fulfilment of all that our native intuitions and parental warnings told us would be—of all that poets and sages, prophets and apostles, taught us in early life. Their words turn out true to the very letter. Not one faileth. We find that God keeps His covenant with us, and rules with a high justice in the earth, and causes all men sooner or later to reap the fruit of their doings. This is the awful lesson of that ancient scripture of Nature and Providence whose leaves are turned over for us by the hand of time. Which of us does not feel in his own individual life, how unerring in its effects is the great law of moral retribution—how inexorably the sentence of our righteous Judge is executing itself upon us without and within—in enfeebled powers, in wasted opportunities, in the secret upbraidings of conscience? We were told it would be so, in our days of unthinking presumption, and hearkened not ; but our sins have found us out and left their sting behind. Time has forced the great truth on our consciousness, and written it in uneffaceable characters on our daily experience. The mingled tares and wheat that we sowed in youth have each sprung up and borne their proper fruit, in the harvest of partial contentment and now unavailing regret which we are reaping in maturer years. Not one folly has been allowed an entrance into our lives, not one sin has been indulged in, not one evil habit has been contracted, without consequences which follow us perhaps to the grave. Even penitence and reformation cannot always stay the outward pain and disorder which wrong-doing brings into the world, though they may restore peace and trust to the soul. When our views are changed, and we are intent on well-doing, and would fain set our hearts and homes right with God, He who guides and governs our mortal lot will not suffer us to forget the sanctity of His law; compels us to feel day by day what a root of evil there is in all sin; and in the yet unextinguished force of vicious tendencies and strong passions, or in the moral feebleness which follows neglect of duty and broken resolutions, allows an awful Nemesis to haunt our life, sometimes through our best affections and holiest relationships to invade our peace and overcast our day, and in tones of terrible distinctness to remind us that the boundaries of right and wrong are irreversible and eternal, and can never be transgressed with impunity. Such are the solemn teachings of time. They humble us, but make us wise. They shew us the true meaning of life. No one who listens to them can doubt that we live under a law which is higher than ourselves—which we did not invent, and all our sophistry cannot annihilate or explain away—which overtakes us at last in spite of all our contrivances to evade it, and avenges itself with an authority which nothing human can resist. If there be one argument for a God and a providence and a moral retribution that is unanswerable, it is that which is brought home to us in accumulating proofs by the witness of time.

And to what conclusion do all these things tend? If the experiences of time have not been wholly neglected and forgotten, they have at least yielded knowledge and worked out in us results which seem to point to something beyond themselves. If this life of ours, looked at spiritually, means anything, it is a discipline—a preparation. Such is the specific effect of time on our mental and moral constitution. It is our great instructor. It trains and developes us. But what is the use of instruction, if not to be applied ? What is the object of discipline, but to furnish out a coming life ? What can be meant by preparation, if there be nothing yet future to be prepared for ? Now the peculiarity of human life, viewed in the individual, is this—that it never rises above the aspect of a discipline and a preparation. It is never followed by a result that seems a natural completion of the mental activity developed in preceding years. Man is ever learning, or at least might be learning, to the last. At eighty or ninety, if the energy dependent on physical organization could be sustained, there is no reason suggested by the mind itself why the acquisitions already made should not become the basis of wider knowledge and fresh discoveries, and new triumphs over ignorance and prejudice and moral feebleness and limitation. Oftentimes, the pure and generous and hopeful sentiments which are the best fruit and highest recompence of intellectual culture, continue to burn on bright and undimmed to the last moment of consciousness, and only go out with life itself. Why then, I ask, this elaborate building up of character by the hand of time, if it is to fall to pieces for ever at death ? Does God in other cases construct thus in vain ? Is it characteristic of His creation to be frustrated of ends which seem evidently designed ? We obscure and embarrass this high argument by bringing too many considerations into view, by incurring unnecessary liabilities, and burdening ourselves with needless proofs. Let us look only at the one point which it is essential to establish. Of primal origins, and intervening developments, and ultimate principles of being, as we know nothing, we may leave them out of view. They are lost in the unsearchable past. They are hidden from us in the fathomless depths of God. But we are conscious of actual powers, and irrepressible aspirations, and marked tendencies; and in these, as patent, undeniable facts, we find a ground of glorious trust and hope. Our moral nature, taken as a whole, is itself a fact, significant and foreshewing. What it suggests through our native instincts and demands from our highest reason, is re-echoed in the voice of history through every age, speaks in all literatures and in all religions, has commanded the assent and furnished the consolations of the wisest and the best, and revealed itself as a reality in Christ. The *how*, the *when*, the *where*, are questions that belong not to us. We know what God, by the constitution of our being and the successive revelations of His providence, induces us to believe, and we can leave the solution of them to Him. We can trust His word that is ever speaking to our souls. His word is truth. It never deceives those who humbly rely on it. How the great principle of human immortality can be realized in its ever-multiplying results—how the infinity of deathless spirits, that are every moment passing through time, are to be disposed of, trained, developed, and allowed to grow in intelligence and felicity, for ever and ever—these are questions which it is easy to raise and impossible to answer; our finite reason is unequal to grapple with them; they involve conceptions too vast for the boldest imagination to grasp. But what are they to God—what are they to Him with whom our planetary system is but a point in space, and a thousand years not as one day, but an infinitesimal of time? Knowing what we do, ignorance on other points justifies the profoundest faith. We cannot comprehend the infinity of God; but that infinity is itself an exhaustless source of devout trust. The spiritual nature which we derive from Him, and which makes us His children—which His providence, acting through time, so carefully nurtures and builds up, and draws onward through successive stages of spiritual development into closer communion with Himself—He will not allow to perish, but will translate in His own time and way, through the brief crisis of material dissolution, with its holy memories and sweet affections, its unexhausted capacities and unsatisfied aspirations, to the glorious company of saints and sages—of those dearer and more precious to us than saints and sages—gathered out of their various stations on earth to their final home with God in heaven!

[Written, 1861; last preached (Octagon Chapel, Norwich), 28th June, 1863.]

XVII.

Evidence of Immortality from the Demand of our Moral Nature.

—+◆+—

Hebrews xiii. 14:

"Here we have no continuing city, but we seek one to come."

THERE are some themes which are as old as the world, and yet will retain their freshness so long as the world endures. No repetition can exhaust the interest which attaches to them. Such are those mysterious fears and longings which haunt the human soul, when it pauses for a moment in the bewildering career of daily life, to ponder on Time and Death and Eternity. Amidst the anxious questionings thus raised within us, where shall we find any solid ground of trust and hope?

Looking for the moment at the connected dispensations of Judaism and Christianity in no higher light than that of remarkable social phenomena, no one can deny that they have thrown a new impulse into the world, and given a more elevated direction to the thoughts of men: first, by infusing a profounder sense of close moral relationship between the human soul and the great invisible Source of Being; and secondly, by determining out of that moral relationship, and not from any abstract theory of the nature and origin of the soul, the retributory character of the higher life which their combined and accumulating influence leads us to anticipate as a moral necessity after death. The immortality of Christian hope has no affinity with the metempsychosis of the ancient sages of India and Egypt, or with the pantheistic dreams of the Pythagorean and Platonic schools. It grows out of a moral root, and points to a moral issue. It is to the Christian a spiritual fact in the grand order of God's moral government, not a philosophical speculation. It is the response to an irresistible demand of our deepest convictions on the moral perfections of God; and what it holds out to us, with a certainty which grows with the growth of our own religious life, is not the dissolution of the individual in the universal soul, but, on the contrary, the intensifying of our respective individualities—the more complete development, through the more exact retribution, of individual worth and individual capacity.

Some important and very consolatory inferences flow from this marked peculiarity of the religious teaching of the Bible.

We now see why it was that the doctrine of immortality formed no part of the Mosaic law. It was the design of that law to withdraw the mind of the chosen people from the fruitless speculations of Eastern sages and priests, about possible changes of being after death, which only fed a superstitious fancy and never touched the deeper springs of human thought and conduct, and bind them in close moral covenant with their national God, and make them feel that their weal and their woe depended on His unfailing moral retributions; that out of this sense of immediate relationship to a just and holy God—needful for a time to be impressed exclusively on them, as their distinction from other peoples, to give it a deeper root in the national mind—there might gradually spring up with the strengthening of their convictions and the widening of their views, the demand for a nobler and completer life than could be realized under the actual conditions of their natural existence. These feelings are vividly expressed in the progressive development of that great idea of a kingdom of God which inspires the utterances of the prophets. We observe in them increasing wonderment and disquietude about the present, and a longing ever more fervent and earnest for a happier future, when their moral anticipations would be realized, and the righteous and the wicked disposed of according to their deserts; till at length, in the latest writings of the Old Testament, we find the expectation of a resurrection of the just dimly shaping itself into view, and gradually taking the form which it completely assumed in the age of Christ, as a vital element of popular belief. But the previous moral training of the people, limited though it was in the first instance, produced an immense effect on the character and influence of this belief. It was in no sense speculative and metaphysical. It was the satisfaction of a practical want of the soul. As it grew out of deep moral conviction, it was brought into the closest connection with life and conduct, furnishing a solution of the darkest problems of Providence, and holding out the strongest inducement to steady persistency in well-doing. In none of the heathen religions, if we except perhaps the old Persian, do we observe it exercising any such practical effect. It had with them a different origin, and its influence, such as it was, fell on a different part of human nature—on the imagination and speculative intellect, not on the conscience and the heart.

We discern further, from this point of view, the close spiritual connection between the old and the new dispensations: how the one prepared the firm, deep, moral basis of personal religion for the spiritual superstructure of the other. Christ took up the belief at the point to which it had been already developed by his prophetic forerunners; and by his own passage through the death of the cross into a higher world, at once gave its true significance and grandeur to the idea of a kingdom of God, and threw open its gates to the universal race of man. Exhibiting life *there* as the development and completion of life *here*, his interpretation of that idea was retrospective in its application; for it declared by necessary inference that immortality was the heritage of all mankind—of all those that had been, as well as of all that were to come. Even in what appear to our more enlarged apprehension of Christian truth the limitations or extravagances of the early belief on this subject, we discover additional traces of the deep moral root out of which it sprang, and the intense moral conviction which it carried with it. We see why it was that, in all the Scripture promises, distinct and positive assurance is given to them alone who, by their partaking of the spirit of Christ, could produce the needful warrant of having fulfilled the moral purpose of existence; while of all the rest the future condition is left in mysterious uncertainty—to be deduced, not from express affirmation, but from a general application to the circumstances of our collective humanity, of the merciful spirit of Christ's religion. We can understand too how, when faith grew out of moral conviction—when it dwelt in the soul as a fact of consciousness—the first Christians should have had that undoubting belief in the constant presence of their risen and glorified Lord—how to their spiritual eye the two worlds, the visible and the invisible, should seem to touch each other—how they should have commemorated the death-day of their virtuous friends as the birth into a second life—how they should have spoken to them and prayed for them, when their devoutest thoughts bore them through the veil into the world of blessed spirits, and they felt with intense conviction that the saints on earth and the saints in heaven were but one family in God. However we may account for its origin, such was the faith of the primitive Church. It is an indisputable fact in the spiritual development of our race; and its perpetuated influence, however enfeebled and corrupted by the growth of opposite tendencies, has changed the whole character of European civilization, and marks off, by an uneffaceable distinction, the religion of heathenism, such as it was, and the religion which simple philosophy has ever been able to evolve out of its intellect, from the religion of Christ. There is the same difference between the aspect of immortality, as seen from the heathen or philosophical and from the Christian point of view, as between a landscape revealed to us by night in a momentary glare of lightning, and the same landscape shining out permanently before us in the clear and steady light of day. There is the same reality in both cases. But in one, it is caught in a transient glance; in the other, it is the object of enduring vision. Now the reason of the difference, as I have before hinted, I believe to be this—that the seat of this hope is placed, in the two cases, in a different part of our nature; in the intellect and imagination, in the one; in the conscience and the pure and deep affections entwined with the conscience, in the other.

Whatever may have been the immediate action of the Divine Spirit, in the first instance, to introduce this great change in the direction of human thought and endeavour, its permanent benefit to us has been, that it has put us in the right point of view for apprehending the true value and immortal issue of life, by fixing our attention and reverence on the moral elements of our nature, and establishing a relation of mutual sympathy —of Fatherly care on one side, and of filial devotedness and responsibility on the other—between the human soul and God. This is one of those truths which, once revealed to the mind, can never perish. It henceforth shines for ever by a light of its own, even though the evidence of the agency by which it was first brought into the world should become dim and fade at last altogether away. Having once gained this high moral point of view, we find in it an argument for human immortality which is unassailable, exhaustless and ever-increasing. Look at life with a Christian eye, and you will see immortality flowing out of it by a natural, I might almost say a necessary, issue.

It is the moral element of our nature which produces what we call character, marks the individual, and determines the fitness and beauty of his life. It is the conformity through conscious volition of the habitual affections and endeavours to the law of truth and right, of honour and faithfulness and love, which places every one where he ought to be in this great system of things, enables him directly to subserve its design and promote its harmony, and hastens the evolution of the grand, progressive Kosmos, ever present to the Eternal Mind, out of the moral conflict and confusion by which the All-wise has decreed that it should be preceded, and which may be among the conditions of its more complete final realization. It is through our moral promptings that we interpret the mind of God, and decipher the meaning and purpose of the mysteries which encompass us. Released from the bonds of moral law—of the provident wisdom, the just and holy severity and the compassionate tenderness, which are the guiding rule of all things, and which here and there we cannot trace, only because their operation is on too vast a scale to be embraced within our finite view—creation would fall asunder, and ancient chaos resume its reign. Our moral sense brings us into contact with what is highest in this universe, that by which it subsists and endures—its wisdom, its holiness and its love. Here we find the bloom, the blossom, the flower of our complex being. Everything else in us, as compared with this—even intellect and genius—appears subordinate and disciplinary. Devoid of moral aim and moral feeling, the most brilliant powers may startle and astonish, excite perhaps admiration and wonder, but they can never strike out a true beauty or yield the highest satisfaction to the mind. What a vital deficiency is implied in any production when we say of it, it is clear, but intellectual and hard. It is the glow of pure and sweet affection, it is the gleam of high and earnest moral feeling, which lends its highest charm to the efforts of genius, and leaves the light of immortality on those few burning words and living touches of the poet and the artist, which shine through all time and draw to them the reverent homage of all hearts, as the revelation of God in our humanity. Our personal experience, if I mistake not, is the same. As we advance in years and get a deeper insight into the true worth of things, we care less for mere talent and those differences of opinion which only afford an opportunity for intellectual display; and we love more fervently pure, simple, genuine goodness in all its forms, under every diversified aspect of belief, condition and pursuit; we find ourselves receding more and more from all strong interest in speculative controversies, to concentrate the whole force of our souls on those deeper truths which concern our personal relations with God, which bind us solemnly to duty, and urge us onward and upward to a purer and nobler life. Is there not something significant in this change of feeling which years bring along with them, that "as the outward man decayeth," we should be drawn away almost unconsciously from the transient and the perishable, and cling more to that which carries in itself the evidence of something imperishable and eternal?

It is certainly a curious fact, that the highest faculties of our nature should be precisely those which seem least to attain their object and work out their appropriate satisfactions within the limits of this life—for they are of such a nature as to create unceasingly with their own self-development an aim and aspiration beyond themselves; while our lowest attributes, if we looked to them alone, might well be thought to have run through their appointed cycle of action and enjoyment in less than the ordinary term of human years. The higher we ascend in our graduated scale of powers, the more we are forced into an outlying futurity for any rational solution of the mysterious purpose of life. He who is only a more refined species of animal, who lives to eat and drink, to dress and amuse himself, has had his fair share of the only happiness he has cared for by the time that he is seventy, and ought to retire without a murmur from the feast at which he has been permitted to sit so long. And if in the most sensual natures there were not occasional indications of something purer and nobler struggling for existence within, our hopes for such, when they lay down their pampered bodies in the grave, would be dark indeed. Even in the somewhat higher vocation of an exclusive worldly activity and a devotion to gain or social position for their

own sakes—as these objects all lie within the limits of
this life, when gained, they may seem to have exhausted
its purpose and leave nothing more to expect or desire.
What is an immortality of love and worship to a man
who has lived entirely for this world? He has schemed
and accumulated successfully—all he has ever lived for
—and he dies, great and rich. To some extent, the
same remark is applicable even to intellectual power
when used for itself alone and divorced from moral
purpose. It is so much force distributed through
society; and excepting so far as it is taken up by individual character and made subservient to a beauty
and a worth beyond itself, it passes from hand to hand
with the mutations of time in ever-accumulating results
of wealth, utility and knowledge, for the progressive
civilization of the race, but giving no sign of the possible destiny of the individual hereafter. As soon, however, as we get into that higher region where heart
and conscience rule, we feel ourselves in possession of
thoughts, affections and aspirations which find no rest
and completion in the objects of this earthly life, and, if
death be the final extinction of our being, seem to fail
of their natural issue and to be cut short of their proper
result. By a strange contrariety to all the analogies of
His providence, the last and most glorious of all God's
works—a reverent, worshipping, loving soul—stands
alone in His creation as an abortion. If this life means
anything morally to the individual, it is a discipline
and an education. And what is the intent of discipline
and education, but to prepare the being that is trained
by it for a state of things yet to come? To moral

culture and development we can assign no limit—certainly not in this life. But what a strange contradiction meets us, if the hope of the Christian is all a dream! When the good man, through bitter and varied experience, has mastered the great lesson of life, and catches at last a glimpse of the true worth and meaning of things; when he has purged off the grosser impurities of his nature, and unlearned his prejudices and calmed his passions and mellowed his affections; when he is best fitted for holy and loving intercourse with his kindred and fellow-creatures, and for deep and peaceful communion with the Father, to whom, through many doubts and fears, he has ever faithfully clung, and whom at length he is beginning to behold in the unveiled brightness of His wisdom and love, with only enough of darkness and mystery left behind to make him long for a completer solution hereafter—just at that crisis, can we suppose it possible that this glorious framework of being should be demolished, that these holy affections should wither away in their first unfolding, and this beautiful light of the soul be extinguished for ever? Nor must this inference be confined to age alone. It is applicable wherever the moral sense and aspiration have been once awakened—nay, wherever we can see that even the possibility of their future development exists.

Then there are the affections—the affections of home, kindred and friendship. What a voice speaks in them of immortality! These form the soul, and determine the character, and make the individual what he is. It is through them that he acquires a sense of what is holy and noble and beautiful, and sees into the deeper meaning of life's mysterious discipline. And as they form the individual here, shaping intellect into its highest use and application—if the individual is to exist hereafter it is certain they must exist along with him to aid his future development, and will be renewed in a finer organization and with an inconceivably more glorious and delightful influence. What a blessed hope is this! May it shine on us for ever! Only recollect that our retention of it must depend on our preserving the moral attitude of the soul out of which it springs. It cannot be grasped by the intellect alone. A Christian hope requires for its nourishment a Christian state of mind. Christ, in his disclosure of our human relationship to God, gave us for ever the point of view from which that star of heavenly promise may be continually seen. Live in his spirit and for his aims; and though clouds may obscure for a moment its healing ray, that blessed light will never go down on your souls!

[Written, 1862; last preached (Northampton),
7th December, 1862.]

<h1 style="text-align:center">XVIII.</h1>

<h2 style="text-align:center">Divine Treasure in Earthen Vessels.</h2>

2 CORINTHIANS iv. 7:

"We have this treasure in earthen vessels, that the excellency of the power may be of God, and not of us."

THE nature we possess is mysteriously complex; and in surveying its mingled elements, it is difficult to draw the line between what is strictly human and what is properly divine. In all ages, opinion has run into extremes on this subject. Some minds, at once profoundly religious and sternly logical—as those of an Augustine, a Calvin, and an Edwards—by resolving all agency into the Divine, reduce to nothing the freedom and spontaneity of man, and have elaborated systems of rigid, consequential necessity, separable by only an imaginary distinction from fatalism itself. Others, again, have looked on humanity as the highest fact of the universe, discerning nothing above and beyond it. They believe man to have the absolute disposal of his own fate through an intelligent application of the laws beneath which he finds himself placed; and regard his intelligence as the last result of a vast and inexplicable phenomenal development. On these deep questions, which have their root in the infinite, I have ever felt how utterly inadequate is our finite logic to their solution; and I have therefore been content to throw myself back on that instinctive common sense of our nature which feels certain that there must be some intermediate view, to meet the apparently conflicting conditions of human existence, though we are as yet unable distinctly to define and firmly to grasp it. Clearly, there are some things given to us at our birth, which form the nucleus and basis of our moral being— our innate sense of truth and justice, our instinctive affections and sympathies, our clinging consciousness of dependence and responsibility. There are some influences, breathed into us subsequently, we know not how or why, but by all men, not wholly imbruted, some time or other felt, which give new force and clearness to our radical perceptions of the right and the true, which inspire us with unwonted courage and trust, open before us unsuspected glimpses into the future capabilities of our being, and carry us out of ourselves into loftier aspirations after indefinite progress. We cannot err in ascribing these brightest moments of our being—these transient illapses of new power and life from some unknown sphere—to the directer influence of the invisible Father who enfolds us continually in the embrace of His all-cherishing Spirit. On the other hand, there are things which we are conscious are the result of our own thought, volition and energy, for the issue and conse-

quences of which, and for the motives which have originated them, we cannot help feeling ourselves personally
responsible. These things we consider human, because
they flow from the exercise of our individual will.

With all the elements of our nature which we recognize as divine, a feeling of certainty and implicit trust
is associated. To doubt them, is to doubt the Power by
which they have been inspired — is to doubt what is
highest in this universe. Distrust here is the worst
infidelity and sin. Only in regard to our own treatment
of these divine elements is there any room for hesita-
tion and doubt, lest we should have wrongly conceived,
or unfaithfully applied, or presumptuously contravened
and violated them. No man of healthy mind can ever
renounce his faith in justice and truth and holiness and
love, and that sublime harmony and beauty which is
the visible expression of their working in outward things.
His doubt relates only to what is human—whether in
his own conclusions and actions he comes up to their
demands and fulfils their obligations, and does not
mingle a large amount of error and frailty and actual
transgression in his dealing with them and application
of them. Under the law imposed on us by God, there
is free space left for the choice of obedience or disobedience. Our noblest function as men is to yield
ourselves up loyally to the high impulses breathed into
us by God. The more we can subjugate to these impulses our animal nature—all the selfishness and the
sophistry that are constantly rising up within us to per-
vert their aim and blunt their force—the more we can
throw our individual tendencies into the great stream of

higher impulse—the more completely we solve the moral problem of our existence by harmonizing the human with the Divine. Notwithstanding the unreasonableness which seems to lie on its surface, there was a deep truth in the old theological dogma, that all which is good in us comes from God, and all that is evil originates in ourselves. " We have our treasure in earthen vessels, that the excellency of the power may be of God, and not of us."

The same mixture of elements that exists in man himself, we find, as might be expected, in the finest products of his mind and hand. In every work of high art, a light confessed at once as divine gleams out on us through envelopments which bear as unmistakeable traces of the limitation and darkness inseparable from everything human. We may even say, the higher the production, the stronger and deeper the inspiration which breathes through it, the more striking, under some of its aspects, will be the contrast between its divine and human elements. In the highest efforts of human genius, we constantly observe an aspiration after something which no language, no human media of expression, can ever adequately reach. The effect falls below the idea. This must be so from the incommensurableness of the finite and the infinite, which shews itself as soon as ever they approximate. The most perfect works in an artistic sense are not always those which have the largest infusion of the divine, excepting so far as the inspiration of the moment carries its appropriate form along with it. As a rule, they owe their general perfection of form to what is human in them, not to what is divine—to taste and skill and mastery over the instruments of execution.

Let us apply this remark to that wonderful literature which we call the Bible. It may help to solve some of the questions which are now so anxiously debated respecting it. In the order of Providence, there are chosen races as well as chosen individuals, endowed with special gifts, sent into the world for a special purpose in the grand, progressive development of our humanity. All the elements indispensable to its growth and completeness have not flowed into it from one source. Egyptians, Phœnicians, Greeks, Romans, Hebrews—all have had their parts assigned them, and done their work. To the prophets of Israel, if we include in the series its consummation in Christ, our nature is indebted for those fundamental convictions and trusts which, far beyond all the wisdom of Greek philosophy, have given it moral stability, and breathed into it noble aspirations and inward harmony and repose. Those ancient seers, at various points of their spiritual experience, came into contact with the living God. Their souls were kindled by this mysterious touch. They caught glimpses of eternal truths, which grew and dilated on their mental vision as they gazed on them. They discussed with ever-clearer intuition the moral relationship of God and man, and the far-reaching consequences that must result from it. Through the darkness and confusion of the present, they dimly traced the outlines of a more glorious future—a distant kingdom of God—the ideal of our human condition—when all men would be united in filial communion with God, and in the bond of fraternal peace with each other. By their brave and fearless teachings they prepared the moral conditions which rendered possible, at the great crisis and turning-point of the world's history, the appearance of a Christ, to realize and exemplify in his own person the union, for which our nature is ultimately destined, between the human and the divine. But these great truths were in no one instance disclosed all at once, absolutely and completely. They were dropped into the world as a prolific seed that was to grow out of our human experience. They came out in momentary gleams and sudden flashes. They were revealed partially and fitfully in their application to particular characters and passing events, and not seldom were darkened and limited by the human errors and infirmities of the medium through which they passed. They were truths which acquired strength, expansion and clearness, by being lived upon. But the light which they brought into the world was of such a nature, that once kindled, it could never go out again. It burnt thenceforth by an inherent vitality of its own, and fed on the natural nutriment which it found in every human soul. The treasure was put into an earthen vessel, that we might know the power to be of God, and not of us. The Divine can only reveal itself through the human; but its human receptacle and vehicle must not be confounded with the Divine itself.

This obvious character of the Scriptures, resulting from the unavoidable conditions of all human intercourse with God, has been more overlooked and disregarded by the mass of Protestants than by the Catholics themselves; and to the obstructions which have thus been thrown in the way of a truly spiritual apprehension of the divine elements of the Bible, we must ascribe the stereotyped rigidity and immoveableness of the forms into which Protestantism has lapsed, and its unaltered relation to the older communion from which it divorced itself more than three hundred years ago. Since the Peace of Westphalia, it has made no perceptible progress. The old territorial landmarks remain as they were then fixed. What was Protestant then, is Protestant now; what was Catholic then, is Catholic now. If Protestantism, as we think, involves a truer principle than Catholicism, and if it be of the nature of truth to grow, there must be something vitally wrong in the Protestant conception of duty, and the Protestant exercise of acquired privilege, to account for this extraordinary result. The old Church, with that easy tolerance of temper which the possession of undisputed power always inspires, delighted to hold in its embrace and apply to its own purposes every variety of culture and talent, and even wide diversities of opinion. When the foundations of sacerdotal ascendency were not endangered, its great men often shielded heretical tendencies from the attacks of the ignorant and fanatical. Within the wide limits of its hereditary system, there was ample room for controversy and the building up of rival theories; and the association of Tradition (which tacitly recognized the progressive character of human thought) with the simple sentence of Scripture itself, for deciding what was, and what was not, religious truth, left a sort of indefinite latitude to free inquiry, which the stricter terms of Protestant creeds effectually exclude. Of many questions that were hotly debated after the Reformation, it is notorious that the grounds had been laid, and the objects defined, and the conditions developed, in the subtle discussions of the Medieval schoolmen. But with the Reformation came a great change, the consequences of which, affecting us to this day, have never yet perhaps been adequately appreciated. For a living tribunal to which men had been accustomed to refer the settlement of their religious difficulties, was now substituted the verbal authority of a book, or rather of a collection of books. The rescue of those books from the hands of their priestly conservators and interpreters, and the conferring upon each individual the right of reading them by the light of his own understanding for himself, was indeed a glorious achievement, marking an era in the history of our race; but it was a privilege of which the multitude were as yet unable to avail themselves, and the benefits of which were intercepted by the prejudices of the revolutionary reaction which had obtained it, and even more by the necessities of the state of things under which it had been won. The throwing off of sacerdotal authority, and the rejection of the traditions on which it had taken its stand, strengthened to intensity by a natural rebound the authority of the Scripture which had come into its place. When a book was delivered to the people as the absolute rule of their faith and practice, which was to supersede all other rules, and which God had sent them direct from heaven for that very purpose, it could not be left open to doubt or question in any part without forfeiting its distinctive character. The very intent of its mission implied its infallibility. It was assumed, as a necessary postulate of its divine authority, that it possessed one uniform character throughout, directly inspired from beginning to end, and that it contained within it a definite, complete and self-consistent body of theological truth, which must be accepted to secure salvation. Individual divines might not put the statement in this broad, unqualified way; but such was the prevalent assumption of the popular Protestantism. Now, here arose a difficulty. The multitude were wholly incapable of working out a system of theological belief for themselves from the multifarious contents of the Bible. Creeds were therefore interposed between it and the popular mind by the leaders of the great Protestant parties—not as superseding the word of Scripture, but as a faithful exposition of it. The expedient succeeded in allaying the speculative fermentation of the first age of the Reformation. As the early enthusiasm subsided, and the new churches took shape and consistency, the mass lapsed into passive acquiescence in the hereditary creed, and let their belief glide without question in the channels that had been prepared for it. Two assumptions henceforth lay at the basis of the popular theology : that every word of Scripture was true, and that every article of the creed could be proved from Scripture. Am I exaggerating the characteristic features of the popular Protestantism in this representation ? Is it not exemplified in the history of Protestant controversy down to the present day ? And when we consider how baseless are the assumptions here involved, and that Protestant sects, almost without an exception, have taken them as their ground of self-assertion and self-defence, can we be surprised at the proverbial sterility of theology ? Is it wonderful that, while all other sciences thrive and grow by striking their roots deep into the rich, productive soil of fact, Theology—which ought to be the queen of sciences, swaying the sublimest realms of thought on the dim border-land of the Seen and the Unseen—by abjuring fact and creating artificial premises of her own, has lost the very power of expanding with the general expansion of the human soul, and is already regarded by thousands as little better, in her actual form, than an exploded tradition of the past ?

The great controversy of the present day, within the limits of Christianity, before which all others fade into comparative insignificance, and into which all others must ultimately resolve themselves, is that which relates to the origin and composition of the Bible, and to the kind of authority with which an honest estimate of its actual constitution justifies us in investing it. Till the premises from which all Protestant disputants draw their conclusions are more precisely defined and substantially agreed on among themselves, controversy, it is obvious, can have no meaning and issue, and the warfare of texts must be interminable. That this is felt to be so, plainly appears from the direction which theological inquiry is now taking in all the higher regions of scholarship and thought. The most eminent men in the Church and Universities in various ways are indicating their conviction, that before the questions which have split up the old Catholicism into endless sects can be even proximately solved, another and far deeper question must first be disposed of. Curiously enough, on the fundamental question of scriptural criticism and interpretation, on which in fact everything else depends, the old creeds by their silence have left open a liberty of opinion which they expressly deny to the subordinate questions logically emanating from it. They tie up the conclusion, without limiting the premiss—not from any doubt as to the extent and stringency of the premiss, but on the assumption that in no Protestant mind could any doubt exist at all.

To persons who have been brought up in implicit reverence for the language of Scripture, and even to some who have renounced the popular view of a verbal inspiration, without perceiving how far that renunciation must logically carry them, these new views respecting the Bible will probably seem liable to two grave objections: first, that they set up the constructions of human reason against the direct authority of the word of God; secondly, that they leave the determination of what is, and what is not, divine truth, to a very vague and arbitrary criterion. A little reflection will, I think, shew that both these charges are more applicable to the theory which advances them, than to that against which they are alleged, and which really furnishes the only solid and enduring basis of religious belief. What, I would ask, are all our Protestant creeds, whether written or simply traditional, but an effort of the logical faculty, often arbitrary in the extreme, to construct out of the mingled elements of the Bible, as well the human as the divine, an artificial system of their own—a work of men's minds, which, when they have completed it, they fall down and worship? It would surely be a truer reverence to surrender our souls with child-like simplicity to the influence of those grander and deeper truths which form the inner life of the Bible—those inspirations of holiness and heroism and love and heavenly trust, which prove themselves divine by their kindling effect on our own higher nature—and dropping, as of no import to us, without any attempt to weave them into a theological theory, the human elements which unavoidably adhere to every historical manifestation, to press on in the work of our daily life towards that spiritual ideal of our humanity which Scripture sublimely images to us in a kingdom of God. Is it not by the living spirit of this eternal and unchanging religion, and not by the theological forms which have encrusted it, that the souls of good men in every Christian communion are really nourished? Is it not by this they truly live? And must not this come from God? What is the constant effect of our human theologies, for which we arbitrarily claim a divine authority, but to stifle this Spirit of God almost to extinction?

But it will be asked, How, on this view of Scripture, are we to distinguish what is, from what is not, divine revelation? What standard will be now left? Are we not delivering up the Word of God to the capricious wilfulness of every self-sufficient interpreter? Before answering this question, let me first ask another. What has been the effect of the received Protestant theory of the Bible? Has a canonical Scripture, assumed to be inspired throughout, enforced uniformity of belief, even as to what are considered fundamentals? Has not every strong mental individuality seen the reflection of its own ideas in Scripture, and derived from that reflection a divine warrant for a new human theology? It is clear, therefore, that should we admit the principle of interpreting the Bible as we interpret any similar collection of ancient books, we should not be quitting definiteness and certainty for caprices of opinion previously unknown; and that whatever might be the results of the application of this principle, we could not be in a worse position than we were before. But I go beyond this, and am prepared to maintain that it is only by a fearless recognition, to the utmost extent to which unquestionable evidence carries us, of the intermixture of divine and human elements in the Scriptures, and by interpreting them accordingly, that we can put any effectual check to the gratuitous license of theological speculation, and bring men back, not indeed to an entire uniformity of opinion, but at least to a substantial agreement in the fundamentals of true religion. Leaving to religious philosophers the question of an archetypal humanity in the Divine Mind, and to physiologists the kindred question of the possible genesis and specific difference of our race—looking at human nature simply as an actual fact, patent in all history and all literature, I cannot doubt that it is one and self-consistent; that it stands by itself as an insulated whole in the system of visible creation; and that the more we extend our acquaintance with its varied phenomena of thought and feeling, and the more freely it is allowed to develope itself, the more conclusive must the evidence of its essential unity become. In the fixed conditions, then, of our own spiritual constitution, we find the ultimate criterion of moral and religious truth. No outward revelation can extinguish the revelation within. God is directly present to us here; and His word written on the heart, is prior to the word written in a book. It is from disregarding this inner light of the soul, and building it over with their own miserable theories, that men have lost themselves in the darkness of endless sophistries and sectarianisms. This light will shew us where the eternal truths of Scripture lie. At its presence, as an infallible test, the divine element will disengage itself, and its human envelopment drop as a base residuum to the ground; and as our nature is ever one, if left to its genuine working—the aberrations of the intellect constantly checked by the deeper law of the conscience and the heart—it will ever arrive at the same practical conclusion at last. We find recorded and uttered in Scripture, what we are conscious has often gone on, though in a less marked and striking way, in the silent depths of our own souls. We are drawn out with an irresistible attraction towards the men who spake and wrought in that strange and mysterious history. As we ponder the words and actions of prophets and apostles, we are unable to resist the conviction that God was in some especial manner present with them and working in their midst. They lay hold of our strongest affections, and carry us away with them into closer communion with the Power in which they lived themselves. They do not so much teach us any new doctrine, as they impart to us a new life, quickening and intensifying what we dimly felt and knew before. We believe because we sympathize. Scripture is a many-sided utterance in forms of marvellous intensity of the same spiritual nature that we possess ourselves. While we judge and accept it by the criterion of a kindred element within our own souls, it re-acts on that criterion, as all higher necessarily act on feebler natures, and by the faith and prayer which it inspires, renders our perceptions of spiritual truth more clear and steadfast and life-giving.

There is one assurance emphatically expressed throughout the Bible which outweighs in value every other, and which, though not always reached, sometimes denied, by philosophy, when once communicated to the soul, shines henceforth in a self-evidencing light of its own—I mean, the assurance that beyond our highest moral aspirations there exists a great Spiritual Reality, towards which, as their infinite counterpart, they are continually tending, which is of kindred nature with our own souls, a living Father, in whose spiritual image we are formed, and of whose perfections, however by us inconceivable, the phenomena of our collective humanity are the least inadequate, because an ever-widening and progressive, manifestation. This is to me the truth of truths, the inestimable distinction of Christianity and the Bible. Let this be well rooted in the mind and become a vital conviction, and all the hopes and trusts and consolations which our weak and sorrow-stricken humanity needs, will grow out of it, and partake of its strength, and gradually cluster round it into a beautiful and organic whole of self-consistent religious truth.

As the Bible represents the permanent conditions of
our compound nature—divine elements in a vessel of
clay—and gives no warrant for the popular assumption
that it is an exceptional phenomenon in the great process of human development, we are justified in the delightful conclusion, that God has never withdrawn from
His people, but is still living and working in the midst
of them; that the light of divine revelation is still
shining in every pure heart; that to all who seek them
in earnest prayer, the fountains of the Spirit are still
open and accessible, flowing into the souls prepared for
them, as they flowed in the age of Christ. Nor let such
a belief be deemed presumptuous. The power is not of
us, but of God. He only asks our faithfulness and self-
surrender to come and take up His abode in our souls.
The Holy One of Nazareth shewed how divine our
nature may become, when it has been subdued by self-
sacrificing love, into unity of aim and endeavour with
the perfect will of God. He was not spared the temptations and trials of our common humanity. He brought
his message to men in an earthen vessel. Through an
earthen vessel he shed abroad the light of the world.
But the vessel was transfigured into glory by the light
which shone through it. The difference between Christ
and us is not that the spirit in which he spake and
wrought was different from that which comes at times
to us; but that in him it shone undimmed through a
pure human medium, serenely in harmony with God;
while in us it is stained and darkened, and broken into
fragmentary lights, by the insubordination and antagonism of our human tendencies to the divine. Let us

subdue these tendencies, and we shall daily grow more like him—increasingly one with him, as he is one with God.

Let us, then, not fear that we shall render impossible a vital unity of the Spirit, or tear asunder for ever the bond of fraternal peace, by calling in question the gratuitous assumptions of the Churches, and laying open the Scriptures, on which they all alike rest their incompatible pretensions, to the freest search of an honest and reverential mind. The courageous service of truth is the highest homage we can offer to the God of truth. To believe in truth is virtually to believe in God. The final sympathy of all good hearts in what is fundamental, is not to be attained by compromise and reservation, but by the largest allowance of mere intellectual diversity. There are truths of unspeakable grandeur and absolute certainty, commending themselves at once by their own inherent light to every awakened conscience, which shine out in the plainest characters, distinct and self-consistent, through all the varied teaching of the Bible: that there is a Living God, the sole Fountain of being, all-holy, just and merciful, between whom and His creature man there subsists a most intimate communion and the most solemn moral relationship; that this earth is the scene on which man is exercised and disciplined, as a subject of the Divine retributions both here and hereafter; that this Living God speaks to us all by the witness of His Spirit in our hearts, when they are pure and quiet enough to hear it, and that from time to time He has sent us more emphatic messages of warning and encouragement through the lips of His chosen servants—holy men and prophets; that there is an antagonism in our nature between its divine and its human elements, which it is the end of our moral discipline to reconcile and harmonize by the subduing influence of high faith and patient self-sacrifice and holy love; and that to shew us the possibility of this union, and reveal the sublime destination of our humanity, God manifested Himself in Christ and dwelt in him, that through him—through his regenerating spirit and the communication of his divine life—we might have peace, and be reconciled to the Father. These are fundamental and eternal truths—involving the very essence of religious conviction and trust—which we should all have more readily apprehended, and been in a better condition to enforce, had we been less prepossessed with our assumed theories; had we been less set on finding our own philosophy reflected in the Bible; had we been content to give up word-cavilling and text-warfare; had we submitted ourselves more freely to the Spirit which breathes through the Divine Word; had we—feeling it presumption in us to determine beforehand how God must communicate with us, and what must be the form and order and measure of His teachings—applied ourselves patiently and reverently to ascertain the simple fact, how God has actually spoken, and what He has really said. This is a lesson which all sects and churches have more or less got to learn. They have all, more or less, without exception, perhaps unconsciously, been guilty of " handling the word of God deceitfully," and wresting it from its true meaning, to subserve their own dogmatic views and extend their own sectarian triumphs.

The two indispensable conditions of a nobler and truer theology for the time to come, are, first, a thoroughly honest use of learning—a fearless resolution of all our theories into their ultimate element—a determination never to ignore or evade whatever criticism, history or science demonstrate to be *fact*, however it may upset our preconceived notions or unsettle our traditional belief; and, secondly, to cultivate with the utmost veneration and tenderness that spiritual element of our being which brings us into living communion with God, and which, though wonderfully nourished and strengthened by the teachings of Scripture, flows from the same divine source, and is only another working of one and the self-same Spirit which uttered Scripture itself. By the first of these conditions we shall be kept from the folly and presumption of constructing theological theories of our own by a forced and artificial systematizing of the heterogeneous materials contained in the rich and progressive literature of the Bible. By the second, we shall be preserved from the intellectual hardness and daring which are apt to overtake the free inquirer, when the balance of his mental constitution is left untrimmed by the counterpoise of reverence and love. Approaching the sublime and mysterious questions which theology involves, from the religious side of our nature, with tenacious adherence to those fundamental assumptions which no healthy nature ever abjures, and of which even the atheist can never entirely divest himself, we shall shew, by the very direction of our thoughts and by the spirit that animates them, that in the disruption of our old prepossessions, in the relinquishment of many things which we once cherished as divine, but which we now perceive are simply human, we are so far from making any assault on religion itself, that we are only relieving it from liabilities and encumbrances which hinder it from putting forth its whole strength, and shining out upon us in the undimmed lustre of its divine purity. Even then we must expect, no doubt, to wound the religious susceptibilities and excite against us the religious hostility of many excellent men. A period of transition cannot escape being a period of uneasiness and conflict. Our encouragement must be found in the reflection that we cannot attach ourselves to a higher service than that of divine truth. No man can be presumptuous enough to expect that his individual efforts should ever be able fully to attain it. But he can be tolerably sure what are the conditions essential to its discovery, in what direction he must look for it, and in what spirit it ought to be pursued. Let him be single-minded, courageous and disinterested, in his search for it, and he will not seek in vain. His mind, with all its weakness and limitation, by its simple honesty will find its fitting place as a link in that mighty chain of thought which stretches through the ages, and unfolds, as it successively evolves itself, the grand purpose of the Eternal Mind. He will, at least, ennoble himself by his ceaseless aspirations after what is noblest in the universe; and by the sweet contagion of love and trust which breathes in every earnest spirit,

and goes forth from every honest life, he will help to
bring men into more brotherly relations towards each
other, and humanity itself into deeper and holier communion with God.

[Written, 1862; last preached (Oakfield Church, Clifton),
4th December, 1864.]

XIX.

The Connection of Christ's Resurrection with Human Immortality.

(A SERMON WRITTEN FOR EASTER SUNDAY.)

MARK xvi. 6:

"He saith unto them, Be not affrighted: ye seek Jesus of Nazareth who was crucified: he is risen; he is not here."

IT is a distinctive mark of our religion that the great festival of Christendom consecrates the belief in immortality. The conviction which transformed the mind of the early disciples—which took away their fears, and changed their Messianic hope from carnal longing into spiritual joy—was this, that their Lord, whom they had seen expire on the cross, was not dead, but risen. This belief, taking possession of the soul, and making things invisible a reality, was the cause of the great revolution which has separated Christianity from heathenism, and signalizes the most remarkable crisis in the spiritual history of our planet. It is this belief, so contrary to what they had before expected—with its marvellous effect on the whole aim and endeavour of their lives, so far transcending what they were previously capable of—which furnishes the strongest argument that the first disciples must have possessed some evidence, whatever that might be, which convinced them that their Master's resurrection was a reality. It may be impossible for us, at this remote time of day, to recover that evidence and say precisely what it was. But it must have existed, and satisfied their minds. Their conduct is otherwise inexplicable; and the intelligent asserter of the great Christian hope will rather insist on this belief, in which the entire history of our religion has had its origin, and call upon the objector to account for it, if it had no basis in fact, than raise doubts and suggest difficulties by attempting to explain and reconcile the recorded appearances, which are so shadowy and so dim, and had best be left in the mysterious obscurity in which they have been transmitted to us. Our spiritual nature welcomes and accepts a belief which is so congenial to the soul; while the critical faculty is constantly puzzled into doubt when it has to deal with historical complexities and contradictions. No one ever came to faith through the weighing of probabilities or the disentanglement of textual difficulties. We believe through sympathy—under the influence of those who believe more than ourselves, and whose pure and loving nature compels us to trust them. There is something refreshing to the spirit in the simple and child-like faith of the first Christians. They believed, apparently, because they could not help believing. Their belief was not an effort of the understanding, but a spontaneous outgoing of the heart. There must have been something to account for this wonderful change in humanity. We meet with nothing like it in the later heathenism or in the later Judaism. From whatever cause it arose, the spiritual eye of those good and simple people had been opened to discern realities which are too often hidden from us. The Spirit of God had re-generated their inward nature, and put them in a new relation to things unseen. In every record which they have left of themselves—in their hymns and in the memorials on their graves—they speak of the world to come with an unaffected, simple-minded genuineness of speech, as if it were as present to them as the world in which they were actually living—as if it were the greater and nearer reality of the two. They speak of departed friends as if still living in the closest spiritual communion with them, hardly separated by the thin veil which divides things seen and unseen. Death was with them, not the hideous spectre which mediæval superstition afterwards arrayed in terror and gloom, but a gentle messenger of release, heralding the birth-day of a new life, which they celebrated annually at the tombs of the honoured and the loved, with cheerful festivals and songs of grateful joy. Compare the térse and polished epitaphs of the Romans with the expressions of Christian tenderness and hope still dimly traceable in the Catacombs, and you will perceive what a new light broke in on our world through the rude and scarce grammatical language of that obscure, unlettered and persecuted people of God. Beautiful gleams glanced at times over the horizon of the noblest heathen thought;

but they were only gleams—gleams that met the aspiring intellect in its upward struggle towards the light. To the unlearned Christian, that light of immortality was the element in which he habitually lived; but it was a light effused from the heart and dwelling in the soul. Between the hurried glances of philosophy and the steady gaze of faith, there is all the difference between fitful flashes of lightning calling into momentary vision out of thick darkness the mountains, lakes and forests of some glorious Alpine scene, and the sweet light of day resting quietly on the same objects and revealing them without excitement as a present, unquestioned reality to the eye.

There is another reason for letting our chief interest attach rather to the profound conviction which seized the minds of the first believers and transformed their whole spiritual being, than to the alleged physical phenomena which are affirmed in the recorded tradition to have produced it, that we thus acquire a point of contact between that primitive faith in the risen Jesus, and the permanent trusts, the inextinguishable aspirations, of our common humanity. There was a time when some men, more zealous than discreet, to exalt the value of revelation, put out, as far as they could, the natural light, and left one solitary star shining over the empty sepulchre of Christ. I cannot imagine any mode of argument at once more unphilosophical and more perilous to our dearest hopes than this. To assert that nature and the soul—God's will without us and within us—announce nothing but final annihilation, and then to attempt to reverse that terrible expectation by the attested occurrence of a single historical event shrouded in the traditions of a remote antiquity, is to risk the belief in immortality on an issue which the failure of one link in the chain of proof, or the discovery of any flaw in the documentary evidence hitherto relied on, may render wholly inconclusive. That God wrought in some mysterious way on the mind of the apostolic age, to produce a strong assurance of the resurrection of the crucified Prophet of Nazareth, I have not a doubt; the whole history of that marvellous time would be to me an insoluble enigma on any other supposition. But I do not, therefore, discredit other indications of the same great law of human destiny and progress. On the contrary, I find a confirmation of the truth of the apostolic belief in what we ourselves of this day, in our holiest and most solemn moods of thought, still occasionally experience. For the stream of the Spirit opened in Christ has flowed down to us, weakened and defiled as it often may be by our carnal affections and our worldly selfishness; and possibly, could we reproduce in ourselves the vivid faith of that first age—could we make an equal surrender of everything to Christ—could we enter into the same direct and habitual communion with the living God—we might attain to the same clear and untroubled perception of things invisible which was vouchsafed to them. Certainly, those who have lived long enough to get some insight into the deep mystery of our present life, must have experienced, more than once perhaps, how death, when it enters our households and breaks up the sweet continuity of a long domestic intercourse, quickens the faith in immortality, and makes us more intensely feel, what we never perhaps seriously doubted, but now for the first time distinctly realize. The words of the young man to the weeping women at the sepulchre are a complete interpretation of the voice of faith within us: "He is risen; he is not here." The very order in which these words are given is significant; the instinctive faith in immortality anticipates the sense of present loss. Heaven, for the moment, absorbs in its glory the dull shadows of earth. In a human soul—in the character which has grown around it—there is something so real, so individual, that we cannot conceive of its perishing. We perceive, indeed, that it is no longer here; but we already believe that it is risen. It can only be removed to another sphere of being, not cognizable by the sense, but distinctly present to the spirit. All who have known death, must know how faith rises with the demand for it; how it awakens into new life, and, as it were, gratuitously proffers to us its divinest consolations, when but for its presence the heart would be utterly crushed and desolate. Few have ever seriously doubted at the bedside of a dying friend, or in taking a last view of the mortal remains which are soon to be closed up forever in earth and ashes and dust. Faith springs up within us, in spite of ourselves, and with marvellous intensity, at such moments. And what are the dreamy doubts of metaphysicians, when confronted with these eternal facts of our living humanity? Can we believe that the just and merciful God, who formed our hearts and breathed into them His own spirit of love, and enriched them with affections which are the source of our purest enjoyments and the ground of our holiest duties, would leave them to find this last consolation and support in mockery and delusion? It cannot be. A voice stronger and deeper than the sharpest logic protests against the possibility of such an issue.

The belief in immortality is closely inwoven with the consciousness of our personal individuality. Now, it is the tendency in some degree of the large, abstract speculations of philosophy, and still more of immersion in the business of the world, to weaken that consciousness, by making us feel ourselves only a part of an extensive organization of connected agencies. The philosopher takes note of great results in their bearing on the general course of human affairs, or he traces the progressive development of cosmical laws and forces till it culminates in man; but in both views the individual is almost lost; he goes for little or nothing. Again, the man of business is apt to forget his humanity in the subserviency of its powers to objects exterior to himself —wealth and power and influence and worldly position; and he measures other men from the same point of view. The soul is an element which never enters into his calculations. It is not supposed to belong to the business of this world. It is relegated to a sphere reserved exclusively for the moralist and the divine. Only in moments when the world's brightness is overcast, and the pride of the philosophic intellect is subdued, and its restlessness is still—only in moments of earnest self-concentration, when great sorrow forces the soul in upon itself, and compels it to ask what and where and why it is—only in such moments does it truly awake to the sense of truths deeper and grander than those by which it has ordinarily lived—only in such moments does it feel, that if there is anything certain, anything real on earth, anything which cannot perish, it is that consciousness of personality which makes it a moral and responsible existence, and connects it by an indissoluble bond with the ever-living God.   And what we feel with respect to ourselves, we feel also with respect to those whom we have lost in the first sad moments of separation. Their individuality rises up with a new force and brightness on our remembrance.   Their soul seems to come nearer to us than ever, though its mortal habiliments have dropped off and are mouldering in the dust.   All that they have been to us and done for us, acquires a sanctity and even a truth which did not belong to it while it was a mere occurrence among the transient incidents of earth, and seems embalmed already in the spirit of immortality.   Their purely mortal lot—its wealth or its poverty—its eminence or its lowliness—its glory or its cross—this has passed away as a dream, and we are willing that it should go for ever.   But that which grew up and was developed amidst the varied discipline of earth—the mind, the character, the personality—its love, its purity, its faithfulness, its honour, its reverence for truth and right, and the sweet affections which bound it in loving sympathy with the Father God and the brother man—these things come to the mind as an imperishable reality, and dwell in the remembrance as a glorified image of the departed. Death has a softening influence on our appreciation of them that are gone.   Of the evil we do not like to speak. We leave them to God, who knows, better than we, what they were, and who will temper justice with mercy. If there have been redeeming traits in their character, it is a relief to dwell on.them, and hope for the best. But of the good we especially cherish all the remembrances which shew that they were good. The small blemishes are lost in the general effect and expression of the entire character. We remember them as we hope to meet them hereafter —the same men and women that we once knew on earth, all the features of personal identity still pre-served, but softened, purified and elevated, by the influ-ences of a higher world and a more glorious society. As a successful portrait arrests with its magic touch, and fixes for ever on the canvas the brightest moments and the happiest looks of a brief earthly friendship, so the hallowed images that dwell in our remembrance of the virtuous dead, mellowed by time and made daily more beautiful by an enduring love, are perhaps a fore-taste and an anticipation of the delightful renovation of intercourse which awaits the good when they meet each other again beyond the grave. The image, though less physically exact, may be more spiritually true, in both cases. The fundamental idea, the great design, as we may call it, of the character, which was blurred and broken by the unavoidable infirmities of earth, passes into a more complete realization, which brings out all the beauty and the truth that were latent in it.

Many a hard-headed man whose mind is wholly occu-pied with the things of this world, will be apt to say, "All this is sentiment and feeling. Where is your proof? Give me a fact; and I will believe." The proper answer is, that this noblest hope of humanity derives its strongest evidence from the moral conditions of the soul itself. It is a trust and a consolation of the inward life; and in the inward life alone can it find the grounds of ultimate assurance. It is a moral recompence, and therefore—to be fully enjoyed, exempt from doubt and fear—it demands a moral culture and implies moral desert. When men insist on physical proof, they ask what has no bearing on a spiritual reality. No evidence furnished by sensible phenomena can establish a fact which belongs to the invisible world alone. The soul believes through a higher witness than that of sense. If more of that gross, palpable, measurable certainty which we justly demand in matters of the present life, were actually attainable and had been vouchsafed to us, not only would it have deranged the proper relation between the two worlds, and wholly unfitted us for our present disciplinary work, but it would have taken from the hope of immortality that moral character through which it exercises its most elevating influence on our present being. It would have become a mechanical impression, and ceased to be a spiritual trust. The doubt or disbelief of worldly and sensual, and even of hard intellectual natures, is entitled to little weight in this question, because it does not touch the proper sources of all religious belief. It is rather what we might expect from the nature of the arguments which they employ and their ignorance of the sole conditions under which such a faith can possibly arise. So viewed, their unbelief may even, by a sort of reflex evidence, strengthen our faith. D'Alembert himself, philosopher as he was, when his own nature had been softened by the recent loss of a friend, bore eloquent witness to the true origin of this consolatory hope, when he spoke of "the precious expectation of immortality" as that "of which the earliest desire must have sprung up, not in a cold and philosophic head, but in a heart which had loved."

The application of the reflections which have now engaged our minds, is obvious. Would you secure the purest consolation and the most effectual support reserved for frail and dying man, cherish, I beseech you, the moral sources out of which they spring. Strong faith in a higher spiritual existence cannot co-exist with a life immersed in the sensualities and ambitions of the world. The cold damps of selfishness must smother the fire of that holy love which is to glow for ever in the clear, bright atmosphere of heaven. If we would bear within us the ennobling consciousness of immortality, let us habitually seek whatever is pure and noble and good. Let us pursue truth and serve humanity with all our hearts. Let us cherish the sacred affections of home in all their tenderness and strength. Let no evil tempers mar them; no clashing wilfulness sever them; no sordid worldliness defile, no low self-indulgence enfeeble or exhaust them. The home is the fore-court of heaven. Yet not for our families must we live alone. This wide world of suffering humanity has claims upon us. Let us strive to better and elevate it. Let us repel by our actions the undeserved reproach, that the hope of immortality makes men dreamy and visionary. Let us shew that it quickens every generous resolve, and invigorates every virtuous endeavour; that it sustains us against opposition, and consoles us under defeat; that it ennobles philanthropy and purifies patriotism, by giving us for the subject of our labours, not mere masses of perishable force, but improvable and immortal souls. Let us recognize the dignity which it confers on our race, by annihilating the factitious distinctions of this transitory life, and concentrating our reverence on those qualities of the heart and life which endure for ever. Let it shew its divine power by making us capable of pain and toil and self-sacrifice in the service of God and man; indifferent to obloquy and worldly loss in the pursuit of a great and noble object; ready, if need be, if freedom or justice or truth demand it of us, to take up our cross and follow our Master to Golgotha. In the grand memories of this sacred day, the Cross and the Resurrection are inseparably joined. How significant is their juxtaposition! What a profound truth does it announce to us! The Cross typifies our earthly life of preparation. The Resurrection opens to us the gates of heaven. We are here, not for ease, not for self-indulgence, not for the gratification of "the lust of the flesh, and the lust of the eyes, and the pride of life"—for these are not of the Father, and pass away—but to wrestle with evil and toil in duty, to deny ourselves, and live for others' good; that out of this conflict we may gain immortal strength; that out of the discipline of this perishable world we may extract the elements of a divine and eternal life; that out of sorrow patiently borne, and temptation bravely resisted, and opportunities faithfully used, we may gather a peace which passeth all understanding, and distil an inward blessedness of spirit which can alone give its true flavour and relish to this mortal life. "Higher, ever higher," is the word that comes forth to us from on high. Immortality is before us. But he who would reach it must struggle and toil to rise. The higher life must be won out of the lower life. Such, my Christian friends, is the appointed law of our being. Be it ours henceforth to fulfil it. The Cross declares our service. The Resurrection assures our reward.

[Written, 1864; last preached (High Pavement, Nottingham),
24th December, 1865.]

XX.

The Work of the Spirit continuous and progressive.

Acts ii. 4:

"They were all filled with a holy spirit, and began to speak with other tongues, as the Spirit gave them utterance."

WHAT was the precise nature of the spiritual change, and the remarkable phenomena accompanying it, which are indicated in these words, and more fully described in the earlier account contained in the fourteenth chapter of the First Epistle to the Corinthians—is one of the obscurest questions of scriptural interpretation, of which various solutions have been suggested, but none with entirely satisfactory result. It is not my intention to enter now into any of these curious but not very profitable inquiries, which belong rather to historical criticism than to the great trusts and consolations of religion; but I shall attempt to shew— what a thoughtful reading of the Bible rarely fails to disclose to us—that under these extraordinary narratives, whether we interpret them as strictly miraculous, or regard them as the mythic representation of a crisis of unusual mental excitement, a grand and permanent law of our spiritual nature is strikingly exemplified.

Through the entire history of the origin of Christianity, in which the enlightenment of the apostolic mind on the day of Pentecost may be regarded as the essential and determining incident, two facts are implied, which must be constantly kept in view, to render it intelligible and self-consistent.

(1.) It is assumed throughout that God is a living, conscious Spirit, admitting the human spirit to direct intercourse and communion with Himself. There is no impassable gulf between God and man. Christ enters the Father's presence, and lays himself on the Paternal bosom, through faith and prayer. All the purest and highest thoughts flow into a human soul from God. It finds in them a life, a quickening energy, which it is conscious does not depend on its own will and effort, and cannot therefore originate with itself. They come not from ourselves, not from below—but from a divine source, from above. Of the greatest word ever yet spoken to our world, Christ said, "It is not mine, but the Father's who sent me." This, then, is the first postulate of true religion—of the recognition of any influence which can in any sense be considered a revelation—that there can be, and that there is, an influx of the Divine into the human.

(2.) The stimulus to this communion with God is constantly furnished by the influence of minds higher than our own. God's Spirit comes to us, in the first instance, mediately through them. But this spiritual awakening does not, perhaps cannot, take place, to its whole extent, all at once. It is deposited in our souls, like a small seed of new life, buried and almost oppressed under the grosser accumulations of an earlier life. Nevertheless, the influence of that nobler personality with which we have been brought into contact is not lost. It has uttered words; it has effused a spirit full of awe and tenderness; it has left behind it an impression, never wholly unfelt, but at first not fully comprehended, the true meaning of which breaks on the soul by degrees, as it experiences, with the silent growth of its own inward life, richer influxes of the same Divine power which breathed that spirit and spoke those words, and in which that deep but dim and mysterious impression had its source. All this is illustrated in the case of the earliest disciples. During our Lord's personal converse with them, their apprehension of his spiritual teachings was slow and dull. An impression was made; but it seemed to have no vitality; it did not fructify. Not till death had wrought a change on their minds, and they looked back on the memory of their holiest Friend with sorrowing regret and reverent love, and they began to realize his unbroken spiritual presence with them from a higher life, did they discern at length the full significance of all that he had said, and done, and been, entered into living communion with him, and were brought under the power of that spirit of truth which guided them step by step into all truth. Such is the idea, veiled under the expressive symbolism of the Pentecostal effusion. It represents—what we must all have noticed and felt—that the effect of the highest teaching, whether by word or act, is not accomplished at a stroke, but comes forth, as it were, in successive revelations of continually enlarging truth, drawn out by reflection and experience, under a divine influence, from the seminal principle at first implanted in the soul.

When I speak of truth, it will of course be understood that I do not here mean scientific truth—a right apprehension of the laws and forces of external phenomena cognizable by the pure intellect—but the inward sense of our personal relation to the Infinite Source of life and consciousness, influencing the affections and the conduct, and constituting what the old philosophy emphatically called Wisdom. Science and Wisdom are perfectly distinct things—often divorced, though capable of subsisting in the closest harmony. What I now wish to call your attention to is this—that when the elements of this divine wisdom have been once imparted to the soul, and imbibed with a simple, honest spirit into as much intellectual light as is already prepared for their reception, they grow and deepen, and expand into unsuspected consequences and wider applications, by the mere force of inward experience, through simple persistency in the spiritual direction which the soul has once resolutely taken. We clearly trace the workings of this great law both in the lives of individuals and in the general history of religion ; and it is distinctly announced in those familiar words of Scripture, "If any man will do God's will, he shall know of the doctrine, whether it be of God or of man." Let our own memories teach us what a fulness of meaning is shed on the impressions of our early years by the reflected lights of experience! New revelations of unsought-for truth are continually opening within us. How many a word, taken in with simple credence by our confiding childhood from parental lips, learned in the sacred lesson, impressed by the voice of the preacher, or associated with the simple melody of some cherished hymn, yields up its hidden treasures of wisdom to the sharpened vision of the soul, when the teaching of years and the deeper witness of the Spirit have had time to act on them, and throws a new light into life, and gives us a further glance into the solemn mysteries which encompass us! We feel in these higher moments of our being that there is no wisdom like that which puts our souls into a right attitude towards God, which reconciles us to His will, and makes us ready for effort and self-sacrifice in His service. We feel that this wisdom of the soul is really exhaustless, having in it an element of the Infinity with which it connects us; and that as through our whole past experience it has ever been revealing to us more and more of the highest truth, so it must still contain much which we do not at present know, but which will be disclosed in that new stage of moral and spiritual being which awaits us hereafter. Simple experience, without any deliberate effort on our part, will teach us much; but when this is seconded by faith and prayer and the answering influence of God's Spirit, it obtains an insight deeper and more searching still.

The progressive work of the Spirit is even more conspicuous in the history of the Church than in the lives of individuals. Theologians have grievously sinned against the order of Providence, and contradicted one of its most obvious laws, when they have argued that the whole mission of Christ was accomplished within the limits of his personal ministry, and that the "gracious words which proceeded out of his mouth," occasional and fragmentary as we see they were, contained in themselves a perfect revelation of the entire range and compass of religious truth. God does not so provide for the spiritual education of our race. Slow and gradual development is the law of His working in the moral as in the physical world. Christ's holy life of oneness with God gave an impulse to the spiritual consciousness of mankind, all the consequences of which did not appear at once, but which it has taken, and may yet take, centuries even partially to unfold. His words, dropped like fruitful seeds into the decaying bosom of the old civilization, deposited in it the elements of a new and higher life which was yet to spring into existence. They struck root in various soils, and shot up in different forms; and in their successive flowerings gave promise of the rich and glorious fruit that they were ultimately to bear. But it was one and the self-same Spirit of God which wrought through all these changes. His omnipresent Love was the sunshine and the shower which cherished the prolific germ, and made it grow, and spread over all the earth, and strike its living fibres into human hearts. It was His Spirit which endued missionaries and confessors with tongues of fire to speak a new language to the world. This living growth of the gospel we plainly discern within the limits of the New Testament itself. It has one form in the Judaic apostles and evangelists, another in Paul, another in John. Again, it had one function in its mortal conflict with heathenism, and another when it became mistress of the civilized world under Constantine. It inspired with an equal but a different zeal the bosoms of Bernard and Luther. It seems almost at war with itself in the cold, dry rationalism of the eighteenth century, and the fervid contemporaneous enthusiasm of the Wesleys and Zinzendorf.

And we who now live are in the midst of another great crisis of its history. Old sectarian boundaries seem breaking down, and old dogmas are losing their authority. But the *spirit* which wrought in Paul and in Jesus, and inspired their words and works—the spirit of love and faith and devotedness—yea, the very spirit which was poured out on the hearts of apostles on the day of Pentecost—is not extinct; in thousands of brave and honest hearts it is active and vigorous still. The very destructiveness, as it may appear to some, of the modern criticism—which, after all, is only pulling down the useless obstructions of the dead letter—will undoubtedly clear the way for a freer and fuller operation of the Eternal Spirit, brought into closer contact with the hearts and lives of men. Channing and Schleiermacher, Arnold and Neander, Bunsen and Parker, with others yet living, despite their undeniable mistakes and shortcomings on some points (for God alone is perfect and unerring), are the prophets of a new era, the heralds of a better time. These great and good men, through simple fidelity to the voice within, as organs of the Spirit of God, from the vantage-ground of a longer experience, saw further and deeper into the ultimate design of Christianity (there is no presumption in saying so), than prophets and apostles themselves, and more completely embraced, in all its possible applications to our new world (which prophets and apostles saw not, and could not therefore comprehend), that gospel of spiritual truth which was given at first by God in the undeveloped seed, but not disclosed in all the fulness of the "bright consummate flower." Jesus himself may be justly thought to have authorized this expectation, when he said to his immediate followers, " He that believeth on me, the works that I do shall he do also ; and greater works than these shall he do, because I go unto my Father."

This belief that the Christian revelation is not completed, but still in progress, and that we shall continually see farther into its meaning and issue, as the Spirit which originally brought it into the world more thoroughly penetrates and sways our own souls, gives a breadth and grandeur to our religious position under God's providence, which is equally lost to the rigid scripturalist who seeks God's present will in the dead letter of an ancient book, and the arid historical critic who interprets the Gospel with the learning of an antiquary as a mere fact of the past. The great thing is to recognize clearly and unhesitatingly the fundamental truth, that the same Spirit which was in Christ and his apostles may be, and ought to be, in us; that it runs through the ages, and will make the Church a living unity to the end of time; that only through this Spirit can we know the deep things of God; that only in His light can we see light. The Spirit sought in prayer, and grasped by faith, still makes us one with Christ and God. It is only through the unintermitted flowing of this Spirit into our hearts, that we can say of Jesus Christ, that he is the same yesterday, and to-day, and for ever. It ebbs and flows indeed with the changes of our human infirmity; but if we are not ourselves faithless, it never utterly forsakes us; and there are seasons when it descends on us with a Pentecostal effusion, which dispels our doubts and our fears, and makes us see all things in the clearness of heavenly light. Sweet indeed are these glimpses of the eternal peace, which come to us from time to time under the burden and sorrow of our earthly lot, to lift us above the world and give us assurance of our final rest in God. Only under the influence of this Spirit does the Bible become to us an intelligible and instructive book—a book for the universal heart, in which the deepest experiences of humanity have recorded themselves. It enables us at once, by a sort of elective affinity, to disengage the spiritual elements of the Bible which are nutritive of the soul, from the historical husk in which the accidents of time have enveloped them. We see that the holy men of former days lived and wrought in the same spirit which is our inspiration now; that they had the same wants, the same aspirations, and the same trusts; but that their conception of spiritual things, deep and real as they felt them to be, was determined by the narrow limits of their intellectual horizon, and took shape from the moulding pressure of their outward life; that had they lived with us, and shared our mental light, and encountered our social problems, their faith would indeed have been the same—the same their love, their self-sacrifice and their devotedness—but these high qualities would have been exercised on different objects, and must have clothed themselves in other forms. It is not the history of the Bible, therefore, nor its dogmas, nor even its examples, that carry with them any authoritative weight to us as religious beings, but only the spiritual life which God has sent into it through the deepest fountains of our humanity, which is ever flowing through it, and must, if we would be true followers of Christ, flow from it into our hearts, and mingle with our life, and make us one in aim and sentiment and endeavour with patriarchs and prophets and apostles and martyrs, and the good and holy men of the Church universal who, in every age and under all the changing conditions of society, have sought for the truth and striven for the right.

The old Protestantism, which, in spite of all the efforts to sustain it, is destined inevitably to crumble away, was narrow and scrupulous in its interpretation of the Bible. It identified religion with theology. It laboured to construct from every part of the multifarious contents of Scripture a perfect system of doctrine, which should authoritatively fix the religious conceptions of mankind, and satisfy all intellectual demands, and be binding on every conscience. But neither Lutheran nor Calvinistic nor Socinian theories have been able to keep their ground, or will ultimately rule the world. The principle on which they separated from Rome was fatal to the claim, which they have all in turn asserted, to mental completeness and mental ascendency. Its inevitable result was the spirit of sectarianism, asserting individual freedom at the expense of ecclesiastical unity, making intellectual differences a reason for the dissolution of spiritual bonds, and having its natural, logical issue in absolute individuality. We have probably reached the extreme limit of this state of things. The strongest present tendencies are rather towards fusion than schism. And the Spirit which, as I have endeavoured to shew, is the one imperishable element in our religion, which connects us with the Past, as it will connect us with the Future, and which has its seat, not in the intellect, but in the conscience and the heart—the more freely it comes into play and dissolves by its genial heat the cold rigidity of the letter—must strengthen all these tendencies, and unite good and earnest men of every variety of theological opinion in closer bonds of fraternal sympathy and co-operation. The Spirit draws us to God as the great object of religious affection and trust; and if that drawing is effectual, if it brings us into vital communion with God, and actually regenerates the soul, it will be of little importance in the eyes of one who has been taught by the Spirit what Christianity really is, through what forms of belief that momentous change has been accomplished. He will simply desire, on behalf of every human mind, that these forms should be such as meet its intellectual capacity and need, and promote its inward growth in holiness and love. He will say to the many friends that he meets in the various persuasions of Christendom, "My brothers, let us each cling to our respective theologies in peace, as reason and conscience demand of us; for I would have no man indifferent to obtaining the clearest conception that he can gain of his personal relation to God. This is a matter on which the individual reason of each must judge for itself, and wherein it is impossible for all of us perfectly to agree. But religion, after all, is better than theology; for it makes us, differ as we may as men, still one in Christ and God. Let the Spirit lift up our hearts together to our common Father in heaven, and bind us all as one loving brotherhood to each other on earth."

It is delightful to think that this view of Christianity places us in the same filial relationship to God as Christ himself. We have the same access to God as he had; and the fountain of grace which furnished him with spiritual strength is not closed to us. True Christianity neither takes us from the world, nor puts God at a distance from us. Both are near to us, in close contact and perfect harmony with each other, when the one is reverently loved and the other innocently used and enjoyed. We should cherish the consciousness that we are constantly living with God. Every pure and gentle affection which sweetens our earthly life, every thrill of blameless delight which wonder and beauty and enthusiasm strike through our sympathizing frame, the high thoughts and generous aspirations of our better moments, the silent consecration of earnest prayer, and the holy calm which follows a resolute effort of virtuous obedience or a victory achieved over besetting sin—all these blessed influences are the breathing of His Spirit and a witness of the omnipresent God. Even our active labours slide into selfishness and sin without the restraining influence of His Spirit. We then think most clearly, and feel most purely, and write most freely and forcibly, when we are conscious of His inspiration. When the sense of truth and right and justice fires our souls, and we remember only what we owe to God, and dismiss every other thought, a new speech is bestowed on us, and we speak with other tongues, as the Spirit gives us utterance. We know that God is present with us, when the spirit of love and trust and sympathy is dwelling in our hearts. Through peace and holy love we seem to have a share in the very being of God himself; and this consciousness, growing out of the deepest feeling of our personality, unites us indissolubly with Him, and may be taken as the surest pledge of our individual immortality.

[Written, 1864; last preached (Free Christian Church, Kentish Town), 3rd June, 1866.]

<h1 style="text-align:center">XXI.</h1>

Spiritual Relationship with the Invisible Christ.

* * *

1 Peter i. 8, 9 :

"Whom having not seen, ye love; in whom, though now ye see him not, yet believing, ye rejoice with joy unspeakable and full of glory; receiving the end of your faith, even the salvation of your souls."

IT is a curious and suggestive fact, that although the Christian religion is founded on belief in a Person, those who first carried it beyond the narrow limits of Judaism, and made it a religion for humanity, had never seen the Person in whose name they preached, had never known Christ in the flesh—but were believers in a glorified humanity, which had been translated to the invisible world, and with which they maintained only a spiritual communion. This was certainly the case with Paul and with those who followed him in preaching the gospel to the heathen—perhaps also with Stephen, who was in one sense his predecessor.

This is a remarkable peculiarity of the gospel, distinguishing it from all other religions ; and is no doubt a chief cause of the ascendency which it has given to things unseen over things seen — in other words, of the profound spirituality of its genuine influence. By concentrating the trust and reverence of its adherents on one who had fulfilled all the conditions of a filial obedience on earth, and then passed, a perfected man, to the final rest and blessedness of the Father's house, it has linked our humanity with Heaven and God in a way that no other aspect of our highest relations possibly could. The spiritual design of our being in this world and in the next is realized to us in Christ. We see in him why it is that we exist. Death is not a severance, but a link—the passage from a lower to a higher state. The dark curtain which hung between the two worlds is rent in twain, and a boundless vista opens out to our view, in which we are permitted to look on the future of the human soul as an unbroken continuity of progressive existence—an endless life of deepening communion with the Father-Spirit of the universe. An idea so vast, and in the mode of its original introduction into our planet so unprecedented, was sure, from the inability of finite minds adequately to apprehend it, to be conceived and presented under various dogmatic forms, many of which keep possession of the popular belief to the present day.

It will naturally be asked, What could have produced all at once so great a revolution in the religious sentiments of mankind ? What could have brought Paul and others to entertain so firm a faith in the divine character and continued spiritual existence of one whom they had never seen or conversed with in this world, and to cherish so profound a conviction of sustaining the closest personal relations to him ? The most satisfactory answer to that question conveys to my mind the clearest proof of the superhuman origin of our religion—in other words, that it came from God and not from men. At this distance of time, and with such a mass of tradition intervening between us and the event, we cannot indeed ever expect to form any clear idea of the psychological experiences which were followed by this effect; we must be content to leave them in the mystery in which they are shrouded; but the effect itself, under the circumstances which accompanied it, seems to me inexplicable except on the supposition of some direct action of God on the believing mind, giving it a witness not previously possessed, and else unattainable, of the realities of the spiritual world. And why, even to the philosophical mind, should this seem incredible ? The condition of our planet is not stationary, but progressive. It has passed, and may even now be passing, through crises of connected change, in which higher forms of being have made, and may yet make, their appearance—in which a new creative force seems to put itself forth, and fresh elements of life to intermingle with the previous system of things. A fact like this, which cannot, I presume, be disputed, finds its only intelligible explanation in the presence of a Power which is anterior to all phenomena, which evolves them, and acts on them, and breathes into them the vitality through which they expand and grow. But can we suppose

God to be thus continually acting on the lower organization of our world, and to remain without any corresponding influence on mind? Great minds, like those of Jesus and Paul, are the selected media through which God from time to time infuses a new spiritual element into the world. They do not constantly appear; for that would be needless, as their life is contagious, and they awaken kindred sympathies wherever their influence spreads. When they have once introduced the truth and the life of which they are the appointed vehicles, their immediate work is accomplished; for they have created a new order of minds which subsist on that truth and endeavour after that life, and find the sure witnesses of a divine source in the response of their own higher nature and the life-long experience of a sanctifying effect. Although, therefore, we cannot explain how these holy persons came into closer communion with God, and obtained their deeper insight into the mysteries of the spiritual world, we can have no doubt of the fact, not only from the profound impression which they have left on the subsequent history of our race, making a new era in the human development of our planet, but also from our own consciousness of a spirit akin to that in which Jesus spoke and wrought, from our deep-felt want in trial and sorrow of the consolation and strength which his religion supplies, from its giving us the right point of view for comprehending the state of things to which we belong, and furnishing us with a key for the solution of its perplexing enigmas. Whatever may in fact have been the origin of our religion, once introduced, it asserts and justifies itself as an influence essentially divine. The profound conviction which lies at the bottom of all true faith, that in Christianity there is some direct intercommunion between the human and the Divine, led, in the natural working of human ideas, under the disturbing influence of conflicting philosophies and a decaying civilization, to those forms of doctrine which seem to many of us now most at variance with simple reason and the conclusions of modern science. But they are, in fact, not so much absolute errors, as the perversions or exaggerations of a great fundamental truth. The propositions that Christ was veritably God, and that two natures, a purely divine and a purely human nature, were united in the one person of Jesus of Nazareth, were only extreme and one-sided forms of stating in definite phraseology, and with limitation to a single individual, the great general truth, that God is always and everywhere dwelling in our humanity. The error was in predicating the whole of deity of the whole of humanity, and bringing them into such close juxtaposition, that the one must logically exclude the other, and in confining to an individual that which, rightly understood, was true of the whole race. But the Catholic Church, as a test of its own spiritual ascendency and as a tax on the faith of its subjects, delighted to reduce irreconcilables within the limits of the same technical formula; and this tendency, fostered by circumstances, became an hereditary vice in the ecclesiastical theology which is not yet expelled. And the ultimate reaction against this tendency has been hardly less mischievous than the tendency itself. In the rationalistic dread of mysticism, it has cut off man from God and set a wide gulf between them, and reduced Christ himself, no longer dwelling in the bosom of the Father, to a thin, bare humanity, specially inspired with a few supernatural truths, and clothed with miraculous powers for their authoritative assertion. An intermediate system, which at the present day finds favour with many thoughtful and cultivated minds, takes up a dogma of the later Platonism, and blends it with the fundamental truth of our religion, that in Christ the relations of God and man are harmonized. It supposes the eternal idea of our humanity to be itself a Person, and to have subsisted from the beginning of all time as the Divine Word in the bosom of the Father. This living Word comes between God and our humanity, the immediate object of our prayers and our aspirations, the bond of our fraternal sympathies, the medium through which we ascend to God himself. It is the divine pattern or archetype of which our humanity in its various forms is the more or less inadequate but ever-unfolding expression—embracing all men and all religions, excluding none from the hope of final salvation, tending incessantly towards a more perfect realization with the completion of the Divine plans, and offering meanwhile to Christians, in place of the vagueness of the ordinary Theism, a concrete, personal embodiment of Deity as the basis of their faith and hope. Of this system it may be honestly conceded, that it is comprehensive and benevolent, and that it completely uproots every remnant of the old Calvinism, which has so long exercised a withering spell over the sweetest and most generous affections of the human heart. We must still, however, ask, what foundation there is in natural reason and in the plainest language of Scripture for its assumption of a second Deity, usurping the functions of the first, intercepting the love and homage which are immediately his due, and relegating him to an eternal inactivity in the boundless spaces beyond the phenomenal. Why should we not go at once to the Omnipotent Father, who is in us as He was in Christ, and cultivate day by day direct communion with the ultimate Source of all that is Divine? I cannot discern one advantage obtained by this system for the formation of a religious character and the cherishing of a devout faith in Christ, which is not as effectually and more directly secured by resting in the grand and simple truth, that our humanity has in it an element of the Divine, and that Christ lived and died to draw closer the bonds which unite it with the Everlasting Father, and to shew us that they are not broken, but strengthened, by death.

I have often thought there was something providential in the very mode in which we get our knowledge of Christ from the Scripture—greatly assisting our love of one whom we have never seen, and in whom, though now we see him not, we may nevertheless rejoice with a joy unspeakable. The holy and loving Jesus, who brought our religion into the world, is rather disclosed to us in a few passing and wonderfully expressive glimpses—a central light beaming at intervals through its envelopment of traditional representation—then revealed in clear and definite outline, with every limb and feature fully displayed. We gather what he was from a few pregnant touches dropped, as it were, incidentally in the ampler record of miracles and discourses, which have possibly taken a hue from the unconscious pen of the biographer. The consequence is this—that the imagination, instead of being anticipated and exhausted by a fulness of detail which leaves nothing to add, and becoming indifferent through too close a familiarity, is impelled by the inspiration which those transient revelations convey, to fill up the sketch from its own highest conceptions of the morally great and pure, and with the growth of the soul itself in holiness, ever penetrates more deeply into the unsearchable riches of the mind of Christ. Nor is this an unreality. It is, on the contrary, the truest reality. Christ discovers our relations with God on that side of our nature where the simplest and purest minds are best able to comprehend and follow him—where lie its love, its trust, its holiness, its unreserved subjection to the Divine will. Such minds know enough of Christ from what is partially revealed, and from their own experience of its effect on themselves, to feel quite sure that the highest conceptions which they can form of love, of trust, of holiness, of absolute oneness of will with God, must have their fulfilment in Christ, and that the further they advance themselves in the Christian life, the more they must know of the spirit of him who introduced it into our world. For these qualities have their necessary adjuncts and consequences, only to be known from spiritual experience; and wherever they are seen to exist in their greatest purity, there we are certain of what must go along with them and grow out of them. Moreover, we think of Christ, not simply as he was on earth, "a man of sorrows and acquainted with grief," tried and tempted as we are, though in all emergencies faithful to duty and God, but rather as one now glorified and perfected in heaven. It is as a dweller in that higher world that our reverent affections rest on him. There we know that all the limitations and obstructions which impede the full development of our religious nature here below, are for ever taken away. There all the sweet and venerable qualities which won the love and reverence of those who conversed with him on earth, and made them feel that a Divine Presence was in the midst of them, have grown, we are sure, and are still growing, into a perfection inconceivable by us. And, therefore, taking the impulse and following the direction which the revelations of the New Testament give to the spiritual tendencies of our minds—in being true to them, we feel that we are true to Christ; and with the full consciousness that we are grasping the deepest reality of our being, we can raise our devout aspirations to Christ as the perfected ideal of our religious humanity in heaven. In a higher sense, proportionate to his spiritual superiority, our remembrance of him, and our deep sympathy with his mind and life, which is faith, are like what we entertain and feel towards some loved and venerated friend taken from us by death. The small details of the earthly career—all that was hard and angular in the inevitable conflict with human sorrow and infirmity—are obliterated—faded and gone for ever; only the grand outlines of nobleness and fidelity and pure unselfish affection stand out to the remembrance, toned down and softened with the mellowing hue which time never fails to bestow; but these alone, with the consecration that has gathered round them, give us, after all, the truest impression of the real man or woman whom we have known and loved here, and whom we hope to know and love more purely and more perfectly hereafter. Such reminiscences are a sort of transition-vision between earth and heaven. They are, perhaps, a dim foreshadowing of the glorified form in which we shall recognize our virtuous friends in another world. The possible future lends its colours to heighten the remembrance of the actual past. We are compelled to anticipate; and that very anticipation is a pledge of immortality. We are not drawn away from a reality that is gone, but we are carried on to a more glorious reality which is to come. All such remembrances have a sweetening, hallowing influence on our own hearts. We welcome, as a lingering presence of the friend who is gone—even as a token that he still lives—the gentle and loving spirit which he breathes over us. And so it is with Christ. Only that in him we see the ideal of our collective humanity in its relations with God, disjoined from the Jewish limitations of thought and speech which attended his earthly career.

Wherever we discern the tokens of religious excellence, there is the spirit of Christ; and in cherishing them, we cherish communion with him. The living Christ, like the living God, is ever in us and around us. He is our humanity harmonized with God. The truest communion of our spirits with him is the recognition in all its forms of the Divine in the human. It is not dogma, therefore, determining with ever such exactness the metaphysical relationship of the Son to the Father, or assuring ourselves by the most unexceptionable evidence of certain historical facts, that makes us Christians ; but it is thinking, feeling, living ourselves—if I may use the expression—into the very spirit of Christ. All patience and gentleness and tenderness, all love and purity and trust and self-sacrificing devotedness, are breathings of that spirit. The child's innocence, the mother's unwearied care and love, the hero's defence of the right and just, the missionary's zeal, the saint's holy and self-denying benevolence, the sage's preference of truth to worldly gain and popular applause—nay, the artist's worship of the divinely beautiful and true—all these are so many manifestations of Christ ; and to acknowledge them as such, to sympathize with them, to love and venerate them, is to hold communion with him. Whatever makes us more deeply conscious of the universal brotherhood of mankind—whatever fills us with hatred of meanness, hypocrisy, falsehood and oppression —whatever fires our souls with a generous zeal for truth and right and justice, for human emancipation and human progress—whatever touches us with a solemn and subduing sense of the presence of the Almighty Father in all the scenes of this beautiful universe and amid the ceaseless changes of our human world—brings us into closest communion with the spirit of Christ, and makes us one with him, as he is one with God. It is to closer and more habitual communion with this spirit that we must look for the regeneration of our humanity. This is the true salvation of the soul. This alone can check our debasing selfishness and our gross materialism. This alone can allay our feverish thirst of wealth, restrain our wild craving for excitement, and subdue to a nobler worship our insane idolatry of rank and fashion. This alone can lead us back to a simple, healthy and natural life, and make us once more true-hearted, genuine, sincere and honest men. A spell benumbs our faculties and blinds our eyes. We are the slaves of a vicious law, and live, without knowing it, in a world of shams and shows. One thrill of genuine sympathy with Christ—one moment of hearty faith in him—would dispel the illusion, and restore to us our moral freedom. It would shew us what and where we are; and open to us glimpses of that grander and more solemn world to which we are all rapidly hastening.

[Written, 1864; last preached (Old Meeting, Birmingham), 16th April, 1865.]

XXII.

The Reconciliation of the World to God in Christ.

2 CORINTHIANS v. 19:

"God was in Christ, reconciling the world unto Himself."

OUR age, whatever may be its faults in other respects, cannot be charged generally with want of earnestness. The last century was marked by a shallow rationalism, which dealt in compromise, was satisfied with half-solutions, and never pushed its principles to their legitimate issue. But now, on all sides, men are awake to the grandeur of the questions that are controverted between them. If there be much doubt (and doubt is the indispensable precursor of the highest truth), there is no scoffing and no irreverence. Men are striving everywhere to be genuine and self-consistent. We see this as well in the renovated zeal of orthodoxy, as in the fearless consequentiality of unbelief. It is not surprising, therefore, that, for the present, opinion should

seem to be taking an extreme form in opposite directions. First, there are those who, in their wish to free
their minds from all gratuitous assumptions inherited
from the past, and to look at the great problems of our
being with thoroughly unprejudiced eyes, regard this
world as a simple fact—a mere system of orderly physical development, governed by universal and undevi-
ating laws, with man for its last and highest product.
Then, there are others, who see in Christianity a rectifi-
cation of the moral disorder of the world, by a special
interposition once for all, creating certain artificial relations towards God, which secure salvation to those who
avail themselves of them, but abandon the remnant of
the human race to hopeless perdition. The former recognize law, order, progressive development, but no
living, moral contact between an invisible Spirit pervading the universe and the finite spirits of men—
phenomena, but nothing behind and beyond phenomena. The latter see, indeed, a God beyond and above
the world, but believe Him to have stepped forth into
the midst of human affairs in one line only of cosmical
development, and for the benefit of a certain portion
only of the human race, leaving all other periods of
history unblessed by the Divine Presence, and all other
members of the human family shut out from the Divine
mercies. But is this our only alternative? Are we
condemned to choose between a Pantheistic and an
Ecclesiastical construction of the universe? Is there
not a view of Christ and Christianity which can admit
the uniform and unfailing law and the progressive development of the one theory, without its godless desti-

tution; and recognize, with the other, the descent of the Divine into the human, and the direct intercourse of God and man, without taking the gospel out of the realm of universal law, without relegating it to a single order of historical events, and limiting its benefits to a portion only of mankind? Let us see.

(1.) Religion in all its forms rests on the assumption of a certain intercourse and sympathy between the human and the Divine. It is the mysterious contact of the mind, which we are conscious of possessing within ourselves, with another and a higher Mind outside our own, though akin to it, and at all times present to it, and enfolding it. Here is the realm of faith. Hence all prayer and all worship. This is one of those primary beliefs which we must be content to take as it is given to us, without looking for any ulterior reason that would logically enforce its acceptance. But, if a primary belief, how, it may be asked, can it ever be lost? To answer this, we must advert, for a moment, to the order of mental development in man. The instinctive affections and primary beliefs lie at the basis of our nature, and furnish the groundwork on which the reasoning faculties build up the progressive structure of materials collected by observation and drawn out into general truths and rules of action by comparison and inference. These reasoning faculties are more properly man's own. Their exercise depends on his will. They are trained and perfected by his personal industry. Here, within certain limits, he is the creator and architect of his own condition. As he progresses in the march of civilization, he becomes so absorbed in the employment of these powers, he finds such interest and delight in applying them to the increase of his knowledge, his power and his wealth, that at last he thinks of himself solely as a productive and reasoning animal. He forgets the ultimate ground on which he stands. The primitive trusts, on which his whole mental fabric rests, are either entirely hidden from view by the vast artificial superstructure that has been reared over them, or have so closely blended themselves with subsequent processes of thought, that it becomes very difficult, in the advanced periods of social culture, to distinguish, amidst the tangled mass of human opinion, the elements originally infused into our nature by God, from the results elaborated out of them by the reason of man. The inherent and hereditary sentiment of religion finds a shelter in systems of rite and dogma created for it by human logic, which stifle its genuine working, while they afford a constant opportunity for arid and unfruitful controversy. Philosophy, on the other hand, growing bolder as it feels more of its own strength, disdains with contempt the consecrated traditions of the past, and attempts to build up a theory of the universe for itself by present observation and in the exercise of its own unaided and irresponsible faculties, trusting to logic alone at once for its premises and its conclusions. For a time, there is a sort of compromise, a hollow truce, an armed neutrality, between religion and philosophy. They exchange words of mutual courtesy, eyeing each other all the while with the profoundest mutual distrust. At length on both sides the mask is thrown aside. Philosophy must be free, and will be fettered no longer by inconvenient courtesies, which keep back the outspoken utterance of its profoundest convictions. Religion, alarmed at the abruptness and vehemence of this divorce from its ancient ally, and seeing no safe and certain future before it, is thrown back with convulsive energy on its old forms of thought and speech, makes vehement efforts to invest them with a philosophical character and significance, and, dimly conscious that there is some great reality behind them, mistakes the hard shell of doctrine for the germ of spiritual life which is still beating feebly within it. Such, in general, was the condition of the heathen world when Christianity commenced its work of spiritual renovation. The philosophers, almost to a man, were Pantheists, for whom everything that could be considered a devotional tie between their own souls and a living God had long ceased to exist, and seemed to be for ever dissolved. Religious natures, such as Plutarch, whom this negative relation to the universe could not satisfy, sought refuge in the New Platonism, which, instead of repudiating, took up again with new zeal the old hereditary faiths of the world; and as some of our modern divines are bent on rationalizing the creeds of the fourth century, and extracting philosophy out of orthodoxy, so those good and pious heathens strove to find a pure and noble Theism in the mythologies of Homer and Hesiod. I do not blame such efforts in either case, made, as I believe they often have been, and still are, with perfect sincerity and deep earnestness. They attest that affectionate clinging of the heart to the great traditions of the past, which is one of the strongest instincts of our

nature, and which no wise religious reformer will ever
overlook, and that want of spiritual solace and support
from some assured and unfailing source, which philosophy of itself is unable to supply. Nevertheless, it is
instructive to observe how Providence met this profound
want of the human soul in the original communication
of Christianity to the world, and what is the lesson
which that great example has transmitted to an age in
many respects so like the commencement of the Christian era as our own.

(2.) The spiritual malady of that time, like the present, was practical estrangement from the great Father
of the universe, on the one hand, through the indifference of the philosophical mind, and, on the other, through
the interposition of a mass of worn-out faiths and forms
between the popular heart and the proper object of
religious trust and worship. Now, how did the gospel
seek to cure this malady, and bring back the alienated
soul of man to its Creator? Not by loftier doctrine, not
by a more refined and beautiful ceremonial, (these were
left to the free development of a progressive intellect
and a more cultivated taste,) not even by better precepts
alone, wise and holy as those of the gospel pre-eminently
were, (for these might have struck the ear, and charmed
the imagination, and excited speculative talk, like the
beautiful ethics of Seneca, without ever reaching the
deep inward springs of the spiritual life,) but by opening afresh in the lower strata of society, where humanity
lay closer to its native instincts, and, worn and jaded
with the carnal fever of the world, was athirst for a
diviner consolation, a copious fountain of the primitive

consciousness of man's intimate relations with God. From the gushing waters in those dark, unnoticed depths, there arose an influence, silent and almost unfelt, like some freshening mist or balmy vapour, which gradually reached and enveloped the intellectual eminences of the world—softening everywhere the arid heart of humanity, distilling into it a new reverence and awe, and calling out the tokens of a hidden life that was supposed to be extinct. It was a transformation, not of the intellect, but of the heart and conscience of the old world. For while philosophy, like the sun, sends down its radiance from above, and parches and burns at the same time that it enlightens, faith ascends from below, out of the simple trusts and genuine intuitions of the popular consciousness, like the fertilizing moisture which clothes the fields with verdure and fills the skies with ever-changing beauty and tempering shade. Christ came, like a divine presence, into a godless world. He infused a new life into our humanity. When the peasants of Galilee gathered round him, and gazed on the calm, benignant earnestness of his features, and hung on his living words, they felt there was some great reality here, which they had never met with before. They felt that never man spake like this man. It was something very different from what they had ever heard from their priests and their rabbis. They felt that through Christ, there was a fresh outpouring of God's Spirit on their souls. He touched springs which had been dormant in them till then, but now vibrated with quick responsiveness to every word that he spoke. They were drawn by sympathy into an indescribable communion of spirit with him. He called out into more vivid consciousness and stronger expression whatever they felt was best and worthiest within themselves. The sympathy which he awakened in them was something which they could not withstand. It was less his doctrine than his life which attracted them; for it penetrated into their own, and made it, they could not but feel, more loving, holy and divine. It was from this quickening source in a Divine humanity—God and man brought once more into living contact and unity— that the renovating power of Christianity went forth; and it owed its earliest successes—its steady propagation against all the apathy and unbelief of the world —less to speech, however eloquent, and still less to writing, however learned and convincing, than to the resistless contagion of a new and a diviner life. There are some truths which are so congenial to our inner nature, that they have only to be distinctly expressed to meet with instantaneous acceptance; and when they are truths of the life, which must be regarded not only as conceivable but as practicable, their realization in a great and noble character adds to their effect, and renders it still more impossible to doubt them. When a man, awakened at length to the moral significance of humanity, looked on the life of Christ, he saw at once that it expressed the true relation between man and God. He saw in its confiding trust, its wide, diffusive sympathy and love, its calm control of every disturbing impulse and affection, its implicit self-surrender to the Sovereign Will both in action and in suffering, and its hope of endless communion with a Father in heaven, the deep secret of human peace and bliss, the conditions of an eternal harmony between the human and the Divine. He saw—if he saw it at all—that there could be no truth beyond this; that, as far as the soul was concerned in its relations with the Infinite and Eternal, this embraced every conceivable requisite for perfect friendship with God. When Christ assured him, that whatever might have been his past weaknesses and sins, he had only to repent and believe—in other words, to enter with all his heart and soul into the spirit of Christ's own life—and the gates of the heavenly kingdom would be thrown open to him, he felt that a load was taken off his soul; that he had entered on a new existence; and that this, too, was a truth which the inward witness of his spirit taught him he could not doubt. So it was, that in the faith of Christ he found salvation, which he had elsewhere sought in vain, from the fears and anxieties and miseries which had incessantly haunted him in the world. Christ's personal presence on earth was, indeed, brief and transitory; but he remained long enough among men to diffuse far and wide the new life which he brought to them from heaven. His followers caught his spirit, and knew, from personal experience and inward change, the greatness of the truth with which they had been entrusted. Their earnestness was like his own, and was equally contagious in its influence. If they were but men, frail and fallible in many respects like those to whom they preached, they were at least sincere—firmly convinced of the grandeur of the cause for which they were labouring; and from their own shortcomings they could always appeal to their great

Master, now in heaven, in whom the ideal of righteousness which they held up before men was realized in
perfection. And the Christian preachers had this unanswerable argument on their side, that the more their
converts practised what they were taught, the more they
must become convinced of its truth ; for the whole
strength of their doctrine was not exhausted in a single
statement, however eloquent and complete, but was in
constant process of verification through the whole of
man's subsequent experience.

It was thus through the power of a divine life, subduing
the soul and drawing other lives into harmony with itself,
that God in that first age of the gospel reconciled the
world to Himself. And so it must be with us now. We
must go back to what is primitive and eternal in the
human soul. We must unlearn our creeds, and let our
worn-out forms and unreal fancies go. We must open
afresh the fountain of God's Spirit in our souls, and let
it send up a new herbage of life through the withered
letter which has so long overgrown it. Let us recognize
the identity of the great spiritual principle which through
all ages, and under all the changing forms of belief and
thought, has breathed a common trust and hope into all
religious souls; and wherever we see men who have seized
that principle, and who grasp it as the highest reality of
their being, let us welcome in them, to whatever sect
or church or religion they may belong, the true prophets of our race, destined by their zeal and their faithfulness to revive among us once more that profound
religiousness of mind in which older prophets and apostles once wrought, and which we must take up again if

we are to carry on their mission and complete their work.

(3.) The very medium through which we gain our knowledge of primitive Christianity, illustrates its proper mode of action on the world. The New Testament exhibits to us, not one uniform, self-consistent type of doctrine—not even one view of the person of Christ himself (for on these points there are almost as many opinions among its writers as amongst ourselves at the present day)—but rather the influence of a great religious life on the moral condition of its contemporaries—an influence diversified in its outward manifestation by the mental temperament on which it fell, by the character of the foregoing education, or by the mass of previously acquired beliefs and opinions which it had to encounter; while in all, whose inmost soul it reached, it brought to pass an effectual conversion to God. Thus, while the heart was purified and the conscience set right with God, no constraint was exercised on the speculative intellect; it was left as it was, and allowed freely to develope itself. This shews the true relation of religion and philosophy. Rightly understood, they can never interfere with each other, because they occupy totally different spheres. Religion has its roots in the profound intuitions of our inmost consciousness, developed by the experience of life and quickened by the outward stimulus of great prophetic souls. It rests on data of its own, as immutable as the Mind which supplies them; and these cannot be affected by any new interpretation of the external universe. The confounding of the provinces of physical inference and spiritual insight

can have no other effect than to corrupt both philosophy and religion. Both, indeed, form parts of one great
system of universal truth; but they are provinces which
lie on opposite sides of our nature; and as we explore
the one with the instruments which logic and mechanical art lend to science, so we penetrate into the other
with the reverent eye of faith. Our spiritual affections
and our philosophical theories always may be—and
when our minds are in a healthy and well-balanced
condition, always must be—in harmony. There is no
natural contrariety between a loving, trustful, reverent
soul, and an honest, truth-seeking understanding. On
the contrary, the profounder our faith—the more deeply
we feel the strength of the foundations on which it
rests—the less are we afraid of any results at which
science, basing itself on facts, may arrive in its reading
of the wonderful Cosmos to which we belong.

(4.) All the great religions that have governed, and
still govern, mankind, have had an historical origin, and
exercised their sway through a long transmission of traditional influences. At the head of them stand such
remarkable personages as a Confucius, a Buddha, a Zoro-
aster. The fact is strikingly significant of the order
in which the Sovereign Wisdom has ordained that the
spiritual development of our planet should proceed; nor
would I refuse to these illustrious names, to which
millions of our race still pay a reverent homage, their
appointed place in the grand, comprehensive scheme of
Providence for the education of our collective humanity.
Nevertheless, when I consider when and where Jesus
Christ appeared in the world's history—how his advent

had been prepared by a long previous discipline of Hebrew prophecy and Hellenic wisdom—how his gospel absorbed and combined and developed the elements of spiritual life and thought that were then loosely floating through the popular mind—how it became the animating principle of a new civilization that has embraced the most cultivated and enlightened nations of the earth—and how that civilization seems destined to become at last the civilization of the entire world—though I cannot but observe that his religion has originated in the same way, and grown up under the same conditions, as all other historical religions, I think I may claim for it, on the evidence of facts alone, a place in the order of spiritual development above them all, and may, without prejudice or enthusiasm, look on Jesus Christ, interpreting his religion by the light of history alone, as the great providential deliverer and spiritualizer of the human race.

(5.) Jesus Christ is entitled to our love and reverence as the primal source of our spiritual life, and as the ideal of our perfected humanity in heaven. It has been wisely appointed that our religion should be so closely inwoven with history. An historical faith widens our views and deepens our sympathies; excludes the isolation and narrowness of spirit that must cling to a worship nursed by the feelings of the present alone; checks by a healthy reverence the caprice and self-willedness of individual speculation; and through the rich and varied associations which it calls up around us, becomes the parent of a beautiful poetry and a consecrated devotion. I have often thought it was something solemn and affecting, when we take our seat at the Lord's table, to let our memories run over the long generations that have passed away, till we come to that upper chamber where Jesus sat with the Twelve and gave them his parting words of love and peace; and then to think of the many good and pious souls that age after age have been comforted in sorrow and strengthened in faith by the same communion of spirit, in which we ourselves still participate, with their risen and perfected Lord. They have long ago completed their earthly task, and are gone to their eternal rest in him. But their memories still enrich and mellow our devotions. They blend our faith with our humanity. They deepen the sense of our immortal inheritance and our human brotherhood, and of that common life in God which alone assures the one and glorifies the other.

> [Written, 1865 ; last preached (Hampstead),
> 14th March, 1869.]

XXIII.

The Faithful Disciple, Performer of greater Works than the Master.

----◆----

JOHN xiv. 12:

"Verily, verily, I say unto you, He that believeth on me, the works that I do shall he do also; and greater works than these shall he do, because I go unto my Father."

THE spiritual union of man with God was the special object of Christ's mission to the world. Its consummation was to be found in the knowledge that Christ was in the Father, and men in Christ, and Christ in men—in the full consciousness that there is only one grand spiritual unity pervading the entire universe. This great change in men's conception of their relations to "things unseen and eternal," was brought to pass through the contagious influence of Christ's own personality. The works which he wrought, and the lasting effects that have resulted from them, were the fruit and the witness of this inmost communion with God. It was thus that he introduced a new life into humanity, which, so far from being weakened, was strengthened and elevated by his translation to an invisible sphere, from which he exercised a purely spiritual sway over the souls of men. The effect of his mission may be described, in short, as intensifying into reality the sense of "things unseen and eternal"—(1) through direct personal communion with the Living God; and (2) through the deepened consciousness of an imperishable life in God, of which death only marks the passage to another and a higher stage of development. And it was a wonderful work, from whatever point of view we look at it, which Christ achieved by the power of his life, and the unmistakeable stamp of divinity that marked his words and acts—even the revival of a spiritual sense in that hardened and carnal generation, making men, to whom God had become a mere name, feel Him once more as a living and immediate Presence, compelling those whose whole being had been absorbed in the gratification of their appetites and the prosecution of their selfish interests, to acknowledge with solemn awe, not as a phrase but as a fact, the moral responsibilities under which they lived, and the inevitable retribution which was awaiting them. In view of so marvellous a change, which was beginning to revolutionize society to its very depths, Christ might well say to his contemporaries, as he still says to us, "Believe me for the very works' sake." He who was so mighty to bring men back to God, proved by the very efficiency of his call that he must himself be a Messenger from God.

But now, observe—a spiritual influence imparted to the world, a new life for the soul, a quickened sense of relationship to things invisible, is something very different from a dogma or an institution. It cannot, like them, be manifested in its completeness all at once. It does not admit of rigid definition and instantaneous development. It is designed for growth and gradual expansion, and may rather be compared to the seed of some flowering plant, which lies buried for a time with its inherent vitality in the bosom of the earth, and requires for the evolution of its full beauty and fragrance the long ripening of the year. It is the animating principle of a vast spiritual organization, which slowly unfolds itself, but is destined to embrace our collective humanity, and will yield ever richer fruits, as the needful conditions and stimulants of their production come into operation. Divine in its source, it descends into the depths of our humanity; and because it blends so closely with our inmost life, with the ultimate elements of thought and motive and aspiration—because it is nothing superficial and transitory, therefore it must, as to its outward form and manifestation, participate largely in the vicissitudes of the subject through which it works; it cannot transcend the limits within which the actual state of knowledge and opinion is confined, nor escape the shadows of superstition and intolerance which ever and anon darken the onward path of our race. It is of the utmost importance to understand clearly this distinction between the form and the substance of religious belief. The sense of filial relationship to a Living God, of His claim to our unquestioning service, and of our only life in Him, which death cannot annihilate—this is a conviction and a trust which belong to the very essence of the Christian faith, and have endured in it through all its changes. But it is obvious that this grand and consolatory faith may be, as it has been, brought home and made real to the individual soul through almost endless varieties of doctrinal conception; and that it admits of almost indefinite expansion into wider views and richer applications, as the intellectual horizon is enlarged, and the obstructions to a clearer vision are taken away. Christ distinctly foresaw this when he said, in the words of the text, "He that believeth on me, the works that I do shall he do also; and greater works than these shall he do, because I go unto my Father." Give men the assurance of an endless life with God and a glorified humanity in heaven, to be won by a life of love and holiness and wisdom on earth, and make that faith, not a name but a power, and it will hardly be possible to assign any limit to the beneficent effects of Christian activity, or to say how much of the evil which deforms our earth will disappear or be transfigured into blessing, and how earth itself thus spiritualized may become a present fore-court of the heaven which is awaiting us. But this anticipation, justified by the distinctest words of Scripture itself, implies that Christ's own power and insight, while he wore our nature on earth, were necessarily limited by the intellectual and social conditions of his country and his age; not, indeed, in the essentials of his message to mankind—the Fatherhood of God and the brotherhood of man, and the ultimate union of the

Divine and the human in the future kingdom of heaven —but in the way in which he conceived and represented these great truths, influenced by the Messianic beliefs of his time, and in which we may even say that it was indispensable for him to conceive and represent them, in order to be understood by those to whom he spoke, and to open any possible medium of spiritual communication between his mind and theirs. We are not, therefore, to look for the most perfect expression of Christianity in the period of its earliest annunciation to the world, or to find the measure of its utmost power in any particular work accomplished by Christ himself on earth; for his true reign did not begin till he had passed into another life; but in the collective results of its ever-widening influence among men, under the guidance of that Spirit of which Christ opened the richest source, and which in its unremitted access to the souls of men makes them, through participation in his faith and love, one with him, as he was one with God. Christ, in the clear light of intimate communion with God, saw the great spiritual realities of existence in the form in which they lay immediately before him, and did the great spiritual work which God put directly into his hand; but he did not see (his own recorded words admit it) what the slowly-unfolding future was needed to reveal; and he could not do what the immutable conditions of human development rendered then impossible. But the seed which he sowed was divine; and God, in His own time and way, gave the increase. His true followers, placed under other circumstances, and freely surrendered to the spirit which he transmitted to them, have been successively accomplishing through the ages what he foretold they should—greater works than he himself had done, because he went to the Father. Intense as was the religious life of the apostolic age, it was still hemmed in unavoidably by Jewish prejudice and pre-possession, till the spirit that was at work in it escaped from bondage into a wider sphere; and as that spirit has slowly permeated the length and breadth of huma-nity, what glorious results has it wrought out—results to which that first narrow field of Palestinian action could not of necessity furnish any parallel—the extinc-tion of serfdom and slavery; the recognition of the sanctity of every human home; the elevation of woman to her just rank in the social scale; the mitigation of the penal code; the extension of education to all classes; the strengthening of the conviction among the educated and the rich that they hold their social privileges for the benefit of the ignorant and poor; and that enlarged conception of commercial relations, once fostered by a spirit of exclusion and selfishness, which has converted them into the natural bonds of human brotherhood and the ultimate securities for universal peace! Adam Smith, our philosopher of the eighteenth century, un-believer as he has often been regarded, was one of the profoundest interpreters of the true meaning of the gospel when he developed for the first time the great principle of Free Trade. And Christianity would gain still greater victories over all that is vile and sordid in the world, if we would seek the evidence of its divinity in the unlimited possibilities of its future action, instead of hunting for it in the worn-out precedents of a time that is gone. This is not to undervalue Christ. It is simply to take his own view of the case. Christ is the source of the motive-power which has rendered these things possible. It is simply to distinguish between the spirit on which all social vitality depends, and the instrumentality through which it operates, and which must necessarily produce greater effects the more it is refined and perfected and relieved from opposing obstacles, and the wider the sphere in which it is permitted to act. Unfortunately, our undiscriminating letter-worship of the books which tell us what Christianity originally was, keeps us back from a full acknowledgment and hearty exemplification of its present and living power. So blind are we, that the very things which are the witness of the historical limitations of an earlier state of opinion—as, for instance, the Messianic conceptions which possessed the popular Jewish mind in the age of Christ—we have actually consecrated into articles of Christian belief, and made the special subject of divine revelation.

The question which I have thus briefly opened is far from being a purely speculative one. It has important practical bearings which deeply concern us all. Feel, realize to yourselves, what true Christianity is — an ever-present sense of your filial relationship to the Living God, and of your imperishable life in Him; grasp this great truth, not with your intellect alone, but with all the faculties of your being, your heart, your conscience and your soul, as an inward, vital power—a spiritual fact which underlies all other facts, and alone gives meaning and coherence to the mysterious universe

in which you are embraced ; and then reflect on the
possibilities of human goodness and human progress
involved in this habitual sense of affinity and intercourse with the all-perfect and ever-blessed Spirit, as
compared with the actual state of Christendom, para-
lyzed with vain conventionalities, cramped by hollow
observances, and spell-bound by superstitious reverence
for the exhausted formulas of some ancient creed. A
living Christendom demands a return to the reign of
the free spirit. Make Christianity a power, and not a
name ; and see what would be the consequence. In the
first place, it would spiritualize all things ; it would
make all things religious ; and would destroy for ever
the pernicious distinction which has wrought so much
mischief between the Church and the world. In whatever is pure, natural, beautiful and good, in the working
of human affections, in the endless varieties of human
character, in all the productions of human genius and
skill, in wit, humour and the playful creations of fancy,
if only seasoned with kindness and purity, not less
than in the graver efforts of heroic enterprize and self-
sacrificing philanthopy, we may find the nutriment, the
material and the expression of the truest Christian life
—vehicles through which the Divine Spirit breathes its
peace and blessing over the world. Then consider our
families ; what a change would come over them if we
could substitute, as their governing rule, the true spirit
of a living Christianity for the slavish spirit of the
world ; if instead of making it the one point, to shine
and be distinguished, to form high connections and
observe with hollow and punctilious exactness the

artificial rules of a heartless respectability, we would turn the thoughts of our children to the exhaustless resources of happiness which are to be found in a simple and natural life, filled with the daily sunshine of the affections, in the sweet courtesies and self-forgetting duties of home, in that spirit of love which is the reflection of the Father's presence in all things, and gives beauty to every object on which it lights, infusing a higher aim and a diviner relish into mental culture and elegant accomplishments, and making their very recreations, as the spontaneous outgoings of an innocent exuberance of life, an unconscious utterance of gratitude and praise!

What is emphatically understood as the business of life—the acquisition of wealth in the various employments of the world — is by many supposed to occupy a sphere lying at the greatest possible distance from Christianity, with which Christianity as such has nothing directly to do. Can there be a more striking example of the unreality of prevalent religious profession?—of the mischief of making Christianity consist in a system of unfelt and unappropriated dogmas, and divorcing it from the world in which we actually live? Our business, as the work on which the strength of our thought and activity is daily spent, ought rather to be the very medium through which we bring out into continual and evident operation the great principles of truthfulness and honour, of justice and humanity, which connect us with the unseen world, and bind us spiritually to God and our fellow-men. God has plainly handed over to us the resources of the world, for the development of wealth and social power; and it is our glory, not our sin—it is a fulfilment, not a violation of our Christianity—to use them nobly and honourably for the purposes for which they were given. I cannot conceive of a man of energy and intelligence proposing to himself a more legitimate, or even a higher object in life, than the attainment of success and eminence in his own line, whether industrial, professional or artistic, and aiming at the acquisition of wealth, not for the purpose of selfish distinction and exclusive advantage, but as a means of social beneficence. For wealth is power; and power exercised in obedience to the laws of God and for the ends which the spirit of Christian love suggests, may exhibit one of the truest manifestations of the religion of Jesus; and Christian teachers, instead of haggling over a great question, and endeavouring to draw modern meanings out of old texts, should say so plainly and at once, and call on our mercantile classes to shew their Christianity less in the forms and professions of the Church, than in the daily work and great business of life.

Political life is often thought to lie at a still greater distance from the realm of faith and love than even the counting-house or the exchange; and possibly for this reason, that the artificial requirements of theology, based on no natural and permanent laws, have been found absolutely irreconcilable with the actual requirements of the world. Released by the disruption of every legitimate bond from the higher influence which should have controlled and animated its course, the science of politics has too frequently been allowed to become a mere system of selfish calculations and ambitious designs, in which justice and humanity have no share; so that to the student of history it has often seemed as if the moral law which governs men, however imperfectly, in the inferior walks of life, had no place in the counsels of their rulers. The fact is, that religion, of which they talked so much, and which became in their hands the pretext for so many unrighteous wars, was to them no reality at all. Happily, it is a proof of the increasing power of a true Christianity, that there have arisen of late, in this country at least, statesmen of a nobler stamp and higher aim; and as the spirit of the gospel prevails over its dead forms, they will multiply, to the blessing of their kind.

Of all human institutions, the Church will benefit most by the transference of Christianity from the reign of dogmatism to the reign of the free spirit. Some apprehend the reverse, and think the overthrow of the old orthodoxies will draw after it the overthrow of the Church. But religion is too deeply seated in human nature, and worship is too natural an expression of religion, to permit us to entertain for one moment so gloomy an apprehension. Only religion will become more natural, and worship more spontaneous. Gifted minds will still continue, as before, to speak words of admonition and consolation to their fellow-men; and, freed from the heavy bondage with which creeds have so long prevented the free play of the human faculties, will assume a higher prophetic function, and give expression, without restraint or fear, to their profoundest intuitions of spiritual truth; while the kindred arts of music and poetry, aided by the softening influences of a chaste and noble architecture, will clothe with a beauty of their own the utterances of prayer and praise.

There is one reflection which can never long be absent from the mind of every thoughtful man : " Why am I here ? and whither am I going ?"　This is a consciousness which perpetually haunts our humanity, and deepens as we advance in years.　We live every moment on the verge of an unseen world ; and the constant disappearance of those whom we have most honoured and loved into the unpenetrable darkness which shrouds the grave, must, without light within from a higher source, throw a cloud at times over the happiest home and the most virtuous soul—yea, darker and sadder almost in proportion as the joint life which has been rent in twain was purer and more loving.　There is no cure for these deepest wounds of the heart but the balm of religion. Here, then, is the special triumph and privilege of the Christian spirit, as strong, as present, now to all who earnestly seek it in faith and prayer, as it was in the first age of the Church—witnessing to the soul of the believer his direct communion with the Father, in whom alone is all true life, and giving him in that solemn consciousness the sure pledge of immortality. Death will seem to him but a momentary break in the grand continuity of the Present with the Future ; all that has made this life glorious and beautiful, destined to become more glorious and more beautiful in the higher life into which he is about to pass—the few golden moments that have illumined his earthly lot beiug transient glimpses of the heaven that is to be revealed hereafter.

He, therefore, who has most wisely used and most richly enjoyed the varied resources of our present existence, drawing out of its material and evanescent elements all the love and all the beauty, all the wealth and power and happiness, which the Spirit enabled him to find in them, as the conditions of a higher blessedness to come—he has best fulfilled the high purpose of his being; he best deserves the name of Christian; he will most clearly discern, as he stands on the silent shore of time, across the dark waters which roll before him, the dim-discovered hills of his future home, and he will be best prepared for entering at once on the full enjoyment of the great inheritance which awaits him there.

[Written, 1867; last preached (Upper Brook Street, Manchester), 21st April, 1867.]

XXIV.

The Personality of God.

———•◆•———

GENESIS i. 27 :

"So God created man in his own image ; in the image of God
created he him : male and female created he them."

THIS remarkable passage contains the root-idea of
the theology of the Bible. It declares that God
and man are of kindred nature ; that the Father
has stamped His own image on His son; and that, consequently, that intercommunion between God and man
must be possible which is involved in the mutual relation of parent and child. This is what divines mean
by the *personality* of God. It is clothing the First
Cause with moral attributes ; enduing it with consciousness and will, and assigning to it purpose and character ;
so that it offers a counterpart to our human sympathies
and aspirations, and becomes an object of reverence,
affection and trust. This belief in the affinity of the
Divine and the human, which has its source in one of
the deepest instincts of our being, gave birth undoubtedly in the early ages of the world to very gross and

anthropomorphic conceptions of God, of which we can trace no indistinct reflection in the oldest records of the Bible. But gross as such conceptions may appear to us in the unqualified strength of their original popular enunciation, they contain at bottom a profound spiritual truth, clearly distinguishable, on a little reflection, from the sensuous imagery through which it rendered itself dimly intelligible to rude and uncultivated minds. These grosser anthropomorphisms had their use and significance in the time and place to which they naturally belonged; they corresponded to the actual capacity for the time being of our slowly advancing race; and they would gradually have expanded into juster and nobler views, had the development of religious ideas been left to its free and unimpeded course. But the spontaneous devotion and poetry of rude ages and simple natures was arrested in its growth by the mischievous interference of priests and theologians. They crystallized it into creeds, in the vain attempt to make that eternal which was only temporal, and fenced it round with the formulas of an artificial science, which took so strong a hold of the religious mind, that they seemed, in the first instance, only to strike a deeper root in the literal scripturalism, in the bibliolatry, as Coleridge called it, of the new life of Protestantism. But this could not endure for ever. The stern Nemesis of Faith is beginning at length to manifest itself. The time for reaction has come, and we are now paying the inevitable penalty of intermeddling with the natural and orderly development of the human mind. Disgust at the coarse and offensive representations of the Divine nature exhibited by the popular creeds, originating in comparatively dark ages, and perpetuated by mere authority into the midst of our present scientific light, is driving men almost unconsciously, in their earnest struggle after a more rational and spiritual faith, into an absolute denial of the proper personality of God, involving them in simple Pantheism, or the identification of Deity with the physical universe, and disposing them to seek in the recognition of mere law, pervading force and phenomenal order, an equivalent for the old faith in a Living God. These oscillations from one extreme of opinion to another, mark the history of human thought. Those who have studied it might have foreseen that, on the first breaking down of the old theologies, such a result was sure to occur. But while we acknowledge the unavoidable operation of this law of action and re-action, we must not suppose that either extreme expresses the entire truth, which lies somewhere between them, nor forget that in the present strong and wide-spread alienation from all human conceptions of God as a Friend and a Father, a great principle is lost sight of, and the hold is relinquished on all spiritual reality. The personality of God, in the sense already explained, as implying a mysterious affinity and intercommunion between the Divine and the human spirit, is the foundation of all religion, involved in all worship, indispensable to all faith and all prayer. We cannot love and reverence mere law. We cannot pour out our souls in joy and sorrow, in contrition and thankfulness, to simple force. There must be a belief in the living sympathy of conscious Spirit to produce anything that deserves the name of religion. Take that trust from the heart of man, and what a wilderness this beautiful universe becomes, peopled with fleeting shadows, and echoing to vast and gloomy vacancy! The instinctive prayer of the human soul, the unbidden ejaculation for help and comfort which escapes at times even from the lips of unbelieving men, the unseen but unmistakeable presence of Something higher and holier than ourselves, which enfolds us with its silent blessing in the dark hour of sorrow and bereavement, that voice of faith which speaks through our collective humanity, and makes itself heard from the earliest records of its existence on our planet, in its simple poetry, its rude art, its quaint but touching usages, in every expression of its deepest trust and tenderest affection—all these things are to me the clear witness of Nature herself to the grandest of all truths, inscribed on the very front of the Bible—that there is a Living God, the Father of our spirits, who formed us in His own image, that we might be conscious of our kindred with Him, and in the sense of it might worship and love and serve Him.

The human soul may be not unfitly described as having two sides—one that is turned to things outward and visible, another which converses with things spiritual and unseen. It is an assumption to affirm that reality is to be found on one of these sides alone. There are phenomena in the inner consciousness of our being, permanent and invariable, of which literature and art in all their forms are the standing witness, which have as marked a stamp of reality on them as any which are made known to us through the senses. What is our indestructible feeling of the difference between right and wrong, between truth and falsehood ? What is our cleaving sense of dependence and responsibility? What is our intuitive perception of the identity of the Power which originates and sustains the order, harmony and beauty of the entire universe, with that which we ourselves are conscious of exercising for the production of the same effects within the limited sphere of our individual agency ? What means our spontaneous clothing of that Power with all the attributes which our highest aspirations suggest to us as inseparably attaching to the most perfect exercise of intelligence and will ? What is the conviction, of which we are unable to divest ourselves, that where an end is pursued, and the adjustment of parts to a whole is manifested, in things visible, there must somewhere or other have been a purpose and a plan in that which is invisible ? Are not these things realities ? Do they not underlie all the great historical movements of our race ? Physical science may ignore them as not coming within the range of its own field of observation. But there they are, in the realm from which its eye is averted—plain and unquestionable — what no oracular utterance of a one-sided philosophy can strike out of the general consciousness and bring into absolute disbelief. To affirm, as has been affirmed from the highest seat of orthodoxy, that God in Himself is wholly unknowable, and that the void can only be filled by the authoritative teaching of the Church, seems to me one of the most irreligious doctrines ever propounded to the world—a desperate attempt to uphold the necessity of a hierarchy at the risk of possible

Atheism. We cannot, it is true, comprehend God in the infinitude of His unsearchable nature; but we know enough of Him through the clearest revelations of our own consciousness, to feel certain that He is something more than a name for unintelligent force and unmoral law — that in His relation to us He is a Spiritual Reality, a Living God. We rise up out of our own self-knowledge, which is the nearest to us of all realities, to the idea of God, the highest Mind, which cannot be disjoined from the sense of our own; and though the vast conception, as it ever ascends and expands, is lost at length to our distinct cognizance in the depths of the Infinite, it preserves, nevertheless, the clearest characters of reality, so far as we can trace it, and we feel that it has a vital root in ourselves. The ascription of moral attributes to God is the most valuable result of this deduction of His nature from our own self-consciousness; for it is an inference which physical phenomena could never of themselves have suggested; though once assumed from the necessary laws of mind, it is applicable to them, and supplies a possible explanation of some of their darkest mysteries. Mere Power, working on a large scale without moral guidance, could only originate confusion and deformity. Truth, justice, holiness and love, seem to me the essential conditions of all fruitful, harmonious and self-consistent action. Without such principles as its basis, I am unable to conceive how an universe like ours could continue to exist. The finest productions of human genius are consummated under the influence of these mental qualities. The highest beauty is the expression of their mingling *quintessence.* Now, what is highest in man must be infinitely higher in God; and the possession of a moral trust in God is an exhaustless source of comfort and support to the soul. In one of his philosophical works, Mr. J. S. Mill, arguing solely from external phenomena, has contended that we have no ground for trust in the continuance of a state of order and well-being beyond what is founded on our past experience of Nature's laws; that it is altogether within the range of possibility that the system of things to which we belong should be broken up and be superseded by another, constructed on quite opposite principles: and on his own theory he is right; for, as I understand him, he leaves no ground for moral confidence in the mysterious Sovereignty under which we live. But let us assume Mind—Mind endowed with every conceivable moral excellence—such as we must assume, if we reason logically upwards from ourselves to God—to be the root and pervading principle of all things, and we pass at once into a feeling of quiet trust and implicit self-surrender to the Ruling Will. We perceive now that actual phenomena do not exhaust the possibilities of the universe, but are only the finite expression of a Wisdom and a Love which infinitely transcend them all; and that whatever changes may occur either in material phenomena or in the condition of the human race, are only stages in the grand development of a progressive universe, which must be in harmony with the fundamental attributes of a just and merciful God, though at present we may be unable to embrace them in any complete system of religious philosophy. Questions are constantly emerging from the inmost depths of our being, which no science can solve, and which find their only answer in religious faith. Science has, it is true, a great and magnificent task to achieve; and it is a mad impiety to presume to say to it, Thus far shalt thou go, and no farther. Science has to shew us plainly what this world is in which we live; how it has arisen and grown; whither it is tending; and what are its possible relations to the million worlds which roll around it and twinkle in remotest space: and when it has laid its demonstrations before us, we have only to accept the result as the ascertained plan of the Divine Intelligence, to adapt our ideas to it, and to believe that it is the wisest and the best. But when Science has done its utmost, it can only have revealed the law of the phenomenal; and there are questions beyond the phenomenal which it cannot deal with, and which nevertheless insist on a reply. I find myself living in a state of things on which science, let us suppose, has shed its fullest light, revealing to me all the laws of succession and co-existence in phenomena which it is possible for human sagacity to discover. But will all this solve for me the deepest mystery of my being? Will this explain to me why I am here, and for what purpose I have been created? Is there not a *why* and a *wherefore* hovering over the grandest solutions of physical science, which it cannot reach, and which sends us back for an answer to the depths of our own spirit, where we can commune silently with God, and find in the ineffable sense of affinity with Him a ground of absolute trust in Wisdom and Goodness which infinitely exceed our own?

The answer that we get from this source will become more distinct and full, as the sense of our own personality is deepened and ennobled. It is observable, that when faith in the Divine Personality, in a Living God, is abandoned, belief in human personality, as an enduring entity surviving the grave, usually goes along with it. When the universe is once divorced from the idea of a living, conscious, intelligent Presence nurturing and developing it in a spirit of parental love, it becomes a mere aggregation of physical forces, and supplies no grounds for moral reasoning about the position and destiny of man; and individuals, with all their deep affections, their earnest longings, and their sublime aspirations, pass into the category of physical phenomena, a mere transient organization of elementary forces, held together for a time by the vital principle, and then broken up and dispersed by death, to enter anew into other and equally perishable combinations. But communion with a Living God strengthens the feeling of our own personality; and while it fills us with the deepest sense of humility and dependence, breathes into us at the same time a profound consciousness of our life in Him, which elevates our self-respect, and will not allow us to regard what we have in common with Him as valueless and mean.

Aspiration after His holiness and righteousness and love—which is the necessary fruit of all true faith—draws us away from too close an engagement with the physical attributes of our being, and concentrates endeavour on the formation of character and the energetic fulfilment of the task of duty which is set before us;

and in all these moral efforts the sense of our personal individuality ever comes out more clear and strong. We feel that the *self* which we carry within us, and which connects us with the Living God, is the greatest and nearest of all realities; and we every day acquire more and more the conviction, that we are in our inmost being something different from, and superior to, the evanescent phenomena that furnish the training and discipline of our immortal souls. Thus the sense of God's personality and the sense of our own act and re-act on each other. As we become ourselves more earnestly moral and more unreservedly devoted to the right and true, as we become in will and endeavour more like God himself, we feel Him more profoundly to be a great spiritual reality, and get a clearer insight into His nature and designs. On the inward eye of the unreservedly devout and holy, revelations of the divinest truth continually unfold themselves. " Blessed," said our Lord, "are the pure in heart, for they shall see God." And it is on this side of our nature that the influence of prophetic minds tells with the most powerful effect. In nothing are we more sympathetic than in our religious affections and our spiritual intuitions. There is always a dormant faculty within us, waiting to open its eye, and behold the Living God. What we might never, in the dimness of our worldliness and our sensuality, have discerned for ourselves, we see clearly and for ever when it is once revealed to us in the light of a prophet's teaching. Hence Christ was emphatically the "Light of the World." He lived in God; and imparting this blessed life to his followers, he said to them,

"Because I live, shall ye live also." The doctrine of the Divine Personality, so sublimely indicated in the opening chapter of Genesis, attained its climax and consummation in the gospel of Christ.

And now let us, in two words, ere we conclude, sum up the meaning and application of this grand doctrine of the Personality of God. Interpreted in the light of this doctrine, what does this world, and what does the life that we lead in it, mean in relation to our affections and our moral principles? Why has God given us souls, and exposed us to sorrow, temptation and trial? Science here is dumb; but the spirit of Christianity, which is identical with the profoundest breathings of our common human heart, replies—For discipline and preparation, for the formation of character, for the development of our individual personality. Shall it be affirmed by science that not one particle of matter ever perishes; that every elementary law operates and has operated unchanged through all worlds and all time? And can we suppose, if we look not to the outward world alone, but blend with it the equally indisputable phenomena of that which is inward and invisible, that the highest and most wonderful reality in this universe— a devout, intelligent and loving soul—shall finally become extinct, and disappear with all that it once contained, amidst the ceaseless flux and ever-changing forms of elementary matter? No; Religion gives us a better hope. This life will not prove one great frustration of all our aspirations after what is pure and noble and good. It is a school of discipline for us all; yea, perchance even for those whom we now regard as the meanest and the worst. For in the meanest and worst, if we knew all and judged them mercifully, there would be found yearnings of human tenderness and gleams of better thought and endeavour, which shew how richly the inward nature was endowed, and forbid us to exclude even these from the hope of final recovery to goodness and God. We cannot believe that the great Parent Mind has made anything so great and noble as a human soul wholly in vain; and why has He scattered these seeds of moral and spiritual capacity so far and wide, if they are never to spring up and bear any fruit at all? And let us not say the prospect is too vast and overpowering to be entertained. We are in the hands, be it remembered, of an Almighty Father. Amidst the darkness which so often overcasts the present transitory scene of things, it is a glorious and consolatory thought, nursed and warranted by the deepest faith, that in the solemn and mysterious process of development which is accomplishing itself through the ages, under His guidance, with whom time and space are nothing, and whose resources are absolutely exhaustless, all things may be tending, here and in other worlds, to the final reconciliation of every soul that has ever lived with its Father and its God.

[Written, 1867; last preached (Upper Brook St., Manchester), 29th December, 1867.]

XXV.

The Losses and the Gains of Age.

———◆———

Jeremiah vi. 4:

"Woe unto us! for the day goeth away, for the shadows of the
evening are stretched out."

POETS from the beginning of time have sung of
old age as the cold and joyless winter of human
life. They have invested it with every repulsive
attribute and mournful accompaniment, and in strains
of the deepest pathos have contrasted its fading decre-
pitude with the blossoming freshness of youth and the
vigorous activity of manhood. There must be an element of truth in these representations, or they would
not have been so generally accepted and so incessantly
repeated. On the other hand, may we not ask whether
this is not, after all, only one side of the question? Is
there not to the religious eye another view of the subject, which yields glimpses of delightful hope and opens
sources of the noblest consolation? Fairly setting over
against each other the losses and the gains of advancing
years, is there not a clear surplus of compensation in

the latter, for the loving and truthful soul, which may well reconcile us to our inevitable fate, and send us down with a cheerful heart into the darkening vale?

What, then, are the undeniable losses which we must all encounter with the change superinduced on body and mind by age? Every one will here revert at once to that decline of physical vigour and enfeebled capacity for exertion, which closes against us more or less many fields of activity that we once delighted to traverse, and which, retarded or accelerated by different circumstances in different men, still marks with unfailing indication the gradual wane of life. Our first experience of this is painful, almost humiliating. We feel that we are no longer what we have been. Nature is as beautiful to the eye as ever, and we love her with as keen a love; but we cannot climb her mountain heights and explore her sylvan solitudes as of yore; we must be content with a more quiet and contemplative enjoyment. The great interests of humanity—its struggles for right, for freedom and for truth—have as strong a hold on our sympathies as ever; and we would fain throw ourselves into them, and help them onward with a strong arm and unwearied foot, as we once did; but we find that the power is gone from us; we must leave the turmoil and the glory of the fight to younger men, and be satisfied with sitting by to advise and deliberate. The mind itself shares in the irresistible change. What it acquired early in life, it holds, perhaps, with a firmer grasp and embraces in a more comprehensive survey than ever; and the fundamental principles which it then imbibed, it will work out, under the guiding lights of a longer experience, into clearer and more harmonious results, and sometimes perhaps find in them fresh and unsuspected applications; but it has not the same facility for making entirely new acquisitions; it has not the same elasticity of adaptation to the altered intellectual emergencies of the day; and the last fruits, the "consummate flower," of an ever-advancing science it must leave to be gathered by younger hands. In early life, the most powerful stimulus to philanthropic effort and many-sided thought was furnished by friends and associates, who had grown up with us under the same mental influences, who participated in our general views and aims, who knew our difficulties and shared our doubts, and were eagerly looking with us for some adequate solution. But time gradually narrows this genial intercourse, and breaks up that delightful hospitality of soul which gave a charm to opening life, and which later intimacies, however valuable, can seldom entirely replace. The companions of the inward man one by one disappear; and we find ourselves comparatively strange and isolated in the midst of a generation with which we have no common memories, whose newest and deepest thoughts we do not perhaps fully comprehend, and by which we are conscious that we ourselves are often misunderstood. The tide of human thought rolls on irresistibly. But after a time we are no longer able to keep abreast of it. It is too strong and too rapid for our failing powers. We make our retreat to the adjoining bank, to take breath, and see those who are less worn and more vigorous dash past us on the crested wave. Man's noblest prerogative is to look before and behind; not to be rooted to the present alone; but the associations which bind us to a loved and venerated Past, are some of the tenderest and holiest which our nature knows; and the rupture of these affectionate bonds, always inevitable, often abrupt and harsh, is one of the sorest trials which advancing years bring upon the soul of man.

There yet remains a still heavier penalty of age—the heavier because it is personal, and comes from ourselves alone—I mean the sense which grows upon us, as we grow in years, of our still cleaving imperfections and infirmities — how inadequately we have fulfilled the great purpose of existence—how we are drawing to the verge of life the same erring and sinful beings in many respects that we entered it. I suppose no one who is really true to himself fails to make this experience; and it is a melancholy and humiliating one. Still, it is the truth, and we must face it. With what pain and self-reproval do we recall the high aims and generous purposes with which we commenced our career in the world, and then remember how weakness, sloth, and perhaps cowardice—the failure of sustained effort and of resolute self-control — have marred and frustrated them, and left, of all the brilliant enterprize to which we so eagerly set our youthful hand, only a scattered wreck floating on the stream of time! Infirmities of temper and errors of conduct, rooted perhaps in our native temperament, which we have so often struggled and prayed against, and which we hoped had been finally overcome, break out anew in our age with mortifying evidence that they were simply kept in abeyance, not wholly subdued, when we have less power to grapple with them, and diminished time and opportunity for effecting their conquest. The future on which we once drew so lavishly, as if its resources were boundless, for meeting postponed obligations—now comes upon us sternly, like an inexorable creditor, with urgent demands for payment which we cannot satisfy. To those who dwell only on the earthly side of our human nature, and do not look beyond patent facts to some higher theory of man's destiny, of which they are but the cipher, this contraction of the future and attendant collapse of hope must come with a gloomy foreboding and significance—and, in the solemn words with which Gibbon checked the rising sentiment of self-exaltation on the completion of his great work, "must tinge with a browner shade the evening of life." It is in such words that we profoundly sympathize with the plaintive regret of the prophet, and are ready to exclaim with him, "Woe unto us! for the day goeth away; for the shadows of the evening are stretched out."

This is one side of the picture. Let us now turn to the other.

The decay of physical vigour and the enfeeblement of the spirit of enterprize is not pure, uncompensated loss. There is a blessing in the deeper calm by which it is followed. If our senses are less keen, the pleasures which they admit are more refined; they partake more of the inward nature and become more spiritual: for out of the accumulated treasures of a wider culture and longer experience, the mind draws up more varied trains of thought and feeling to enrich and ennoble the associations which they excite. Do not the golden words of our favourite authors—the passages of the poets that we have loved from childhood—glow with a diviner beauty and yield a deeper meaning the older we grow, and the more we can bring to their interpretation the results of the life which we ourselves have lived? So long as we can see and hear at all, does nature wear a less or a more lovely aspect to the quiet eye, and music breathe less or more enchantment into the listening ear, of age? Even when eye and ear are closed, memory still survives to fill the invisible palace of the soul with the brightest visions and the sweetest melodies; more bright, perhaps, and more sweet, through the idealizing influence of the soul itself, than ever entered through the grosser aperture of the outward sense. Deliverance from the excitability and restlessness which are the almost inevitable accompaniments of the energy and enthusiasm of opening life, is an infinite gain for the understanding of what is deepest, and the enjoyment of what is holiest, in this vast universe of God. The passions are more obedient, and imagination is less seductive; and through the dispersion of these sensuous vapours, the inward light shines out more clear and strong. Calmly collected within itself, the soul discerns, as it were intuitively, what was so often hidden from it before—the grand and vital distinction between the transient shows and the imperishable realities of things—between right and expediency, between benevolence and weakness, between a genuine reverence for humanity and a servile truckling to its passions and prejudices, between the fluctuating dogmas of sects and schools and the eternal truth of God. And the fruit of all this, in every well-ordered age, is *moral wisdom*, by far the most precious result of the experience of life; less dazzling than the dreams of youthful hope—less fertile in resource, less redundant in energy than the unworn strength of manhood—but with deeper insight into the solemn mystery of our being, with principles more firmly fixed and convictions more strongly grasped, with a more limited range of objects, indeed, but with a steadier aim, a more single purpose, and a profounder trust.

We miss painfully, it is true, with the advance of age, the loved associates of earlier life who year by year are taken from our side. But we must not live too exclusively in the past; the present and the future have undiminished claims upon us. We must strive to keep up bravely and cheerfully with the onward movement of the generation to which we belong. The noblest attributes of humanity never perish—its love of truth, its sense of justice, its zeal for right, its compassionate intercession for the down-trodden and the wronged. These are to be found, if we will look for them, in every changing phase of human society; they ask our recognition, and call for our sympathy and our help. Only we must not confound these permanent realities with the different forms of speech and modes of action which from time to time they take up. We are all too prone to assume that truth can only be advanced, and good done, in one way and in accordance with our own cherished formulas. The forms of thought and the applications of principle are ever-varying and progressive; while beneath them all there is a latent substratum of ultimate moral aim and deep intuitive truth, which undergoes no change. Wherever there is clear evidence of earnestness and sincerity in any human soul, however strange the diction in which it clothes its purpose may sound in our ears, and however novel and startling some of its modes of procedure may seem to us—if you will look candidly through these outward manifestations to the inward vitality contained in them, you will find the same fundamental principle at work which we in our days of vigour, and the worthiest of our fathers before us, ever aimed at in our highest efforts and our holiest moods. The fervour of youthful enthusiasm may need the corrections which riper wisdom can furnish, and which years will infallibly bring with them. But where there is a good and pure heart—where there is a noble spirit—never doubt of the final result. Rather draw a new freshness into your declining years—a freshness the more sweet because it is of the soul itself —from a cheerful participation in the new interests that are springing up around you, and a cordial recognition of the new spirits that are rising into life to deal with them. Whatever years may take from you, let them not rob you of your faith in humanity and your sympathy with the generous and noble-minded young. Even for them that are gone, time brings with it a hallowing influence, which glorifies them in our memory. If they have been good, we think of them not altogether as they were on earth, but as we trust they have now become. The little infirmities of temper and eccentricities of conduct which marred the perfect fruition of earthly intercourse, have all disappeared in the general remembrance of what was noblest and loveliest in their character; just as in a successful portrait, any blemish or imperfection of the outward features is lost and dissolved in the radiant glow of the predominant expression. And this may perhaps, after all, be the truest image of departed friends—what best represents their real, inward self—what will alone survive the mysterious transformation of the grave, to become the subject of higher spiritual intercourse in heaven. It is with this higher influence that the memories of the virtuous and the venerable who have been taken from us accompany us to the grave; their spirit seems to draw nearer to us as we advance in years, and the reality of their unseen being to be more deeply felt. Surely this is a compensation to religious age for much that it has lost.

If those who have passed away, but to whom our natural affections still fondly cling, were wild and erring in their earthly career, we cannot indeed without irreverence suppose that the judgment of a righteous God will fail at last to overtake all unrepented, unforsaken sin, or that anything can arrest the inevitable course of retributive law; but we also remember, that the chastisements of a Father are never prompted by vindictiveness, but always spring from the highest and holiest love; that they are always inflicted with a healing and restorative design; and that when the soul awakes to seriousness, and understands what it has been and done—as it must do in the revelations of a life to come—they will descend on it with at once a chastening and a renovating power, and, if Will can only be rectified and strengthened, may build up slowly and painfully, but still with sure effect, the dilapidated fabric of moral and spiritual life. Such, at least, are the consolatory hopes on which age, softened and made humble by the deep consciousness of personal imperfection and frailty, delights to dwell; and this is a holier and happier frame of mind than that spirit of harsh judgment and unqualified condemnation in which those who have not yet learned to know themselves are always so ready to indulge. It is a compensation to age, under the humiliating sense of infirmities and sins which the discipline of years has not sufficed to expel or subdue—not indeed that it becomes less painfully sensitive to the eternal distinction of right and wrong (for this would be the most fearful of penalties, rather than a blessing), but that it imbibes a deeper and tenderer sympathy with our common humanity in its endless shapes of sorrow and sin—that it judges an erring brother, as a brother, with a merciful, though not with an indifferent or undiscriminating, compassion; that, identifying itself with the great family of man—feeling how we are all beset with temptation, and oppressed with weakness, and prone to fall—it does not isolate itself from the general lot in proud and haughty self-sufficiency, but with a quiet trust that all this trial and discipline may be slowly preparing the way for some greater ultimate good, ventures to hope the best for all men, even the worst, lends its aid, in every way still possible to it, for their moral redemption and elevation, and sends up a daily prayer to the Fountain of all good for help and deliverance for itself and for them.

After all, I am free to confess that, as the matter

strikes my mind, if the consolations of age were furnished by this terrestrial life alone, considerable as I think they would still be, they would hardly suffice to counterbalance the undeniable ills which attend it, and repress the melancholy which steals over the deepening consciousness of irreparable loss. Hence men, in whom the religious sense has ever been cultivated at all, are drawn by the natural feelings of age into closer communion with the one ever-present and undying Friend, whose outstretched arm sustains them when earth is already crumbling beneath their feet, and whose Spirit whispers deepest peace to the soul when the unsubstantial pageantries amidst which it has lived are fast fading away. The felt decay of the physical almost compels them to draw, as they have never drawn before, on the spiritual. They now learn through their own weakness and insufficiency, that there is no strength and no peace like that which only God can give. A failing strength is supplemented by one that is unfailing. A short-sighted wisdom surrenders itself to the guidance and disposal of One that embraces and is equal to all things. Unspeakable rest and quietness of soul is the consequence of such a faith as this. If our faith were perfect, our peace would be perfect too. One result of life's experience becomes increasingly clear to us with years—what has been achieved by it in the form of character—the development of the mysterious *I*. *There* it lies before our reflective consciousness—that strange and mingled compound of good and evil, with latent capacities for action and enjoyment which have never yet been fully drawn out, built up out of instinct and habit, impelled by will, enlightened by reason and controlled by conscience—the most wonderful product known to us of the all-inspiring and creative energy of God. No thoughtful man can fail to ask himself, as he approaches the close of his earthly existence — Must this, too, which constitutes myself — this mysterious continuity of consciousness, thought and will, which makes me one responsible unity from youth to age— must this, too, be dissipated with the material elements of its outward vehicle, which are in ceaseless flux, and in the course of a few years are entirely changed—this spiritual essence and energy, which is God's mightiest agent in working out the great idea of His visible crea- tion—this wonderful instrument of power and beauty and truth, which bears on it no indication of having completed its mission, but rather of having only ac- quired a fitness for a higher one yet to come? I know how easy it is to declaim on this awful subject; how readily science can raise difficulties which mere science cannot meet; what truths there are, lying in the very depths of our moral being, which faith grasps intuitively as certainties, but which the subtlest human logic can- not adequately demonstrate. My trust is in the Living God, my Father; and that trust age deepens and justi- fies. Compelled by the necessities of my mental consti- tution to believe in a Sovereign Mind, the Fountain of right and truth, and the Author of the moral law, I can- not conceive of any limit to the essential perfections of His nature. Into childlike faith in His infinite wisdom and infinite love, I resolve all my doubts and difficulties and fears. If I cleave to Him, I am sure He will never forsake me; I am sure a Father will never forsake His child. The part of a wise man, therefore, is, not to indulge in vain, speculative dreams, or to be over-anxious about what we are not yet permitted to know, but to cherish a healthy trust and a filial love, to forget himself in the higher interests of humanity and truth, and to throw his whole soul into the effort more clearly to know and more faithfully to accomplish so much of the Divine will as is yet revealed to us. Then, in this daily contact with spiritual realities, a holier light will be kindled in the soul, and we shall be brought step by step to a nearer view of the truth. We shall aim at that profound and constant religiousness of spirit, making the whole universe a temple, and life itself one silent, unbroken prayer, of which both the possibility and the beauty have been so wonderfully set forth in the brief but precious glimpses that have reached us of the ministry of the Prophet of Nazareth. Such a spirit will bring us into habitual communion with the Living God; so that when this mortal life flits from our faltering grasp, we shall lay hold of His eternal strength, and find an imperishable heritage in Him.

[Written, 1867; last preached (Upper Brook St., Manchester), 3rd January, 1869.]

XXVI.

The Immortal Future mercifully veiled to us by God.

Psalm lxiii. 7:

"Because Thou hast been my help, therefore in the shadow of
Thy wings will I rejoice."

IT may be reasonably objected to enthusiastic views of religion, that they disturb the proper relation of things seen and unseen; that they overset the balance of the mind, fill it with dreams, and unfit it for active usefulness. On the other hand, the danger of most people—especially of those who live in the world, and entertain what are called rational opinions—lies in the opposite direction. They are too much engrossed by the world of sense, lose sight of the spiritual world which lies beyond it, and have scarce a perception of the grand and awful verities which are disclosed, through the veil of God's visible works and providences, to the enlightened eye of the religious mind. It is ever the part of a wise man to understand his position, fully to comprehend the circumstances in which he is placed, to keep them steadily in view, and to order his whole course of life in reference to them. This is, in fact, the proper character of wisdom.   Without this habitual realization to our inner consciousness of all that concerns us, of all that is in preparation for us, and of the thousand contingencies to which our being is hourly exposed, there can be no peace of mind, no feeling of moral security, no calm and cheerful enjoyment of life.   What, then, *is* the actual state of man on earth ?   Let us clearly represent it to ourselves.   We breathe; we live; we think; we form plans; we toil after a distant future; we meet with success; we encounter disappointment; we suffer pain; we taste of happiness.   Such is the mingled web of our existence. Through this alternation of influences, treasuring up experience as we proceed, we live on, from day to day, from year to year, till we die.   But is this all ?   Does this brief chapter of accidents complete the story of man?   Do we never ask ourselves, in those silent vigils of the spirit when it communes with itself and with God, For what end am I created ?   How must I interpret the enigma of my existence ?   How may I best fulfil the purpose it reveals ?   We evidently belong to some vaster system of things, from which our frail and apparently evanescent being derives its meaning and coherence, all the provisions and tendencies of which we are at present prevented from seeing by the interposing shade of sense, but in reference to which alone can we find any rational solution of the doubts which perplex and the contradictions which assail us, in speculating on our nature and our destination. Open your eyes on the world. Observe what is daily occurring in it—events which leave no impression on the mind, *because* they daily occur, yet in themselves full of wonder, pregnant with a thousand deep suggestions to the thoughtful spirit. Take up a newspaper, and turn to the column which gives its stated chronicle of births and deaths—the brief epitome of human history—the table which records, with almost barometric precision, the daily influx, and the daily discharge, in that vast tide of generations which rolls on and on, with ceaseless roar and undying echoes, through the hollow vault of time, heedless of the prayer, unchecked by the science and energy, of man, sweeping all before it, relentless and resistless, into the deep abyss of eternity. With what calm indifference does the eye glance over that record of mortality! and yet what a story is unfolded in it! In those few lines, the diverse fates, the uncertainties and accidents, of human life will all be found. Within their short compass, the dread mystery of Providence is contained. There death, the great reality which awaits us all, stands revealed in awful clearness. There are recorded, side by side, the peaceful exit of exhausted age, and the sudden blight and fall of blossoming youth; the slow consumption of life by lingering disease, and its instantaneous extinction by accident or the visitation of God; the thronged and honoured obsequies of the benefactor of his kind, and the silent interment, from which memory turns shuddering aside, of the self-destroyer. All these things are before us. They make up the history of our race, in

the most interesting and solemn event which befals it.
Chance seems to dispose of them; but we are sure that
no chance is there—that it is but the semblance of it,
the result of our ignorance and limitation; we are sure
there is a meaning and a purpose in all these things,
though it may surpass our present knowledge to discover fully what it is—though we may be compelled to
refer our deep persuasion of its existence to boundless
faith in the wisdom and goodness of the Eternal Father.
In truth, while religious wisdom will ever cherish a
sense of its relation to a higher and more wondrous
system of things, with which death is our mysterious
medium of communication, and in which improving and
virtuous minds will, we trust, be permitted hereafter to
take a part—while it will shrink from spiritual deadness
as the most fatal disease that can prey upon the human
soul—it is still benevolently ordered for us, that our
belief in the spiritual, and in a future after death, should
be left to be cherished by faith and devotional feeling,
by a thoughtful interpretation of the signs which God
has impressed on His visible creation, and by cordial
sympathy with the doctrines of His accredited mes-
sengers and prophets.   In tenderness to our weak
vision, God has drawn a veil between us and the
world of spirits.   Its unclouded splendour would over-
power us.   Were we to look upon it with our present
faculties, we should die.   And therefore has God spread
out the shadow of His wings over us, that the mind,
yet tender and sensitive, might grow up into healthful
strength beneath them, and then finally, when His shel-
tering pinions are upraised to allow free action to our

matured powers, might soar forth undazzled into the clear brightness of celestial truth.

I have already remarked that happiness and true wisdom depend on our rightly conceiving the state in which we live. Death is an ever-approaching reality. We must learn, then, to face it calmly, to blend it with all our prospects of futurity, and to see in it, as in every other appointment of God's providence, some proof, which we shall hereafter more completely understand, of His unfailing care and love; some wise provision for the greater future improvement and happiness of His children. The visible scene which encompasses us on earth has been thrown around us by the hand of God, and is wrought over with lessons of heavenly truth, full of hints and warnings and suggestions, which reveal its duty and destination to the serious mind, and may be reduced, by reflection, to a clear and positive significance. Through types and dim foreshadowings we gain as deep an insight into our future being as it is desirable for us to possess; but the light of heaven streams through the mystic characters, and gives us proof of its own unclouded radiance beyond them, and fills us with the delightful trust that the lessons now faintly traced to the mental eye, and the truths at present only half developed, will hereafter be drawn out into promi-nence, and set before us in all their glory and their strength. In the mean time, we may rejoice in the assurance that this light comes to us from God; that He gives it us, as we seek it in sincerity, and are capable of it; and that by it He is illuminating our earthly path, and aiding us to reach a higher stage of

intellectual and moral excellence. This is our ground
of hope and trust towards God. Amidst the comparative darkness of our present state, and the uncertainty
of our continuance in it, we can look up with filial confidence to our Father in heaven and say, "Because Thou
hast been our help, therefore in the shadow of Thy
wings will we rejoice." Of all the foundations on which
human peace and comfort can rest, the best and surest
is the simple, childlike faith of the gospel—that God is
our heavenly Father—that we are placed on earth to
prepare for heaven—that heaven is our home—the end,
the crown, the consummation, the grand and final reality
of our being. Nothing can be added to a faith like this.
It exhausts the deepest wants of the soul. It offers
everything that is needed to quiet apprehension, to
allay our doubts, and to give us inward peace. We are
encircled in the arms of a righteous and loving Father,
who simply asks our wills and affections, and will bestow on us in return the rest and blessedness of His
eternal mansions. For the tranquillity and satisfaction
of the mind, philosophy can suggest nothing better than
such a faith. With all its discoveries, it cannot go
beyond it. It can but dress it up in new phraseology;
devise for it wider applications; and gather round it
fresh illustrations and new analogies from the ever-
expanding field of scientific vision. Philosophy must,
at last, pause reverentially before it as an ultimate
fact, fixed deep in the immutable constitution of the
human mind—the only solid basis on which can be
reared a clear, intelligible, self-consistent theory of
God's spiritual universe. Happy they who have this

faith deep-enshrined in their inmost souls! Let them be grateful for it, and cherish it, and rest in it. It outweighs in value every other possession of our outward or our inward life. It is a light in the soul itself, which sheds its lustre on the external world. It is like the air of heaven, diffusing health and vigour through every vein of the moral man. It reveals the constant presence of God; and, unfolding a glorious future, it deprives the grave of its horrors, and enables us to walk with unabated cheerfulness, though we see our fate, and feel that death is close at our side.

There are, however, some minds which find themselves able to grasp more firmly, and apprehend more clearly, the assurances of faith, by associating them with the general aspects of Divine providence, and bringing to their aid considerations drawn from the structure and working of human nature itself. They build on faith; but reason and free speculation furnish the materials of the superstructure. To such minds the following suggestions are offered, in the belief that they will render more perceptible the accordance of faith with the strongest tendencies of our present being, reconcile us to death, and give the future and invisible a deeper and more solemn influence over our whole cast of thought.

(1.) Every meditative mind raises itself by reflection, above the multitude of individual impressions which flow in upon it from its daily experience and observation, to the conception of some great idea embodied in these impressions, connecting them together as a whole, and indicating the common unity which they combine to express. In the springing up of such an idea within us, we find out the *meaning* of life. Every one who exercises his reason at all, catches glimpses of this meaning; but the wise man alone, whose final convictions repose on deep faith in God, reasons it out, as far as he can trace it, to his own satisfaction, and governs his whole life in accordance with it. Now, the peculiarity of the idea which is suggested by the contemplation of life, is that of incompleteness—or I should rather say, of *incipiency*. We are evidently in the beginning of a system. We are living in the midst of rudiments. What we perceive might be, if tendencies were worked out to their natural results—what our moral feeling, our sense of justice and fitness, tell us ought to be—is not in fact accomplished. The shadow of it dimly flits before us. Our mind discerns on every side a thousand types of order and beauty, imperfectly developed in the various forms of moral being; but the realization is wanting—the completion is yet to come. Is not this the reflection which at once presents itself to us on a survey of life? And if life be under the government of a wise and good God, does not this reflection carry in it an implicit assurance that there must be some more glorious future for the soul of man—some undiscovered scene of good, hidden from us by the visible and the present, which is awaiting our liberated spirits, and into which death is the appointed door of admission?

(2.) This persuasion is strengthened by our perceiving that, if we put our minds and characters into voluntary harmony with the obvious order and design of the universe, we experience a sensible progress, a moving on from strength to strength in the knowledge of ourselves, and in the power of interpreting the outward world, with the continuance of the providential discipline through which we pass. Our very follies and transgressions, if not persisted in, furnish, in the lessons which they have yielded, the elements of future wisdom—beacons and landmarks for our future course—nay, in some men perhaps, the indispensable conditions of a more rapid advancement. To the thoughtful, life is one great lesson, of which the fruits are continually accumulating. But why do they accumulate, if there be no distant object to which their possessor can hereafter apply them? Why should man, taught by the experience of many years, be then best able to turn the gifts of Providence to their true account, and find out the secret of happiness that is hidden in them, when he seems on the point of parting with them for ever? Why should there be such a treasure of practical wisdom in the bosom of age, if it is to perish altogether in the grave? Propose such questions distinctly to yourself; revolve in your mind the possible solution of them; and the answer most obviously suggested will bring the strong support of unprejudiced reason to the gospel assurance of life and immortality.

(3.) Reflection on our own minds must convince us that we are under the direction and superintendence of a higher Mind; and from the unity of plan and tendency perceptible in all things—from the good that so obviously predominates in creation, encountering evil at all points, and constantly triumphing over it more and more—we are equally sure that that Mind must be

one and supreme—infinitely wise, powerful and benevolent. We are certain, moreover, that we, from our
intellectual and moral endowments, are related to that
wonderful Being, and have an interest in His favour
and blessing, which He can, and which He will, withhold
or confer, according to the spiritual fitness or unfitness
of His creatures to receive and improve it. With the
designs of that great Being, so far as they are revealed
to us, let us heartily ally ourselves, aiming, under the
impulse and guidance of His Spirit, after all excellence
and the production of the greatest possible good. Thus
we become the children of God. Thus we put ourselves
under the protection of an Almighty Father. Thus we
have Omnipotent Wisdom on our side, through all the
changes and accidents of existence. Nothing can separate us from Him. Nothing can divorce the derived
from the primal Spirit. Nothing can tear the children of God from that parental embrace which enfolds
heaven and earth. We are ever in a Father's hand. In
life and in death, we cannot doubt that He will dispose
of us for our highest good. Do you really believe in an
Almighty Father? that He loves you—only more wisely
and more purely—as you love your own child? that life
is His gift? that death is His appointment? Stretched
upon your dying bed, with earth and all its cherished
objects receding from your eyes; what can you require
for support and consolation more efficacious and sustaining than a faith like this?

(4.) Let us reflect on ourselves. We have liberty of
action; we can submit ourselves to the Divine law; and
pursue with a free choice that which we feel to be right.

We plainly see that there is a progress in all things, bearing them on to higher ends and more glorious results. The Spirit of God is working around us and within us, drawing out into clearer view the great and wondrous design of His creation. Nothing is at rest. All things are moving on and on. Now, *we* are not like the plants and the lower animals—passive, unconscious instruments in the hand of God. We have will and thought. We can work with God and for God. We can spontaneously and deliberately mingle our efforts in the great stream of progress, and contribute our share of influence to its volume and impulse. In this lower world, God works the greatest changes *through* us.

And is there no token of immortality in all this? Shall the most precious and beautiful instruments of God's power—not simply the general form and nature and mind of man, but that concentration of consciousness and intelligence which exists by itself, alone and incommunicable, and constitutes individual character—after a few years of service, be broken up and laid aside for ever? Shall those indomitable energies which have subjugated Nature, extracted her secrets, and made her do the bidding of men for the fertilization and enrichment of the earth — that ever-teeming imagination, which, instinct with the great ideas of truth and beauty, has clothed them in forms of immortality—those large and generous sympathies which have embraced the interests of myriads, and prompted heroic efforts for their deliverance from oppression and their restitution to the rights of humanity—and that high conscientiousness, which has preferred poverty, neglect and oppression, to the utterance of one false word or the sacrifice of its inherent sense of right—shall these noblest products of the Creator's hand, these brightest emanations of His Spirit, these best expressions of His own divine excellence, vanish at last out of existence, with the mechanical instincts of the brute? Shall the intellect of a Plato and a Newton, the sanctity of a Baxter, a Fenelon and a Channing, and the large-souled benevolence of a Howard or a Clarkson, dissolve into the elements, like the sap that once circulated in the cells of submerged forests, or the vital breath that animated, thousands of ages ago, the gigantic monsters of a primeval world?

In questions of this kind we are necessarily thrown back on faith ; we cannot demonstrate; we cannot compel by force of logic the assent of a mind unwilling to believe : and yet I confess to you, Christian friends, there are moments in my existence—as I doubt not there are in yours—moments too, I believe, we shall all admit—the calmest, happiest, holiest that we experience —when these considerations come with such a force into my mind, and bring with them such an air of truth, such an aspect of authority—rise up with such resistless influence and persuasiveness from the very depths of my moral being—that I cannot but receive them as the voice of God himself— the sweet and clear-tongued promise of our destined immortality. Do not misapprehend the bearing of my argument, as though I claimed this promise for the pre-eminently wise and virtuous of our race alone. These are the more advanced members of the great family of God; and the presumptions offered by reason in favour of an hereafter centre more conspicuously in them, because they stand out above the rest of their fellow-creatures, and exhibit with peculiar distinctness the great design of God in man. Yet they only shew what *all* are intended to become; they are but first in that great career which all are destined to pursue; and the belief, of which we most clearly see the reasonableness—the promise, of which we most strongly feel the appropriateness, in reference to them—descends from them with cheering, animating influence on all in every sphere, however lowly, and with whatever amount of inward gifts and outward opportunities endowed, whose minds are earnestly turned to God and goodness—who are governed by the same pure and holy principles, and aspire after the same high objects. Immortality is promised to all the good. Goodness—inward, earnest, practical goodness, actuated by the love of God and man, is the only preparation for heaven, the sole means of encountering and disarming Death. That last enemy cannot be overpowered and deprived of his terrors by the subtleties of doctrine or the strength of fanatical assurance; but at the presence of Goodness he lays aside his grisly aspect, and puts on a smile. Meet him we must; there is no shunning his approach; he crosses our path at every turn. But let us address ourselves with full purpose of heart to God and goodness, intent on duty and usefulness, and we shall not fear. At whatever hour, and under whatever form, he presents himself—in age, maturity or youth, in our chamber or in the world, amidst the press of business and in the flush of health, or under the tortures of lingering disease—we shall be equally prepared for him. We shall recognize in him a messenger from God, to give us our dismissal from earthly trial, and conduct us to our eternal rest.

[Written, 1845; last preached (Pendyffryn, North Wales), 4th April, 1869.

The last sermon preached by the writer, who died 28th May, 1869, in the seventy-second year of his age.]

C. Green & Son, Printers, 178, Strand.